Created and Directed by Hans Höfer

INSIGHT GUIDES
Vienna

Produced by Wilhelm Klein
Edited by Dr. Heinz Vestner
Photographed by Christian Hager
Translated by Susan James

HOUGHTON MIFFLIN COMPANY

APA PUBLICATIONS

Vienna

First Edition (5th Reprint)
© **1993 APA PUBLICATIONS (HK) LTD**
All Rights Reserved
Printed in Singapore by Höfer Press Pte. Ltd

Distributed in the United States by:
Houghton Mifflin Company
2 Park Street
Boston, Massachusetts 02108
ISBN: 0-395-66253-2

Distributed in Canada by:
Thomas Allen & Son
390 Steelcase Road East
Markham, Ontario L3R 1G2
ISBN: 0-395-66253-2

Distributed in the UK & Ireland by:
GeoCenter International UK Ltd
The Viables Center, Harrow Way
Basingstoke, Hampshire RG22 4BJ
ISBN: 9-62421-070-5

Worldwide distribution enquiries:
Höfer Communications Pte Ltd
38 Joo Koon Road
Singapore 2262
ISBN: 9-62421-070-5

ABOUT THIS BOOK

Postwar Vienna has had an image problem. Once the European capital of music, the center of an empire and the most important city in Central Europe, Vienna has become a backwater. It was divided for many years, like Berlin is still divided, between east and west by political authority.

Now, once again, Vienna is a vibrant city, reborn with a generation of new leadership and cultural creators. Its old look remains–a "Capital looking for an Empire"–and that is part of its charm. And that is the reason why Vienna was one of the first urban centers to be profiled in the *Cityguide* series from Apa Publications of Singapore. For the serious traveler, the *Cityguides* are a handy companion that can transport you down the busy boulevards and into the special nooks and crannies often overlooked by standard tourist publications.

Cityguides are the natural extension of the special brand of travel literature founded by **Hans Höfer**, a native of West Germany, with his first book, *Insight Guide: Bali*, in 1970. Since then, the *Insight* series has expanded to comprise an entire library of prize-winning travel literature with each book marked by fine writing, great photographs and fresh, frank journalism. The books all reflect Höfer's training in the Bauhaus tradition of book design, typography and photography. To maintain that standard, Höfer gives responsibility for each edition to a single editor who gathers articles and pictures from the best available local writers and photographers.

Wilhelm Klein, an author who has already written several books for Apa Publications, is the project editor for *Cityguide: Vienna.* Apart from *Burma* and *Burma the Golden,* he has also written and taken photographs for *Continental Europe, East Asia, Nepal, India* and *Rajasthan.*

He describes himself as a "Viennese in exile", one of the many who left their home town in the 50s and 60s to make their fortunes in foreign parts. In the early 80s, he realized that his home town had changed completely and Vienna was once again a city which he could love and live in.

Klein found his photographer in **Christian Häger**, another "Viennese in exile" who runs a successful advertising studio in Frankfurt am Main. Häger learned photography in Vienna, where he still knows every alley and every hidden corner that he explored as a boy. For this book, he traveled often to Vienna, staying for several weeks at a time.

In Vienna they say that **Dr. Felix Czeike** has turned over every stone of the city center at least once and is as familiar with past ages of the city as one of us would be familiar with the present. He is Hofrat, a professor at the university, director of the Wiener Landesarchiv (archives of the federal state of Vienna), general secretary and president of a variety of historical societies and president of a variety of historical societies throughout Austria. Czeike has published 45 books and more than 700 articles in periodicals and newspapers.

The introduction to a book like this ought to be written by someone who can view the city from a slight distance. Our "Viennese foreigner" is **Dr. Lonnie R. Johnson.** Dr. Johnson is an American from Minneapolis, who graduated summa cum laude from St. John's University in Minnesota. He obtained his PhD in 1983 from the University of Vienna. Since 1979 he has been Associate Director of the Institute of European Studies,

Klein

Häger

Czeike

Johnson

Kohout

the oldest of such institutes for American undergraduates in Austria. Together with Inge Lehne, he wrote *Vienna–The Past in the Present: A Historical Survey* in 1985, and in 1987 he published *Introducing Austria: A Guide of Sorts*.

Younger authors were needed to track down the "New Vienna." **Dr. Jutta Kohout** studied history and political science in Vienna and graduated there in 1980. Today she is a free-lance journalist and contributor to the German magazines *Stern* and *Geo* and the German edition of *Cosmopolitan*. She knows Vienna inside and out: the pubs, museums, discos, theaters and balls that make it the "city of many dreams."

Dr. Andrea Schurian also studied political science and lived for some time in New York and on the West Coast of the USA. Schurian was born in Klagenfurt and is Viennese by choice. She works for Austrian television making cultural programs and documentaries. Her special field is European and particularly Austrian and Viennese culture. She has written for *Town and Country*, *Vogue*, *Geo* and *Merian* and also for many international art magazines.

Dr. Günter Treffer, who has studied in Innsbruck, Vienna and at the University of Pennsylvania, is one of those cosmopolitan people that only a city like Vienna can produce–evidently European, but at home all over the world. He has been an editor and a publisher for various well-known houses and as an author has written books about Vienna, its surrounding countryside and its history. His contribution covering the suburbs of Vienna and the surrounding country round off this book.

However, contributions from the main authors don't make up the whole book. **Dr. Helmet Zilk**, Mayor of Vienna, was a teacher, professor of education, TV author and journalist, before becoming program director of ORF (Austrian television) in 1974. In 1984 he was elected Mayor of Vienna for the first time and he won the re-election in 1987. Dr. Zilk wrote about a subject which has been dear to him since childhood–the Viennese woman.

Friedensreich Hundertwasser is more than a world-famous painter–in Vienna his main interest is in "Green" city architecture. In 1958 they called it "leaving the mould to grow," now it's recognized all over the world as "Green Policy." Hundertwasser has written the contribution on new city architecture.

Ludwig Hirsch is poet, singer and storyteller in one; he is what every Viennese would like to be. For this book he wrote his alternative, rather grimly "dark grey" guide to Vienna.

Special thanks to **Susan James** who translated the German version of *Cityguide: Vienna* to English. James was born in West Germany and spent her childhood moving between West Germany and England. She has held numerous professions–a teacher, researcher, proof-reader, journalist, magazine editor and translator.

Providing valuable assistance to James is **Irena Marner**. At the age of 25, Marner did her M.A. in German, English and American literature at the University of Regensberg in Bavaria. For the past two years she has been busy building up her own literary agency, but has also worked as a free-lance editor, translator and journalist.

—Apa Publications

Schurian

Treffer

Zilk

Hundertwasser

Hirsch

LUDWIG HEINER

ZUCKERBACKER

HISTORY AND CULTURE

PEOPLE AND THEMES

MAPS

PLACES

TRAVEL TIPS

VIENNA, CITY OF MY DREAMS

If you get too close to one of the masterpieces in the world famous collection of Vienna's Kunsthistorisches Museum, one of the guards inevitably will reprimand you to step back from the picture, but he does not see the beauty of the painting. The Viennese often seem to treat their city with the same disinterest or familiarity that museum guards show for great works of art. Confronted day in and day out with a beautiful city that fascinates and mesmerizes foreigners, the Viennese absolve their daily routines without paying too much attention to the spectacular setting. However, if you happen to walk on the grass in one of Vienna's many parks, one of the locals may feel compelled to tell you to get off.

Despite the fact that Vienna is one of the most intact ensembles of historical buildings in the world, it is far from being an open-air museum. Nonetheless, Vienna suffers and benefits from its reputation for harboring a thousand-year-old collection of artifacts carried together by innumerable hands and crowned with all sorts of Imperial paraphernalia that serve as a constant reminder of those days when the city was not the capital of a small Central European state of 7 million, but the **kaiserliche Haupt-und Residenzstadt**, the "Imperial Capital City and Residence" of the Habsburgs who ruled an empire of over 50 million.

Today, Vienna's politicians never tire of praising all of the indisputable contemporary merits of the city. They stress its importance as a home of a number of United Nations organizations, assorted other international agencies, and its role as a neutral meeting ground for East and West. Still, it's the city's Imperial past that interests most visitors, much more than its present geopolitical function as a capital of a neutral state between two rival blocks. One of the most reliable and well-worn accesses to Vienna is its Imperial heritage. Two of the city's most popular attractions, the **Vienna Boys' Choir** and the **Lipizzaner**, were founded by the Habsburgs. The boys still sing in the **Court Chapel** and the horses still prance in the **Spanish Riding School** on Sunday mornings. Virtually all facets of the Habsburgs' lives are on display: scepters, crowns, and coronation gowns in the **Imperial Treasury**; armor and weapons in the **Weapons Collection** of the Kunsthistorisches Museum; exquisite dishes and cutlery in the **Court Table and Silverware Depot**; carriages and saddles in the **Imperial Coach Collection**; how and where they lived in the **Imperial Apartments of the Hofburg** in the inner city

Preceding pages: Konditorei Ludwig Heiner; the Vienna Boys' Choir; Ball in Hofburg; view of St. Stephen's Cathedral in winter. Left, entrance to the Stadtbeisel.

as well as in the former summer residence of the **Schloß Schönbrunn Palace**, and the place they all came to rest, known as the **Imperial Burial Vault** or **Kaisergruft**.

The Habsburg which seems to overshadow all others is **Emperor Francis Joseph I**. The grandfatherly regent with mutton-chop sideburns, inevitably dressed in a uniform, and stooped with age still appears everywhere in the city. Nowadays, his persona dominates the postcard stands and adorns the T-shirts, coffee mugs, plates, and key chains at the souvenir shops. The Vien-

product, a series of concentric rings which can be read like the cross section of an ancient tree, starting with the historical core of the inner city.

Vienna's city government spends a tremendous amount of time and energy convincing the Viennese that they are living in a modern city, but only the satellite projects on the outskirts are convincing examples of this claim. For the inner city and its adjoining districts, modernity is then visually limited to the ground floor store fronts, individual buildings erected after 1945 to fill the holes

nese, with their innate sense of decorum, have branded this special branch of the souvenir industry dedicated to his immortality as **Kaiser-Kitsch**.

Well over half of Vienna's buildings predate the 20th century, and the patchwork of architectural styles and monuments, ecclesiastical and profane, ranging from the Middle Ages to 19th-century history and Vienna's particular version of art nouveau, **Jugendstil**, give the city of Vienna an anachronistic and eclectic touch.

Despite all of the artifice that has gone into making Vienna what it is today, it is perhaps best to look closely at the city as an organic

the war had torn in the cityscape, or in its subterranean, like the city's subway system, the U-Bahn, which has been internationally acclaimed for its design. Its construction also unearthed a series of archeological finds—Celtic graves, Roman ruins, and an early medieval chapel.

A walk along the **Ringstraße**—the boulevard that encloses the inner city is lined with noble edifices like the University, City Hall, Parliament, the Museums of Art and Natural History, the Imperial residence of the Hofburg, and the Opera, all of which are somewhere between grand and melancholy—is perhaps one of the best ways to develop a feeling for the monumental gravity of Vienna as a former seat of power.

However, there is also a Vienna for visitors, who are not specifically interested in the Imperial artifacts of the crown-and-coffins-and-palaces approach. The visitors, mostly want to capture a specific atmosphere instead: the waltzing and conviviality, the **joie de vivre**, and the innocent hedonism of the good old Imperial days: a leisurely afternoon in a coffeehouse, an opera or an operetta, maybe a ball, an evening in a wine cellar or at a **Heuriger**, one of the many

smoothly, which, in turn, makes them feel like they are being rushed.

This is one of the peculiar charms of Vienna. The city is leisurely, as if it were resisting the 20th century demands for efficiency, and by those standards, it is a bit old fashioned.

Vienna does, however, have a nightlife, a relatively recent acquisition called the **Beisel** scene. The Beisel, an expression in Viennese dialect borrowed from the Yiddish word for house, used to be a well-worn, shabby and small neighborhood establish-

places on the outskirts of the city where vintners serve locally produced wine in a rustic atmosphere.

But too much wood paneling, too many polished brass fittings, an immaculate black and white marble floor, or waiters who are too polite or agile are signs either of an imitation for tourists or of a traditional institution which has been "renovated" and "revitalized" to death. These kinds of places are not comfortable enough for the natives who, unlike many foreign guests, are only unnerved when everything runs too

ment where simple people enjoyed simple food and drink at modest prices in an equally modest atmosphere. However, prosperity killed this traditional institution which the younger generation now has rediscovered and adapted to meet its contemporary needs. And adapted they were: either left in their original state (for the nostalgic, genuine atmosphere), or restored impeccably (the antique-snob appeal method), or redecorated in the latest neo-New Wave, postmodern style (for the trendy crowd). Add some music and the Beisel is complete.

For some people, the "Beisel scene" is an alternative to an evening at the opera, a

Left, Schloß Schönbrunn. Above, two buskers.

15

theater or a concert, established features of Vienna's incomparable palette of cultural offerings. But there are alternatives to the "standard" Viennese menu of attractions, alternatives for those who are not too fond of whipped cream.

The allegedly more sophisticated approach to Vienna has a different focus—a necrophilic fascination with Vienna at the turn of the century which, on occasion, reaches the dimensions of a death cult. This approach involves pilgrimages to selected birthplaces of our modern sensibility. Freud

vocative eroticism to existential frankness. Like so many composers before him—Haydn, Mozart, Schubert, Beethoven, and Brahms—Mahler composed and suffered in Vienna, a city where an artist's death traditionally has been the prerequisite for local recognition.

As an experience, "Vienna 1900" has added a new aesthetic dimension to the conventional pleasures of Vienna; as a trademark, it has become so popular in recent years that it has encroached upon the city's old Imperial image.

opened up the abyss of the unconscious in Vienna, and why should you childishly enjoy the gold and glitter of the Imperial Apartments when you can anguish on the very spot where the founder of psychoanalysis had his famous couch? Austria, like most other countries, has its own national "founders of modern architecture," and the buildings of **Otto Wagner** and **Adolf Loos** actually appeal more to many people than Germany's Bauhaus or France's Le Corbusier. The restrained design of Viennese **Jugendstil** is less frivolous and contrived than many other forms of art nouveau. The nudes of **Gustav Klimt** and **Egon Schiele** range from pro-

Most tours of Vienna are complete without a visit to one of the working class districts that sprung up on the outskirts of the city in the course of the 19th century. A comprehensive tour, however, would have to include these neighborhoods because they show how the great majority of the Viennese once lived behind the city's Imperial façade. The squalor of the past has been replaced by a standard of living which, in historical comparison, has improved enormously, but which, by most Western European standards, is in many cases somewhere between substandard and modest.

In the working class districts, visitors

16

inevitably notice large, sometimes mammoth housing complexes, somber and spartan in design, that are too old to be contemporary, yet too new to fit into their older surroundings. These buildings are an optical bridge to post-World War I or "modern" Vienna, the first major city in the world to be governed by a socialist municipal administration. During the "interwar period", the Municipality of Vienna erected some 60,000 living units to tackle two chronic Viennese problems: housing and health. Rhetorically stylized into being "palaces for

curiosities exert a particular charm on foreigners, the Viennese sometimes seem to treat their city in a matter-of-fact way, but this is only feigned indifference. They love and hate Vienna. With foreigners or on those rare occasions when they leave the city, the Viennese spend most of their time praising or defending Vienna, but among themselves or at home, they love to complain about their city—and each other.

Like the city itself, the Viennese have a sunny and a dark side, and in both cases the sunny disposition is a commercially exag-

the people" by their socialist patrons, the largest "interwar" housing complexes were named after leading revolutionaries. They now enjoy the status of monuments to the progressive social welfare programs of the "interwar" era circumscribed as "Red Vienna". If you have ideological reservations about visiting the housing complexes named after Marx and Engels, you can visit the one named after a less radical revolutionary: George Washington.

Born and raised amidst all of these monuments and attractions, the landmarks and

gerated cliché. The Viennese soul is delicately, perhaps even frivolously balanced between light-heartedness and disregard, equanimity and cynicism, sentimentality and brutality.

Helmut Qualtinger, the late Viennese cabaret artist and actor, ironically captured the passion that goes into being Viennese: "The Viennese can't stand it in Vienna; but they can't stand it anywhere else, either." But a song the Viennese love to sing at the Heuriger, usually prefaced by a few glasses of wine to increase its profundity, is equally Viennese as well: Vienna, Vienna, just you alone, you are the city of my dreams..."

Left, Karl-Marx-Hof. Above, at the foot of the pillars of Parliament.

17

The area around Vienna has been inhabited for many thousands of years, but the actual history of the city begins when the Romans advanced into the Celtic Kingdom of Noricum. Here, the Romans built a line of fortifications along the banks of the Danube, as a protection against the German tribes. The main camp in this area was Carnuntum, at the point where the road from Poland to the Adriatic crossed the Danube.

The second flanking fortification was where part of the city center of Vienna is now, at Vindobona, next to a Celtic settlement that lay in a good strategic position. A civilian town grew up next to the camp. Somewhere around A.D. 400 the fort was destroyed by Germanic tribes.

The Roman walls remained intact until the 12th century and up till that time had protected the developing settlement, which had its centers to the north of the Hoher Markt (Berghof and St. Ruprecht's Church), at St. Peter's and at Maria am Gestade. Fortified villages grew up outside the gates, among them trading settlements between Wollzeile and Fleischmarkt and near todays Weihburggasse.

Vienna was first described as "civitas" (town) in 1137. In 1147, St. Stephen's Cathedral was consecrated, in 1155, the House of Babenberg set up its residence in Vienna (Am Hof), and in 1189, Frederick Barbarossa rested in Vienna on his way to the Crusades. Towards the end of the 12th century, an expansion of the city took place that would shape the development of Vienna for centuries to come. A new circular wall surrounded it. The district around the Neuer Markt was built in the time of Duke Leopold VI to absorb the trade in goods coming north from Venice. At that time the whole area between the Kärntner Straße, Graben and Kohlmarkt was built up. At the beginning of the 13th century Vienna was a fully developed city with a center and suburbs, the most important city north of the Alps after Cologne. Leopold encouraged trade, gave Vienna city rights in 1221 (at the head of the city council was a city magistrate), invited Catholic orders, whose churches (Teutonic Order of Knights, Dominicans, Minorites) can still be seen today, into the city, and founded the Michaelerkirche. Vienna developed into an important trade and cultural center, praised by the Minnesinger poets.

After the death of Duke Frederick II in the battle of the Leitha (1246), the Bohemian King Przemysl Ottokar II and the King of Hungary, Bela IV, both laid claim to the masterless Austrian inheritance. The wealthy Viennese merchant families backed Ottokar, whose policies of support for the cities seemed to offer them advantages. In 1273, a German king was elected, Rudolf I of the house of Habsburg, who ended the quarrel by giving Austria and Styria to his sons Albrecht I and Rudolf II after the defeat and death of Ottokar in the battle of Dürnkrut in 1278. The Viennese were placated in 1278 with a city charter, and a mayor has been at the head of the city council since 1282.

Albrecht reduced the economic privileges of the city considerably in 1281, and provoked a rebellion by the citizens which he could only put down with great difficulty in 1288. In 1296, the city's rights were reduced even further and considerable restraint was placed on the political activities even of the wealthy families.

The Habsburgs completed the building of the new castle begun by Ottokar II (Schweizer Trakt of the Hofburg) and encouraged the completion of the Herrenviertel (Herrengasse). Despite repeated efforts they could not overcome the mistrust of the Viennese citizens for a long time. However, from the beginning of the 14th century, on Vienna's precedence over other cities in the Habsburg domains was undisputed.

The Gothic city

The bird's-eye view by Jacob Hoefnagel,

Previous pages: View of Vienna, 1483. Left, Rudolf IV, the Founder.

THE BABENBERG RULERS

Leopold I was the first Babenberg ruler. The Babenbergs did homage for the core of Austria (known as Ostarrichi from 996—the name Wenia for Vienna first appeared in documents dating from 881) in 976, and under Margrave and Leopold III they added Vienna to their domains in 1135. Leopold III avoided taking sides in the disputes over who should be crowned Holy Roman Emperor until a majority of princes supported Henry IV. Leopold then married Henry's sister Agnes and consolidated his position in Austria.

He was highly regarded by the church and

last decades of Babenberg rule. In 1190, Walther von der Vogelweide stayed in the city, in 1227 it was another poet, Ulrich von Liechtenstein. In 1192 Richard Lionheart was captured just outside Vienna on his way back from the Holy Land. A ransom of 50,000 pounds of silver was demanded and was minted in Vienna.

A new coin—the Wiener Pfennig—was minted specially for the occasion. The Babenbergs built a new city wall with strong towers with this money. It protected Vienna until the 16th century. The building gave the opportunity

eventually canonized in 1485. In 1137, Leopold IV signed a treaty with the Bishop of Passau which allowed St. Stephen's Cathedral to be built. In 1155, Henry II "Jasomirgott" (the nickname is said to refer to his favorite exclamation, roughly "so help me God"), who had lost the dukedom of Bavaria due to the reconciliation of the Emperor with the Guelfs, moved his residence to Vienna and built a castle "Am Hof". In 1156, Austria was promoted to a dukedom ("privilegium minus").

Henry invited Irish monks from Regensburg and built them a monastery outside the city, which he intended for the burial place of his family (Schottenkloster in the Freyung). There were many cultural and political peaks during the

for an expansion which counts as a notable example of far-sighted city planning.

Duke Leopold VI was held in the highest esteem by Emperor and Pope and acted as intermediary in peace talks in 1230 at the peace talks of San Germano between the Emperor Frederick II and Pope Gregory IX. During the Duke's rule, Vienna was a very popular place for tradesmen and Minnesänger poets. The city charter of 1221 gave the citizens a trade monopoly that lasted around three hundred years and led to the blossoming of trade.

Frederick II made Vienna into an "imperial city" and temporarily withdrew it from Babenberg rule. With the death of Frederick in 1247, the Babenberg dynasty died out.

dating from 1609, is often described as the "last picture of the Gothic city". The narrow, high-gabled town houses still predominate, with the spires of Gothic churches, most of which were still extant, soaring above them. The only change made had been to the fortifications, in 1529. A Renaissance wall had been built, following Italian models, and its mighty bastions were a familiar sight in Vienna right up until 1857. Gothic styles in the arts and the rule of wealthy merchant families in the political and economic arena are typical for the 14th to the 16th centuries.

(1359), he founded the University in 1365 and instigated economic and social reforms. In 1396, the Dukes passed an order in council which gave craftsmen and tradesmen equal standing with the great merchant families and saved Vienna from the bloody civil wars that convulsed many German cities at this time.

In the 15th century, we can already see a clear picture of the city. The humanist Aeneas Silvius Piccolomini (later Pope Pius II) left a description of the city, and authentic drawings were produced in 1470 and 1490.

The 14th century brought the consolidation of Habsburg rule, running parallel with the completion of the Old City (1304-40 building of the Gothic choir of St. Stephen's, 1330-39 building of the Augustinerkirche next to the Burg, from 1330, building of the "jewel of Gothic architecture", the church of Maria am Gestade began). The dominant personality among the nobility was Duke Rudolf IV, the Founder, who laid the foundation stone of the tower of St. Stephen's

It was not a good time for the mayors, however. Following the example of other German Imperial cities, they wanted to pursue independent policies. Konrad Vorlauf was executed in 1408 for being on the losing side during an internecine Habsburg struggle, and Konrad Holzer, darling of the people, suffered the same fate in 1463 as a result of bad tactics. The unhappy persecution of the Jews in 1421, which was set in motion for the most trivial reasons and yet led to the destruction of the Jewish quarter; the confused events of the 40s and 50s, when the Emperor Frederick III quarreled with his brother Albrecht VI, and was besieged by the Vien-

Left, Walther von der Vogelweide. Above, Vienna in the 15th century.

ST. STEPHEN'S CATHEDRAL

The southern tower of St. Stephen's Cathedral is 450 feet (137 metres) high and can be seen from far away. The Cathedral in the center of Vienna has become a trademark of the city, and is both a magnificent example of a church built in several stages and the most notable building of the High and Late Gothic periods in Austria.

Frederick III (tomb in the Choir) got the Pope to make Vienna a bishopric in 1469, Charles VI had it made an archbishopric. From then on St. Stephen's has been the Archbishop's cathedral. The oldest Romanesque building was put up from

ated by Duke Rudolf IV (known as the Founder). The tomb of Rudolf and his wife can be seen in the choir. The "Albertine Choir" was built from 1304-40, the Main Aisle (by Hans Puchsbaum) with its well crafted side arches from 1359-1440 and the southern tower, completed by Hans Prachatitz, from 1359-1433. Work ceased on the northern tower, it was begun in 1469, and completed in 1511. The high roof with its glazed tiles plays a large part in the overall impression and harmoniously combines the architectural styles of various periods. The Cathedral is rich in valu-

1137-60, at that time outside the city walls. It was a three-nave basilica with two fortified towers. A late Romanesque building on the same ground plan followed in the 13th century (1230/40-1263). The west front and door, "Riesentor" or Giant's Doorway, a magnificent portal built around 1240, and the two towers, "Heidentürme", are all that remains of last late Gothic buildings put up in a German-speaking country.

Albertine Choir

The Heidentürme mark the width of the Romanesque cathedral. Work started on the Gothic Cathedral in the 14th century; the Romanesque building had been gutted by fire. Work was initi-

able works of art, among them the Dienstbotenmadonna (Virgin of the Servants - 1340), the Wiener Neustädter Altar (1447 - the triptych altar on the left in the Choir) and the Late Gothic pulpit by Anton Pilgram (c. 1500). Pilgram left his portrait carved on the pulpit—he is the man looking out of the window. His portrait can also be seen on the late Gothic organ base. In April 1945, the Cathedral caught fire during the fighting. The collapse of the late medieval roof destroyed the famous Gothic choir pews of Wilhelm Rollinger (1487). The "Pummerin" (Boomer), the biggest bell in Austria, which was smashed as it fell from the tower, was recast in 1951. St. Stephen's Cathedral is not only a great work of art, but also a symbol of the Austrian nation.

nese in the Hofburg in 1462, even though he had presented them with a new coat of arms in 1461; Vienna was occupied by the King of Hungary, Matthew Corvinus (1485-90)— all these events mark the more notable stage of an eventful century.

In the **16th century**, the whole of Europe was shaken by the Protestant teachings of Martin Luther and the threat of the Turks. In 1529, the Turks, led by Sultan Suleiman, reached the walls of Vienna for the first time, and the city only survived due to the early onset of winter. After this, Ferdinand I deliberately moved his residence to Vienna in 1533. Noticeable social and architectural changes followed the settlement of court personnel and the increased presence of nobility in Vienna.

The remainder of the 16th century was marked by the building of the Renaissance wall with its bastions, which was completed in the 60s. The image of the walls with their glacis (area in which building was prohibited) in front and the unregulated course of the Danube appeared in many pictures produced in the following years. On the other side of the glacis the suburbs developed, mainly inhabited by craftsmen and tradesmen, and further out by peasants. Since all financial and labor resources went to the building of the walls, there are few Renaissance buildings within the city area.

In the second half of the century disputes with the Protestants became more and more acrimonious. In the 70s, under the tolerant Emperor Maximilian II, Vienna was almost 80 percent Protestant and, for a short time, even had a Lutheran mayor. Maximilian's successor, Rudolf II moved the Imperial residence to Prague, and Vienna temporarily lost its position of precedence.

The glory of the Baroque

The Emperor Ferdinand II was rigorous in his suppression of Protestantism. His motives were mainly political rather than relig-

ious—loyalties of a monarch's subjects, opposed royal absolutism, and might even harbor republican tendencies.

Thanks to the fanatical involvement of the Jesuits, the first half of the 17th century saw an overwhelming victory for the Counter-Reformation. Under Cardinal Melchior Khesl a number of orders were invited to Vienna. Their churches still remain among the attractions of the city today. In Leopoldstadt the Carmelites and the hospital order of the Brothers of Mercy settled. The Augustinians built the Rochuskirche on the

Landstraße, on the Wieden the Paulites settled, as did the Servites in the Roau —and that's just to name a few. In the city center new churches were built by the Franciscans, the Dominicans and the Capuchins (including the Kapuzinergruft where the Habsburgs are buried). The Schottenkirche received its Baroque façade and the Jesuits built an impressive church next to the Old University which they ran. The Ghetto in Leopoldstadt was assigned to the Jews in 1625, but religious bigotry closed it again as early as 1671.

The "advance of the monasteries" is contemporary with the breakthrough of the Roman Baroque style in architecture. Its

Left, central aisle of St. Stephen's. Above, Kärntner Straße c. 1470.

THE TURKS AT THE GATES OF VIENNA

In 1529, a Turkish army, under the command of Sultan Suleiman himself, first besieged Vienna. Bad weather forced the Turks to withdraw and raise the siege.

The war with the Turks in the 17th century reached its peak in the 70s, but Europe was divided. The Sultan had renewed his alliance with France, but the Pope, together with Leopold I, had gained military help from the Empire. However, the defenders of Vienna had no real chance until the Polish King Jan III Sobieski joined this alli-

By September, the city's situation had become desperate. Mines had torn great gaps in the wall, ammunition and provisions were running out, casualties were higher than expected, epidemics broke out, Liebenberg died. But the Turks were also showing signs of wear.

The last desperate strength of the Viennese was only just enough to fight off the final large-scale attack by Janissaries on September 6, in which the Löwel bastion collapsed. At last, unhindered by the Turks, the relief force arrived on the

ance in 1683.

In 1682, the leader of the Hungarian army rebelled against Habsburg domination, Imre Thököli, asked the Turks for help. This provided the Turks with the excuse to send an army.

The Grand Vizier Kara Mustapha had gathered a huge army to march against central Europe. The advance guard arrived outside Vienna on July 13, 1683. A few days later, the whole city was surrounded by 25,000 tents. The Emperor and a large part of the population had fled. The Turks made their main attacks against the Burg and Löwel bastions. Would the 17,000 defenders, led by Mayor Johann Andreas von Liebenberg and City Commander Ernst Rudiger von Starhemberg be able to hold out against the 300,000 besiegers?

Kahlenberg, a hill in the Vienna Woods, unaccountably left unoccupied by Kara Mustapha. On September 12, 1683, after the Capuchin monk Marco d'Aviano had held his famous Mass, it went into the attack along a broad front.

Perhaps the battle would not have ended in quite such a clear-cut victory if Kara Mustapha hadn't made the fatal mistake of simultaneously storming the walls once again. After bitter fighting the Turkish front, not least due to pressure from Polish cavalry, began to give way. Soon the Turks were trying to save themselves in headlong fight, leaving uncounted piles of spoil for the victors. The Pummerin, the great bell of St. Stephen's, was cast from the melted-down bronze of captured Turkish guns.

high point is the façade of the Kirche Am Hof, which is probably the nearest to resembling Roman models. The early Baroque style (c. 1600-1680) was formed by Italian architects, sculptors and painters. The building of palaces remained well behind that of churches.

The Thirty Years' War (1618-1648) passed Vienna by almost without trace—the Swedish army once approached the city (1645) but did not attack it. The mayor and the city council became more and more dependent on the rulers—no noteworthy

Charles VI (1711-40) and his daughter Maria Theresia (1740-80) into a "Mecca of the arts". Nobility and commoners burst out of the confines of the fortified city into the airy suburbs and outskirts. Vienna had never seen such building activity before. The era of the high Baroque (c. 1685-1750) is characterized by a passion for building which had its roots both in the spiritual and material worlds. The court, aligning itself with European power struggles, the church, strengthened by the defeat of Protestantism, the nobility, which had acquired massive

political disputes developed. Daniel Moser, the most prominent head of the city, was one of the Emperor Ferdinand II's most loyal followers.

The last years of the 17th century saw important events: a catastrophic outbreak of the plague (1679) and the second siege by the Turks (1683). The victory over the Turks is marked by a change in the architecture of the city. The "Imperial city", freed from military threat, developed as the residence of

wealth—the need to impress which had seized all the upper echelons of society led to the wish to glorify recent victories. In these times of uncertain currency and few opportunities for economic investment, this was also a lucrative way of investing capital.

The Baroque style, with its feeling for life, its stress on the eternal, and its splendor and show, met all the conditions. The city center began to change fundamentally, the suburbs were improved. A Baroque metropolis of European stature arose out of this mighty symbiosis of the temporal and the spiritual, involving all branches of the arts. Under Leopold I (1659-1705), the first of the

Left, the Turkish siege of Vienna, 1683. Above, the Kohlmarkt, 1784.

"Baroque Emperors", Vienna became a center for European music and theater. The architectural style of the high Baroque was no longer in the hands of the Italians, but in those of two great contemporary architects, Johann Bernhard Fischer von Erlach and Johann Lukas von Hildebrandt. Fischer, with a touch of genius, knew how to transform the Baroque of the south into an art form that suited the Viennese mentality. His most superb works were created for the Emperor: the Hofbibliothek on Josefsplatz (National Library), the Böhmische

Hofkanzlei on Judenplatz and the Hofstallungen. His most notable work is the Karlskirche, commissioned by Charles VI during the plague of 1713. He also built palaces for the nobility, for the families of Batthyány-Strattman, Schwarzenberg and Trautson among others. Some buildings were completed after his death in 1723, by his son Joseph Emanuel, who also designed the Reichskanzleitrakt of the Hofburg.

Hildebrandt, the second great individualist of this era, worked mainly for Prince Eugene of Savoy (Belvedere, Winterpalais) and for the nobility, which overwhelmed him with contracts (the palaces of

Schönborn, Harrach and Daun-Kinsky). For the court, he created the Geheime Hofkanzlei (now the Federal Chancellery) as well as St. Peter's and the Piaristenkirche.

The city administration had the Town Hall built in the Wipplingerstraße by Anton Ospel. Sculptors (such as Georg Raphael Donner or Balthasar Permoser), fresco painters (such as Daniel Gran, who decorated the Hofbibliothek, Franz Anton Maulpertsch, who painted the Piaristenkirche, and Johann Michael Rottmayr, responsible for the Karlskirche), as well as countless painters and plasterers were responsible, together with the architects, for the image of "Viennese Baroque".

Under Maria Theresia, who had Schloß Schönbrunn built, Vienna developed into the capital of an absolutist centralized state. The mayors were demoted to assistants to the rulers, the citizens began to lose interest in local politics.

Culture and science were considerably influenced by the French, who came to Vienna in the entourage of Maria Theresia's husband Francis Stephen (Emperor Francis I). It was this Emperor, too, who intervened actively in economic policy to encourage domestic production. From the 50s onward the Baroque style, also under French influence, gradually transformed into Rococo—the most noticeable example in the city center is the Aula of the Old University.

Emperor Joseph II (1780-90), who as his mother's co-ruler was responsible for making Vienna a garrison city, has gone down in history as the initiator of a massive work of reform. The "Edict of Tolerance", the dissolution of some monasteries (which caused Pope Pius VI to make a rapid trip to Vienna), the reforms to the magistracy, highly influential in Vienna, which completely abolished city autonomy, are the most remarkable measures taken by his government, along with laws passed to further science, technology and education, and also the

Above, Johann Fischer von Erlach. Right, Maria Theresia as a young woman. Following page, Napoleon in Vienna.

Maria Theresia And Schloß Schönbrunn

The daughter of Charles VI, Maria Theresia, is known to Europe through the "Pragmatic Sanction" that allowed the female succession, through her defensive wars against the Prussian King Frederick II and her political reforms within the country. The Pragmatic Sanction was the major political project of Charles VI's reign. The edict was published in 1720 and accepted by the estates of all the Habsburg countries by 1722, but Charles had to make broad concessions to other influential European powers to win their support. The central targets for her reforms, which cleared the

who had planned a "Super-Versailles" on the height of the Gloriette, couldn't be afforded. In about 1700, work started on the modified building on today's site. Then, in 1743, Maria Theresia gave her architect Nikolaus Pacassi the contract to expand the palace into a summer residence. Only the entrance façade now remains of Fischer von Erlach's original design. Pacassi's most important change was building the Große and the Kleine Galerie into the central section, by which he lost the balanced high Baroque symmetry, but gained an incredible dynamism. Decoration and

way for an absolutist centralized state and therefore strongly influenced the position of Vienna, were adminstration, law, the police, economic, financial and currency policy.

Men such as Kaunitz, Haugwitz and Sonnenfels were among her advisors. Her husband, Emperor Francis I (1745-65), gave the economy considerable boosts by encouraging industries to settle in the country and strengthening the arts and sciences by inviting French artists and scholars, to whom he entrusted the expansion of the court collections.

The expansion of Schönbrunn is bound up with the personality of Maria Theresia. The original design by Johann Bernhard Fischer von Erlach, one of the leading architects of Baroque Vienna,

furnishings turned Schönbrunn into an important major work of Austrian Rococo. Pacassi's successor Johann Ferdinand von Hohenberg created another typical late Rococo interior in his Schloßtheater. However, his plans for the park establish him as a leading architect of classic late Baroque.

The final version of the palace had 1,500 rooms, the Gloriette (a fake temple), a palm house, formal gardens, a zoo and the Schloßtheater, in which Mozart and Haydn performed new works by Imperial command. The gardens were opened to the public by Maria Theresia's son Joseph II, the reforming Emperor, who also opened the Imperial gardens of the Augarten and the hunting preserve of the Prater.

founding of the Hofburg Theater as a national theater company. The run up to the new century is marked by the French Revolution, Napoleon's claims to power and the defeat of Rococo by classicism.

The Metropolis of Europe

The 19th century had a turbulent start. Napoleon took over Vienna twice (1805 and 1809) and resided in Schönbrunn. The battle of Aspern in 1809 was his first defeat, but could not influence the outcome of the war. The Emperor Francis II had taken up the Austrian crown in 1804 and laid down the crown of the Holy Roman Empire in 1806. The confusions of war did not pass Vienna by without trace. The population suffered an oppressive housing shortage and rising costs of living.

The enormous sums of military expenditure had thrown the state finances into disorder, and in 1811 this led to state bankruptcy and a currency collapse, from which the economy of Vienna took more than 20 years to recover. Because of this, the city lost its value as a partner for its rulers and was put under strict control. The mayors were forced to take what orders they were given and lost status in the eyes of the population.

On the surface the position of Vienna was more gorgeous than ever. In 1814-15 the "Congress of Vienna", attended by statesmen and diplomats from all over Europe who were trying to divide up the legacy of Napoleon, met here. The splendid celebrations lasted for months, and with hindsight the slogan "The Congress is dancing" was coined to cover this period. The well-balanced mixture of discussions and entertainment is usually seen as a formula for success. The period of time up until 1848, dominated by State Chancellor Metternich, is classified either as Vormärz or Biedermeier, according to your political point of view. Vormärz equals police state, censorship, loss of civil rights. Biedermeier refers to middle class comfort and the blossoming of the arts. The first notable buildings in the neo-classical style were created, among them the Albertina, the Technische Hochschule and the

Münzamt. More and more often the survival of the Renaissance fortifications was called into question. The area of the bastion blown up by the retreating French in 1809 was used as the site for the Burggarten and Volksgarten. In 1817, the remaining bastions were opened up as promenades and the fortified character of the city was lost. Making use of private transport, the citizens also had the opportunity to take outings into the surrounding countryside, particularly into the Vienna Woods. A few suburbs developed into summer and health resorts. Innovations came in the 20s and 30s: 1823 saw the opening of the Danube steamship company, 1828 the building of the first gasworks, 1835 the first exhibition of manufactured goods and 1837 the opening of the first railway, rapidly followed by others. The swift spread of the steam engine also effected the replacement of outdated forms of manufacture by early industrial factories.

The economic revolution made social problems more serious. Poor conditions of work, low wages, rising prices, frightful housing conditions and a lack of political rights finally led to the revolution of 1848, in which the middle and working classes at times fought together for the same aims. After the repression of the revolution by the military there was a period of neo-absolutism. In 1850, the government decided to combine the suburbs (as far as today's Gürtel) with the city center for administrative purposes. The city was divided into eight districts and now had a population of 431,000. In 1857, the Emperor Franz Joseph ordered the demolition of the fortifications and the building development of the surrounding glacis. The creation of the "Ringstraßenzone" occupied the most famous architects in Europe for decades. It was a work of civic architecture unparalleled in its homogenous nature anywhere in Europe.

In 1861, the community council, Gemeinderat, was for the first time elected again. However, only a limited section of the population (less than one per cent, all privileged property owners) was elegible to vote. The political and intellectual outlook of the Gemeinderat was liberal. The most notable

BIEDERMEIER CULTURE

The term "Vormärz", literally means "before march", and refers to the political situation before the revolution of March 1848. "Biedermeier" is made up of the adjective "bieder", meaning worthy, respectable, and a little boring, and the common surname Meier. A rough translation would be "good citizen Meier".

If you separate the Biedermeier period from the contemporary negative political events of the Vormärz, you will get to know a period which, despite its European dimensions, has a particu-

striking children's portraits. However, social problems often appear in the subject matter. Music was dominated by Beethoven and Schubert and by the "fathers" of the Viennese Waltz; Strauss and Lanner. The Gesellschaft der Musikfreunde (Society of the Friends of Music) and the Viennese Philharmonic Orchestra, together with composers and music publishers, laid the foundations of Vienna's fame as the classic metropolis of music.

Franz Grillparzer (1791-1872), was the lead-

larly Viennese aspect. The middle classes were kept out of politics and could hardly engage in trade either. They withdrew to their private sphere and, in their salons, concentrated on culture. Architects, Kornhäusel among them, built houses and villas whose ornamental façades still stand out when you look at the city, but also built the first big apartment blocks. In sculpture, Zauner and Marchese were active making monuments to the rulers, as was Klieber with his well-crafted ornamental sculptures.

Painting was a favorite art form of the Biedermeier. Waldmüller achieved European status with his landscape and genre paintings. Amerling was the most sought after society portraitist, Kriehuber founded the art of portrait lithography, Daffinger painted miniatures and Fendi produced

ing poet and dramatist of the day, and has been when compared to his German predecessors, such as Goethe and Schiller. His reputation rests on his 12 tragedies and one—unsuccessful—comedy. His work looks back to the achievements of classical dramatists, but offers new insights into the actions and motives of characters and a new realism.

Along with Grillparzer, F. Raimund and J. Nestroy predominated in literature. Theater blossomed, and various places of entertainment were much patronized. A busy social life and the maintenance of a comfortable home were ideal conditions for a cultivated lifestyle. Furniture (many pieces designed by Danhauser), paintings, porcelain and silver, clocks and painted glass are still to be seen in museums and antique shops today.

mayor of this period, which lasted up until 1895, was Cajetan Felder (1868-78). In the 60s and 70s, apart from the building of the Ringstraße, considerable improvements to the city's infrastructure were undertaken. The water supply was improved, the course of the Danube was regulated, the Zentralfriedhof (central cemetery) was built, but the building of the new Town Hall and the opening of a new park, the Stadtpark, were also notable events.

After expansion to the south of the city (1874) various suburbs (Bezirke 11 to 19)

were incorporated in 1892. Practical developments were however left to the Gemeinderat, already dominated in 1895 by the Christian Socialist Party led by Mayor Karl Lueger (1897-1910). There were radical changes of economic direction (the building of the city gasworks and electricity stations, the communal ownership and electrification of the trams), further improvements to the water supply, and also the first policies for

Left, Franz Schubert—painting by Moritz von Schwind. Above, 1848—Graf Latour is lynched by the mob.

dealing with social and health problems. These developments continued to be financed by loans, so that the city ran up debts of threatening proportions. In 1905, Lueger obtained a foothold on the opposite side of the Danube by incorporating Florisdorf (Vienna 21), but also declared a green belt of meadows and woodland around the city. In 1910, Vienna had more than 2 million inhabitants. The Social Democrats in opposition demanded a general franchise, but this was not implemented, as Lueger was worried that he might lose power. The second half of the 19th century was architecturally influenced by Historicism, from which the Viennese Secessionism of the turn of the century (Wagner, Loos etc) split off. The work of notable representatives of the Second Viennese School of Medicine (Billroth, Hyrtl, Skoda and others) and the blossoming of other sciences (Sigmund Freud and others) made Vienna world famous. The great composers (Bruckner, Brahms, Mahler), the "Golden Age" of Viennese operetta (Strauss, Millöcker, Suppé), followed by the "Silver Age" (Léhar), the excellent ensembles of the Hofoper, opened in 1869, and the Hofburgtheater, which moved into the theater on the Ring in 1888, the innumerable poets (Zweig, Werfel, Hofmannsthal), painters (Makart, Feuerbach) and sculptors, as well as the Künstlerhaus (from which the Secession broke off, led by Klimt and Kolo Moser, in 1897), the Musikverein, the art academies and other institutions—all of them, financed by nobility and the upper middle classes, shaped the times which have gained legendary fame as "Ringstraße Era" and "Fin de siècle".

Vienna, capital of the Republic

After the end of the First World War, profound political and social changes took place. The general franchise, introduced in 1919, gave the Socialists an absolute majority in the Gemeinderat, which has only been interrupted (forcibly) once since that time, by Fascism (1934-45). Vienna was also split off from the Federal State of Lower Austria and since 1922, it has been both city and

EMPEROR FRANZ JOSEPH AND THE RINGSTRASSE

In 1916, the Emperor Franz Joseph's funeral procession took him to his tomb after a reign of 68 years. It left the Hofburg and crossed the Ringstraße, then followed the Franz-Josephs-Kai to the city center and St. Stephen's Cathedral. This Ringstraße had been Franz Joseph's very own project; in 1857, he had given instructions for it to be built in the often quoted document "Es ist Mein Wille..." (It is Our will...). In 1859, he approved the plans, in 1865, he performed the official opening ceremony in 1879. The procession meant a lot to him because it coincided with his silver wed-

existing buildings as the construction took place in the area formerly occupied by the Renaissance fortifications.

The State Opera House (Staatsoper), in an early French Renaissance style, was the first building to be completed. Other notable buildings are the Naturhistorisches Museum and Kunsthistorisches Museum, (both in a neo-Renaissance style, the neo-Gothic Rathaus (Town Hall) and the Votivkirche, the University (built in Italian Renaissance style), the Burgtheater (in the same style but with touches of Baroque), the neo-

ding anniversary celebrations.

However, the glories of the Ringstraße often led people to forget that the Emperor hindered Vienna more often than he helped the city. Architects from the whole of Europe answered the monarch's call and came to Vienna to take part in planning and building the Ringstraße area. The Dane Hansen came from Athens, the South German Schmid from Milan, the North German Semper from Zurich. Together with the Viennese Hasenauer, Ferstel and many others, they didn't want to miss out on the opportunity to prove themselves in the design of a whole city district, especially as the site was in a central area (between the city center and the suburbs), but—in contrast to Paris and, later, Rome—on land free of

Hellenistic Parliament, the Stock Exchange (a mixture of Neo-classical and Renaissance) and the Central Law Courts (German Renaissance). Although many historical styles, fitting in with 19th-century taste, were used, the Ringstraße did develop as a whole, a series of buildings, protected as part of Vienna's heritage, and unique in Europe: more so as most of the damage done by World War II could be repaired. The impressive buildings of the Ringstraße area have kept their attraction for visitors.

A generation of architects influenced by history, joined in the Stubenring by Secessionists, has here built a monument both to itself and to the upper middle class of this period, who moved into the palatial apartment houses.

Federal State. The period of time, up until 1934 is known throughout Europe under the name of "Red Vienna". Vienna's achievements in the field of communal housing and in programs for improving health and easing social problems aroused the interest of other European cities. The names of Mayor Karl Seitz and City Counsellor Julius Tandler became famous outside Austria's borders, synonymous with the successes of the socialist administration, which would not be moved off course either by repressive measures of the government or by the world

economic crisis. Escalations in paramilitary confrontation led to civil war in February 1934. It was the first struggle between democratic and fascist forces in Europe. After its victory, Austrian Nationalism under Federal Chancellor Dollfuß put an end to Vienna's progessive policies. The mayor was arrested and the democratically elected Gemeinderat dissolved. Vienna was put under a government commissar and lost its independent status.

During the following four years new goals

Left, Emperor Franz Joseph I as a young man. Above, memorial plaque in Karl-Marx.

were set. Above all, the social housing program was immediately stopped. Austrian Fascism led smoothly into the occupation of Austria in March 1938 and Nazi dictatorship. The photos circulating throughout the world showing the Heldenplatz in Vienna with Hitler holding a mass meeting of his supporters unfortunately often meant that the numerous "others" who didn't accept developments are forgotten. They were often persecuted for religious or political reasons and imprisoned in concentration camps. Vienna was greatly expanded, though most of the new incorporations were abolished once more after 1946. Despite Nazi plans, Vienna was spared major changes, as there was not enough time available before the outbreak of the Second World War. The violent extermination of the Jewish part of the population and the almost total destruction of the synagogues of Vienna in the infamous "Reichskristallnacht" should never be forgotten, just as we should remember those driven into exile and those victims who lost their lives resisting Hitler. Vienna was bombed and suffered considerable damage, most of which could be repaired. The public buildings were rebuilt in their original styles.

After the liberation of Vienna in 1945— St. Stephen's Cathedral caught fire during the fighting—and the end of the Four Power Occupation, in 1955 the Austrian Constitution was renewed and Austria's continuing neutrality was declared. Much work has been done in Vienna since then, but care has always been taken to combine tradition and modernity. Vienna doesn't want to be a museum city, but the whole of the town is a place of special interest.

Vienna wants to be a human and an environmentally conscious city. Pedestrian precincts and parks have been laid out to that end, as well as the leisure parks on the newly created Danube island and in the Vienna Woods, where the countryside is protected by law. Today, Vienna presents itself as a city standing between East and West, conscious of its cultural past and welcoming visitors with the same charm possessed by the people of Vienna.

A LIVELY AND LIVING CITY

Sounds in society

While there were no celestial violins playing in medieval Vienna—they hadn't been invented—undoubtedly there should have been celestial lutes. The Minnesänger, trobadours of the German language, used their schmaltzy hit songs to gain a foothold in the chambers (and hearts) of the ladies, turning the whole of Vienna city into a lively musical circus.

A well-known pop star of the time was Walther von der Vogelweide with his romantic moon-in-June songs. These medieval songsters were definitely not on the fringes of society. From 1288, they were represented by the Brotherhood of St. Nicholas, later, with all social propriety, by the appropriate ducal office. The Minnesänger not only laid the foundations of Vienna's musical reputation, but also for modern musical societies and trade unions.

Music and Vienna; that's no cliché, but a true description of the city. From the cradle to the grave, the Viennese are accompanied by music. In the concert hall listening to the Philharmonic or drinking Heuriger and swaying to typical Viennese Schrammel songs—life and love in Vienna is governed by music. In his book *Wien - Brevier einer Stadt,* Gottfried Heindl enthuses over the city's singing soul: "The art of opera, symphonic creation and popular song have been united in the musical city of Vienna to form a perfect historical, social and geographic trinity." Music, which is not subject to any of the prejudices of class, is an integral part of social life. Even the imperial rulers of the House of Habsburg occasionally grabbed quill and music paper and tried their hand at composition. A start was made in 1637 by the Emperor Ferdinand I. He was followed en suite by the Emperors Leopold I, Joseph I and Charles VI. The great mother of Viennese female self-confidence, Maria Theresia, put majestic emotion into her voice when she trilled her father's arias. In 1762, she presented her subjects with the first

performance of *Orpheus and Eurydice* by the innovative German operatic composer Willibald Gluck, who had deserted his home in the Upper Palatinate in favor of the musical world of Vienna. Before his burial in a state tomb in the Zentralfriedhof, he managed to give Maria Theresia's children a quick introduction to the art of fine sounds.

Maximilian I showed signs of the typical Habsburg fascination with music, at least on

the level of organization, when he founded the Hofmusikkapelle in 1498. Centuries later, His Majesty Franz Joseph had evidently lost this particular imperial trait. The Emperor, who, by his own reckoning, was "spared nothing", snored quietly into his beard in the new opera house on the Ring and added his own imperial voice to the critics who grumbled at the building designed by August Sicard von Sicardsburg and Eduard van der Nüll. The gigantic opera house, place of pilgrimage for the international music scene and the highest paid voices, was the first monumental building of the Ringstraße era. Confronted with this massive noisebox in 1869, the cheeky Viennese rhyme: "Der Sicardsburg und der van der Nüll haben beide keinen Stül (Sicardsburg and van der Nüll both have no style)!" Indignant, van der Nüll committed suicide, and Sicardsburg was evidently so upset by this criticism that he died shortly afterwards. Shocked by the mortality rate among his architects, the Emperor, following the motto "Let's not make waves", took every oppor-

concisely sums up the history of Viennese culture: "All the rivers of European culture flowed together here. It was the essential genius of this city of music to resolve all contrasts in harmony, to make something new and individual, something Austrian, Viennese."

All notable European composers have at some time moved to the imperial city, either temporarily or permanently. Once the re-

tunity to give his expert opinion on opera: "It was very nice, I enjoyed it very much."

Only a very small part of Viennese music actually comes from those born in Vienna. This is the most typical characteristic of the Viennese. Slavonic, Hungarian, Bohemian, Italian and Jewish ingredients not only made up the Viennese art of cooking and baking, but also refined the native sound. The Austrian author Stefan Zweig, in his brilliant autobiography *Die Welt von Gestern*,

Left, Brahms' memorial in the Zentralfriedhof. Above, Karlsplatz, with Musikfreundehaus.

form of opera, created especially for the Viennese stage, was under way, Mozart, the child prodigy from Salzburg, set out on his road to musical success. Franz Schubert, the more gentle composer of the Biedermeier, presented Vienna with the legacy of his Lieder. He wasn't without rivals; other leaders of the Lieder-scene were the Styrian Hugo Wolf and Robert Schumann. Anton Bruckner from Upper Austria played the organ like Johann Sebastian Bach from Eisenach, but didn't confine himself to sacred music. Following Johann Strauss' "Golden Age" of operetta, the Hungarians Franz Lehár and Emmerich Kálmán and the Vien-

THE CLASSIC VIENNESE TRIO

In the years from 1779 to 1827 three non-Viennese and their "Viennese Classicism" entered musical history. Wolfgang Amadeus Mozart was born in Salzburg and had traveled throughout Europe as a child prodigy, making a short stop to visit Maria Theresia, who was delighted by the six-year-old's piano playing, and shortly afterwards, showing signs of his genius in his first compositions. Torn between fizzing temperament and deep depression, this vigorous bonvivant reformed opera and the Singspiel.

The second of the Viennese Classicists was

own compositions.

Mozart asked the question: "Every, nation has its opera, why shouldn't we German speakers have our own?" In the Figarohaus in the Domgasse you can see where Mozart withdrew in order to initiate a new era in the history of opera with *Figaro*. Several plaques with Beethoven's name honor a number of houses in Heiligenstadt, on the Mölkerbastei and in the Schwarzspanierstraße, where, almost completely deaf, he spent his last years. The house where Haydn died is also a museum. The three composers have fulfilled the

Joseph Haydn, a farmer's son from Lower Austria, whose strong faith came out in his oratorios and masses. The Rhinelander, Ludwig van Beethoven later received "Mozart's spirit from Haydn's hands". He was the first to replace the minuet with the scherzo in his symphonies. These were three very different personalities, who succeeded in combining Baroque sounds with those of the Rococo period and with elements of folk music to form their own very special musical legacies. During their lives they were loved—Beethoven by his patrons among the nobility, for instance—but also despised and subjected to wicked intrigues, like the eccentric "Wolferl" Mozart, who despite his successful operas usually barely managed to scrape a living out of his

most important condition for their posthumous Viennization—they died in Vienna. Mozart died at the age of 37, impoverished and lonely. His last resting place is in a mass grave, probably in the St. Marxer cemetery. His tombstone in the Zentralfriedhof, Vienna's top address for the prominent deceased, is a mere cenotaph. Thirty years later, the Viennese gave "their" musician Beethoven an ostentatious funeral.

Joseph Haydn found his final resting place in stages. In the Haydn-Park in the 12. Berzirk a memorial stone marks his first grave. Eleven years later his body was moved to Eisenstadt, the first town in which the composer worked. In 1954, the skull, owned by the Vienna Musikverein, was also moved there.

nese Robert Stolz took charge of the "silver" remake. Both gold and silver works are still enthusiastically applauded in the **Volksoper**. In the early 20th, century Arnold Schönberg, Alban Berg and Anton Webern enriched international music with their thematically ingenious twelve tone system.

Today, in this UN city beside the greyish-blue Danube, romantic imitators work alongside old traditionalists, moderate modernists alongside radical innovators. Electronic music is still well represented with resounding names such as György Li-

all over the world, Jo Zawinul's sound "Viennises", international bands such as Falco's *Kommissar* spread itself around even in the US pop charts. "Art reaches its peak wherever it becomes a matter that concerns all the people", said Stefan Zweig, philosophizing. In Vienna this is the case in music more than in any other branch of the arts. This city is the permanent dwelling place of the Viennese and those who (would like to) consider themselves to be Viennese, and its **Staatsoper** (State Opera House) is a magnet for the most talented musicians in

geti, Friedrich Cerha or Ernst Krenek.

It should be obvious that musical entertainment is definitely not dominated by boredom-inducing disasters. When the well-known Heuriger musician Schmid-Hansl died just before the New Year, it made the front page of all the newspapers. The "Spitzbuben" (rogues) spread traditional music of the old school among the Heuriger drinkers. But Austro-Pop and Austro-Jazz make the top of the international charts too. The Vienna Art Orchestra often goes on tour

Left, Haydn, Beethoven and Mozart. Above, Yehudi Menuhin in the Konzerthaus.

the world. It was one of the last victims of the bombs of World War II. When it was reopened in 1955 with Beethoven's *Fidelio* the whole of Austria followed the performance. The opera house is a national shrine to culture. In other areas critics may complain about state overspending, but even the most economy-conscious critics shut up when it comes to the Staatsoper.

In what it has to offer, the opera house on the Ring can certainly compare itself with the Metropolitan Opera in New York, with Milan's La Scala or London's Covent Garden. When international box office stars such as Placido Domingo or Mirella Freni raise their voices, young people in particular scramble for the last few standing room tickets after queueing for hours. The Viennese standing room audience is more reliable than the music critics in the daily papers. They boo without mercy at anyone who misses a note.

The **Musikverein** was built in 1870 by the Ringstraße architect Theophil Hansen as a masterpiece of the Historic style. Here, in between tours, the Vienna Philharmonic, the most famous music-makers in the city, offer a special delight every year. In cycles of ten

Symphonic Orchestra, Vienna's second famous orchestra. In contrast to the Philharmonic, they will occasionally play modern and jazz pieces. This well-balanced mixture of classics and hot jazz draws a great variety of music fans to the **Sophiensäle**.

There are *Star Wars* too, because the Viennese fans only like those who promise quality—and stick to it. If you want to find out whether the Viennese Liedermacher scene is all we Viennese say it is, pop into the **Metropol**, the **Kulisse**, the **Rote Engel** or the **Stadthalle** from time to time. If you

concerts each, they delight the ear of their exclusive audience. Tickets are only available—and fiercely fought over—on the black market. The conductors who perform with the Philharmonic are as peerless as the orchestra. As well as Claudio Abbado, Maestro "Lennie" Bernstein or Carlos Kleiber will occasionally take up the baton. The second monument to musical tradition is the **Konzerthaus**, built in 1913. It has one large hall and two smaller ones dedicated to Mozart and Schubert. Here classics and rock music are played.

At home in the Konzerthaus—whenever they're not on a world tour—are the Vienna

want exact details of times and performances, take a look at the listings magazine *Falter* first. It's less intellectual, but more emotional. If you get to know the top Viennese product of music, you have a good chance of simply enjoying yourself—and, if you listen closely, picking up some tips for future trips into the city. As John Lennon, in love with Vienna, sang in the *Ballad of John and Yoko*: "Made a lightning trip to Vienna, eating chocolate cake in a bag." Well, there you are!

Constructive or neo-geometrical, wild, expressive, pastiche, literary or just plain different—in the early 80s the young paint-

THE WALTZ KING

Delegates from Europe, even from Russia, had come to the city on the Danube in 1814 to work out a European peace deal at the Congress of Vienna. And it worked! "The congress is dancing!" noted the eager chroniclers and were upset about the love of pleasure demonstrated by the new society dance at the Habsburg court: the most well-born ladies pressed themselves into the arms of courtiers, princes, statesmen, diplomats and spies. And in public too, devil take it!

This "frivolous" couple dance, which, so outraged the Puritans was none other than the Vien-

collapses and revolutions, social changes, twelve-tone music and the Blues. His soft, delicate musical blossoms still float over Vienna and every year, during the ball season, they fall on the city like a reviving summer rain.

Johann Strauss the Younger, director of music for the court balls in the years from 1846 to 1870, expanded the little waltz of the Biedermeier period to symphonically orchestrated chains of waltzes, whose sensuous prelude the erotically charged dance duet was fittingly compared to the steps leading up to a grand palace. His waltzing

nese waltz. One of the most prominent composers of the time, next to Joseph Lanner, was the bandmaster Johann Strauss. However, it was his eldest son, born in 1825, who went down in musical history as the master of the three-four time hit: Johann Strauss the Younger, unsurpassed Waltz King from his debut in 1844. He was a most successful bandleader and traveled extensively in Europe and even in America (in 1876), playing his waltzes to enthusiastic audiences. Any pop group could grow green with envy at his lasting success: his compositions have survived political

Left, Franz Schubert. Above, Johann Strauss in concert.

tone are the acoustic equivalent of one of the many facets of Viennese emotion and therefore, also part of the conservative principle behind Viennese charm. The waltz was and is the audible sign of a perfect world which visibly no longer exists. The genius and creator of this world was Johann Strauss Junior himself, whom Richard Wagner described as "the most musical mind of the 19th century". This composer, now commemorated by a memorial in the Vienna Stadtpark, also refined the art of popular theater, evident in the Singspiele and musical sketches, to the heights of the "Golden Age of Operetta."

His *Fledermaus*, written in 1874, is put on every New Year's Eve in a splendid production by the Vienna State Opera.

THE VIENNA BOYS' CHOIR

Their mouths open wide, their voices rise higher and higher; no dubious notes pass their lips, no weakness of voice disturbs the ear. They're all standing up straight in their blue and white sailor suits, side by side, note by note. Following parental and possibly their own ambitions, driven by their teachers into the highest ranges of the human voice, the Vienna Boys' Choir is as much a symbol of the city as St. Stephen's Cathedral and the Donauturm. They are part of the schedule for all important visitors

Schubert discovered his liking for Lieder. The present home of the Boys' Choir is as rich in tradition as their history. They rehearse in the Palais Augarten and also get through a normal school curriculum. Their home, a small hunting palace on the Danube island of Wolfsau, was built in the 17th century and is also home for another top Austrian product —the world famous Augarten porcelain.

The Palais was an exclusive place of entertainment until well into the 19th century. Here

to Vienna, and they travel the world as the youngest ambassadors for Viennese culture and clichés. Ninety-six bright clear voices, tested at primary school age for suitability and the right (i.e. Austrian) nationality, are divided into four choirs—musical representatives of a long tradition. In 1498, the Emperor Maximilian I wanted to extend the range of his court musicians by adding about 20 high-voiced choirboys. In the course of history a number of remarkable child voices from the ever expanding Boys' Choir became composers of genius.

Joseph Haydn sang top C here, and Franz

Left, statue of Peter Altenberg in the Café Central. Above, The Vienna Boys' Choir.

Wolfgang Amadeus Mozart, Ludwig van Beethoven and Johann Strauss picked up their batons to please an illustrious public. Now, in their rare moments of free time, the choirboys run about in the park.

Their Sunday outing to the Hofburgkapelle is something of a busman's holiday, for here, honoring God and delighting the (paying) visitors, they sing hymns during mass.

Nature brings an end to the career of every member of the Vienna Boys' Choir. Once his voice deepens with puberty, no boy is allowed to spoil the sound of the choir. However, a boy is not thrown out when his voice breaks. He finishes his school days in the Augarten, in the special home, the Mutantenheim for those whose voices have broken. He returns to normal life.

brush wielders stormed the Viennese (and subsequently the international) galleries and collections. There was a fireworks display of young talent. Now they work behind the Baroque facades of the houses, keeping their paintpots on the boil and getting the highest prices for their flights of fancy. Interest in painting has altered dramatically since that time, too. In early years, only the artist's best friends, a few select collectors and professional scroungers would turn up at a vernissage. Nowadays, opening parties are crammed with hundreds of birds of paradise,

earnest managers and attractive baronesses. The young artists' greatest success was to give the lie to the market forces which, in the 60s and 70s, tried to declare the painting on board or canvas to be definitely and finally out. Now they all live peacefully alongside (and sometimes with) each other: video artists, sculptors and other three-dimensional artists, conceptualists and painters.

Vienna's first painting was done in the Gothic style. The portrait of Rudolph IV, painted around 1365, is the second oldest head and shoulders portrait in Western art still in existence. It can be seen in the Diocesan Museum. But even then paintings were not without their rivals in the art world. Glass painting and stained glass provided the Viennese with their first superlative works of art and the busy labors of the court craftsmen brought them international fame. A remnant of this time, the Habsburg Window, fills St. Stephen's Cathedral with delicate light. The artists of the next generation wrestled with the real world through the medium of courtly, spiritual, blue-blooded Gothic painting. Biblical events were often only a foreground distraction for a background scene of Vienna. Art and nature formed a typically Viennese symbiosis, finally crowned by the Danube School in the early 16th century.

The arts scene

High and Late Baroque brought international tensions back into the art world. The imperial city of Vienna exerted a magnetic attraction on artists all over the world. Viennese masters traveled to study their Flemish and Italian idols. You can see Baroque masterpieces free of admission charges if you go to the churches and look at the frescos. Take Johann Spillenberger for instance, who was particularly impressed by Titian and Tintoretto. He painted the *Holy Family* in the Dominikanerkirche and *St. Anne* in the Augustinerkirche. Martin Johann Schmidt, generally known as "Kremser Schmidt", whose works can also be seen in the Kunsthistorisches Museum, painted the frescos in the Karmeliterkirche and the Melkerhofkapelle. The pompous Baroque imagery was perfected by Franz Anton Maulpertsch. He took the reality, the opulent, extravagant lifestyle, and exaggerated it to realistic yet fantastical, theatrical works of art.

In Baroque times it was mostly the nobility who took pleasure in paintings. In the Biedermeier period the more comfortable middle class taste was for small canvasses and watercolors, still life and family portraits. The artistic movement of the Vormärz

Above, Pallas Athene above the Minervabrunnen. Right, concert in the Musikverein hall.

"EVERYBODY DANCE THE WALTZ"

When this clichéd imperative is shouted out with great feeling on the last Thursday during Fasching (Viennese carnival), the elegant restraint of permed ladies and well-dressed gentlemen turns to crazy chaos as they dance on the spot to waltz music, gently decadent, with heavy jewelry swaying in time to the music.

Dinner jackets hung with medals scratch necks draped with pearls; merciless high heels dig into innocent feet. The scene swirls and bubbles like a cauldron, it's a magnificent fairground, a display of human vanities: the Opera Ball! Showtime!

in seven dance halls. Gaming tables round off the nonstop entertainment on offer.

The Opera Ball! A magnificent successor to the even more magnificent Court Opera Balls which delighted imperial Vienna from 1877 on. However, the end of the nobility meant that the balls also came to a democratic end. The Opera Ball was not revived until 1935, and that was bad timing! World War II put an end to the good times when the Opera House was bombed. This most magnificent ball, the essence of "noblesse oblige", wasn't held again until 1965. It's held

For one champagne-soaked night the Opera obeys only its own rules. The most important is to see and be seen, possibly by one of the many TV teams hunting for extravagant ballgowns and dinner jackets among the VIPs. They get enough of those in front of the camera. The King and Queen of Spain let themselves be intoxicated by waltz tunes, Prince Philip attempted a dance here, and the star tenor Luciano Pavarotti squeezed his enormous if resonant bulk into a starched dinner shirt for this ball of balls. Highly animated enjoyment and small-talk are flung together in the dignified Opera House, which disguises itself for this evening as a great palace of pleasure, with 24,000 carnations piled up in towering bouquets and with jazzing and waltzing orchestras playing

every year, but it is expensive.

A 2,000 schilling ticket is positively cheap. A table costs you between 3,000 and 10,000 schilling. If you want to be able to withdraw to the privacy of one of the 150 boxes, you'll need to fork out between 60,000 and 130,000 schilling. It's undeniable that the opening ceremony at 10 p.m. can be seen most comfortably while drinking champagne in one of the boxes. Eighty white dresses, their owners with tiaras in their hair, float beside young men in tails, sweaty hands in white gloves. *Jeunesse dorée* makes an entrance into the adult world. Every year about a thousand hopeful couples apply to Opera Ball organiser Lotte Tobisch for the opening dance. For most of them it remains a dream.

painted pictures that were a reaction to academic Neo-classicism. One of their notable winners was Ferdinand Georg Waldmüller, whose meditative landscape idylls were later used as models by the Impressionists.

But before Impressionists and introverts gained a hold over Viennese studios, the pseudo-Baroque splendors of the Gründerzeit came into fashion in the second half of the 19th century. A decadent, extravagant lifestyle was reflected in decorative, colorful art, as in the Makart style. No-one else had more influence over the art of

the Fin de siécle than the glittering personality, Hans Makart. An oracle in matters of taste, ennobled as State Artist by the Emperor, he decorated the new magnificent buildings along the Ringstraße with Rubenesque frescos. This sensual painter reached the peak of his personality cult when he designed the celebrations to mark the silver wedding jubilee of the Emperor and Empress in 1879. All along the Ringstraße, Makart organized a magnificent fancy dress party, a choreographed masterpiece in the style of the "German Renaissance". The

Left, the Opera Ball. Above, Arthur Schnitzler.

professional and craft associations marched in historic costume, the artists accompanying them were put into Rubens-style clothing. Makart's exaggerated aestheticism even impressed the young Gustav Klimt, but this Makart imitator soon found his own style. The academic Künstlerhaus—an association of Viennese artists and meeting place for the Ringstraße art world—would not stand for new developments within its walls, so in 1897, 19 rebellious artists founded the Vereinigung bildender Künstler Secession (the Association of the Secession of Pictorial Artists). The association building was designed by co-founder Joseph Olbrich and given a cupola in the shape of a leafy treetop—which earned it the disrespectful nickname of "Krauthappel" (cabbage top). From now on things were busy in the art world. Klimt was the president of the Secession until the Klimt-Gruppe split up in 1905. He laid the basic foundations for one of the most varied and exciting scenarios. Egon Schiele, Austria's model expressionist and nowadays a quick starter at multi-million auctions, had no quarrel with the Secessionists at the beginning of his artistic career at least. Oskar Kokoschka, poet and painter, developed the linear elements of Art Nouveau into color-intensive landscapes, allegories and portraits. The pictorial creativity, the abstract and geometrical experiments of the Secessionists and also of artists such as Anton Kolig or Boeckl, came to an abrupt end at the time of World War II.

Kitsch took the place of art in the exhibition halls. What had previously counted as "art" was now called "entartet"—estranged, decadent. Jewish collections disappeared along with their owners and were found, if at all, only many years later. Many artists who escaped the extermination machine preferred never to return. The first post-war generation of artists stood in front of this ghostly heap of rubble, confronted by imperial attitudes which under the Nazis had been patched up into that blind faith in authority which is all too often trivialised as "respect", and made an attempt at cultural regeneration. One of the first to take avant garde artists under his wing was by profession a

THE BURG

"No illegitimate children are allowed on the stage, and kings must always be good", the intellectuals sneered in 1845, when censors tried to turn the plays written for the "Nationaltheater nächst der Burg" into inoffensive little plays.

Censorship has been out for a long time. But kings, even if not good, must at least be well played. Of course people talk about the play too! And about the director, yes they do! And nowadays often about the setting as well. But the most important thing for the Viennese is the cast. The acting! The cult of the actors at the Burgtheater is

In the theater on the Michaelerplatz "well-crafted translations" and "German originals" were performed, while a new theater was being built on the Ring, following designs by Karl Hasenauer and Gottfried Semper. Even Ernst and Gustav Klimt picked up a brush in order to paint part of the ceiling, decorated in an opulent imitation Renaissance style.

On October 14, 1888, the financial and social elite of Vienna streamed through the gold-topped gates to the official opening, led by Emperor Franz Joseph and his sideburns. The play was

traditional—and has some justification. This is where top stars have celebrated the high dramatic art. Even today the cast lists are filled with famous actors: Klaus Maria Brandauer, Gert Voss, Erika Pluhar. And all the rest of them.

"Burg" is short for one of the oldest theaters in the world. The first lady of the "Burg" was Empress Maria Theresia. In 1741, she granted the use of an empty ballroom in the Hofburg for the "Theater nächst der Burg". Her son Joseph II actually took charge of the theater himself for a short time. His Majesty the director promoted the theater to "Nationaltheater" in 1776 and gave the actors the rank of court official. The reforming Emperor forbade curtain calls, a prohibition which is still respected today.

Esther, by the Austrian classic playwright Grillparzer. The first reactions were of humorous complaint: "In Parliament you can't hear anything, in the Town Hall you can't see anything and in the Burgtheater you can't hear or see anything." The grumblers were right. Ten years later the auditorium was adapted to improve the poor acoustics. The "Burg" was seriously damaged during the war—a fire in 1945 left the theater with only the shell—and was restored in the early 50s. Artistic quality wasn't damaged by this intermission lasting nearly 10 years, and neither was the ever-entertaining party game of sneering at the current director. It's not meant to be snide, not at all. It's simply the other side of the Viennese theater world's heart of gold, that's all.

priest. Monsignore Otto Mauer was, in his secondary job, in charge of the **Galerie nächst St. Stephan**, the most important postwar forum for artists. Today the Galerie—now under secular direction—still deserves praise for its support of modern art. An enormous exercise of will-power and talent led to an avant garde scene, which had no reason to fear comparison with other nations, emerging from the postwar cultural vacuum.

Within Austria they were often still condemned as *enfants terribles*, but abroad, himself and others with black or monochrome curtains, painter of crucifixes and, on top of all that, individualistically self-taught, can get collectors at home and abroad to pay a high price per square centimeter for his works. Friedensreich Hundertwasser's rainy day dark colors, spirals and onion domes decorate walls all over the world too.

Creativity

More traditional and much less criticized paths have been followed by the develop-

their works hung in galleries and museums. The Aktionisten, provocateurs par excellence, only upset bigotted purists nowadays. In the 60s they would have called the police in, but in the spring of 1987, only vigorous participation by the mostly youthful audience marked Nitsch's use of the Secession as a background for splattering, smearing and painting in blood and red paint.

Arnulf Rainer, constructive destructivist, hand and finger painter, programming cover-ups and retouching of photographs of

Left, the Burgtheater. Above, theater at the Spittelberg.

ment of the Viennese "Fantastic Realism" since the 60s. The public had fewer problems understanding those works than with the abstracts of Maria Lassnig or Oswald Oberhuber, for instance, or with the dry, abstract sculpture of Karl Prantl. In the works of the *Phantasten* you can see whatever you want. In the orgasmic colors of Ernst Fuchs or Arik Bauer you can see figures and allegories, and in Rudolf Hausner's work there are no problems in recognizing the creator as "Adam".

Now, however, Vienna is without its own style. Creativity is an individual process, which can be publicly observed in the art galleries. The newcomers to the art market are as varied as the forms of artistic expression. Not all of them can keep up the standard to a ripe old age—either artistically or financially. But there are plenty of reasons for excitement. Who will make the grade? The tin can sculptor Erwin Wurm, or the paper sculptor Heimo Zobernig, the Old Master of the "Neuen Wilden" Siegfried Anzinger or his contemporary Hubert Schmalix, the "geometrical" Gerwald Rockenschaub or Herbert Brandl, who lays it on thick? We shall see. You must go and see

ated, mannerist, theatrical language. But you shouldn't disturb the sacred cows. No Viennese theater performed her criticism of the world of art and patronage. *Burgtheater* was staged only in Germany. And yet, literary reflections of reality have a long tradition. In the last century, Franz Grillparzer, a sort of Austrian copy of Goethe, was delighted by squabbles over the succession and versified them into *Bruderzwist im Hause Habsburg* (Brotherly Strife in the House of Habsburg), which is still performed today with appropriate pathos. The anonymous

them, in the galleries of Vienna, where as a rule, a new star rises over the artistic horizon about once a month.

From the Burg to Spitelberg

"Well, really!" and "Is she allowed to do that?" Snorts of indignation and sharp paragraphs of scorn poured down on the Austrian author, Elfriede Jelinik. In her satirical piece *Burgtheater* she looked at the house of the same name on the Ring and particularly at its most famous dynasty of actors. She looked for skeletons of the Nazi past in their cupboards and packaged her finds in exagger-

epic poet who wrote the *Nibelungenlied* in the Middle Ages, kept to the realities of the Dark Ages in his verses. Karl Kraus, the sharp-tongued chronicler and critic of his times, dumped his whole loathing of the intellectuals, artists, warmongers, dimwitted monarchs and political parties of the new 20th century into *Die letzten Tage der Menschheit* (The Last Days of Mankind).

Karl Kraus showed a certain amount of *Schadenfreude* when, concerned not only about poor interpretation but also the sheer size of his drama, he remarked that it could probably only be performed by some theater on the Moon. Thomas Bernhard, probably the best known contemporary Austrian literary talent, also seems to be plagued by doubts about appropriate staging of his dramas. This talented Lord High Complainer to the nation, whose novels and plays give Viennese society and politics the expected bad report, has only been performed since director Claus Peymann swept through the Burgtheater with the thoroughness of a German new broom. Before this, Bernhard had refused to let his plays be performed in Vienna. Then, he had *Ritter, Dene, Voss*, which was written especially for the top stars

ensemble search for the causes and the after effects of the Nazi years. The works of authors, from the period between the wars are being scanned with particular care for definitive statements. What's in a name —the favored writer of the *Jura Soyfer Theatre*, which sets up its stage in the open air near the Spittelberg, is Jura Soyfer. He wrote during the First Republic—melancholy, political, popular comedies for the proletariat.

Naturally Austrian literature does exist outside the theater. But Viennese poetry, particularly between the 16th and the 19th

in Peymann's team of comedy actors, peformed in Salzburg and then in Vienna. Peter Turrini also writes plays critical of society. His latest work, *Die Minderleister*, a tragedy of unemployment set in Austria's deprived region of Styria, had hardly been typed up when both the Vienna Festival and the Akademietheater snapped up the rights to the premier of this committed political work. Political committment features in the repertoires of most small to medium companies. In the *Kreis*, George Tabori and his

Left, inscription on the Secession. Above, staircase on the Museum of Modern Art.

century, was almost exclusively dramatic. The Viennese, still often illiterate, were offered snippets of culture in the theater. A number of theaters shot out of the ground. November 30, 1709 saw the birth of the new Kärntnertortheater; in spring 1788 the theater in der Josefstadt, still a center for middle-class audiences today, opened its doors for the first time; in 1801 the Theater an der Wien was opened, in which Peter Weck now stages his continously sold out song-and-dance musicals. The Habsburgs desired that the language of the stage should be predominantly Viennese. The main difference between the Viennese style and the

WAGNER AND LOOS

In the middle of the architectural amalgam of ostentatious monuments to the Ringstraße era and contemporary top drawer kitsch there is an aesthetic affirmation of functionalism: the Postsparkassenamt (Post Office Savings Bank), built from 1904 to 1907 by the Viennese architectural genius Otto Wagner. The architectural manifestos of modernity had changed Wagner's own heavy Historicist past into a creed of rationalism: "Nothing that isn't useful can be beautiful". Enthusiastically hailed by the intellectuals of the "Junges Wien" movement as one of the "greatest

turned after four years in the USA, to embark on his plain and simple designs. His first success was the decoration in 1899 of the "Café Museum", popular with artists. It was done without Fin de siécle plush or Art Nouveau fads. The café soon gained the name "Café Nihilism", and Loos gained the reputation of an exciting newcomer in the field of architecture. Although fond of women, he designed the "American Bar" in the Kärntner Durchgang some years later, and the female population of Vienna was up in arms. Women were not allowed into the little mirrored

generals" of architectural innovation, he left his native city a number of pieces of futuristic architecture. Still influenced by Art Nouveau, he built apartment blocks along the Wienzeile.

He improved the Stadtbahn with stations designed in loving detail. He designed defence structures, houses and furniture. Less compromising than Wagner in dealing with the decorative tradition in architecture was his colleague Adolf Loos, some 30 years younger. He was an architect and also a brilliant and provoking critic. In the absence of sufficient contracts, Loos at first realized his revolutionary ideas of architecture as an expert author. He sneered at Vienna, with its palaces and highly ornamental façades, as a "Central European village" to which he had re-

bar. But that didn't last long.

After only five weeks ladies sat sipping spirits at the elegant bar. A bigger and longer-lasting scandal was provided by this most elegant utility fanatic when he designed the office block in the Michaelerplatz. Clever use of space and exquisite, rhythmically and mathematically proportioned materials instead of stucco and curlicues—and right opposite the Hofburg, dumped right under the Emperor's nose! "House with no eyebrows!" "The Hideous House!" the conservative critics raged. Loos' employer stayed calm—and Loos was proved right. Today they're all on the sighseeing tour— the palaces and the Hofburg as well as the architectural works of art by Wagner and Loos.

German poetry of didacticism and reason lay in a melancholy tendency to dreaminess and poetic isolation. Ferdinand Raimund, fairytale-teller of the Biedermeier period, imagined the protagonists of his magical plays out of Vormärz reality and into wonderful (and somewhat kitsch) fairylands. At the same time, Franz Grillparzer allowed the question of mutability to dissolve in *König Ottokars Gluük und Ende*. Adalbert Stifter filled his novels with Romantic studies of landscape and people. His contemporary, Johann Nestroy lent an ear to the ordinary people of the suburbs and in his cyncial sketches he fantasized the moral triumph of a poor honest craftsman over the corrupt nouveau riche and slimy officials. His piece *Der Zerissene,* offers a study of Viennese character still valid today: "Jetzt möcht' ich sehen, wer stärker ist: i oder i." (Now I want to see who's the stronger: me or me.) Later, Kraus also documented his schizophrenic literary existence as an optimist in *Die Letzten Tagen.* Kraus' contemporary, the poetic doctor Arthur Schnitzler, just about perfected the inner monologue in *Das Weite Land.* Today, the novelist Peter Handke writes monologues about his continual journeys into his own inner self, while Barbara Frischmuth's trilogy—beginning with *Die Mystifikation der Sophie Silber*—keeps up the mythic poetical tradition of a Raimund or Richard Beer-Hofmann and develops it into a feminist manifesto for the 80s.

Author! Author!

The flowering of countless literary talents turned Vienna, especially at the beginning of this century, into a splendid garden of authors. The "Junges Wien" movement even refined newspaper feature writing and criticism. Many an art critic today still borrows from the language of Peter Altenberg or Egon Friedell. Articles, anecdotes and quotes by and about Viennese coffee house literati are on the reading list of today's

generation. For instance, Hermann Bahr, doyen of the literary scene, is supposed to have searched eagerly for "Loris", who had reviewed Bahr's play *Mutter* in stylistically mature language and with sparkling intelligence. "Loris" was unmasked: he was the grammar school boy Hugo von Hofmannsthal. Arthur Schnitzler, attending his first poetry reading, wrote: "For the first time in my life I had the feeling that I was in the presence of someone who was born a genius. Never again in my life would I feel this way so overwhelmingly again." Hitler and his

thugs brutally turned intellectual Vienna into provincial Dullsville.

Books were burned, the authors, mainly Jewish, driven away. In exile, Stefan Zweig and his second wife committed suicide together. Those who had survived the Nazi terror often stayed in the countries that had offered them refuge in their hour of danger, for instance Manés Sperber, Elias Canetti or the poet Erich Fried.

Hilde Spiel became a traveler, commuting between exile and home, and only a few returned permanently to the city where Hitler had cruelly realized his threat: "Vienna is a pearl, I shall give it a setting which

Left, Loos' house in the Michaelerplatz. Above, Art Nouveau staircase in the Wienzeile.

is worthy of it." H.C. Artmann was one of the first after the War to separate the German language from its Austrian neighbor: Many manifestos of Austrian independence and sorrowful analyses of the past followed. Nowadays, all forms of the language are at home in the theater: West German slang, Viennese colloquial speech, the dialect of the suburbs or cultured upper-class "Schönbrunn" German. In the Vienna English Theatre they even speak perfect English. More than 50 theaters and independent theater groups make for a busy repertoire.

Even the Empress Maria Theresia knew that: "You have to have spectacle, otherwise you simply can't live in such a great residence." A truly wise pronouncement by a wise monarch, fitting not only for its time, but also for today's tourist industry.

Treasures and curios

Admittedly, for some people the whole of Vienna is a big open-air museum. There are the Baroque palaces, and there is the broad spectrum of Viennese characters, from the "court" official who is neither court nor courtesy to the caretaker who doesn't care,

who, as permanent tourist attractions, have refined the art of complaint to its pinnacle in the Viennese version of *Raunzen*. Around five hundred monuments litter the streets of Vienna for you to view free of charge—impish cherubs pressed against hefty palace gates; busts of artists in marble, white as whipped cream; gigantic imperial statues; chiselled hero-worship. Once you've seen, you'll understand. Of course Raphael Donner could only do justice to himself and his Baroque fountain at the Neuer Markt in the open air. Neither would the magnificent majesties of Peter and Paul Strudel fit into a cramped little museum.

Apart from the open air attractions, there are large numbers of artistic temples, all with the proper atmosphere, in Vienna. There are those that even the Viennese don't really know. There are rumoured to be barely a thousand regular local visitors who take an interest in the collections of art or curios, which are certainly up to the highest European standards. However, there are many millions from abroad or from the provinces who come to enjoy the local collections.

In the course of history almost everything that nature and the human race have created has been collected. Art, absurdities, stuffed extinct animals, tools and household articles, relics of the entertainment industry such as the circus, funeral parlors or the theater. How many cities have their own theater museum with varying displays? The largest collection of the graphic arts in the world is in Vienna. The drawings—from Dürer, Raffael, Michelangelo right through to Schiele—are kept in the **Albertina**.

In the early 19th century, the Belgian architect Louis de Montoyer altered the old Palais Taroucca. The main room was decorated by Joseph Kornhäusel. The core of the art collection of the Goethemuseum of the Goethe Association—this is the official name—came from the private collection of Duke Albert of Saxe-Teschen. The drawings and etchings from the imperial Hofbibliothek eventually found their way into the Albertina as well.

About 9,200 chronological devices tick, chime, strike and stop in the **Uhrenmuseum** (clock museum). The most valuable piece is an astronomical clock, nine feet (three meters) high. The most astronomical thing about it is the time needed for the hand to circle round the dial once. You'll need to have patience; it takes 20,964 years!

Johann Nestroy, fearless cynic and critic of the Vormärz period, was during his lifetime afraid only of two things: being bitten by a dog and being inadvertently buried alive. He wanted to ensure against the latter by using the death knell. On his death, a string was to be laid from his coffin to the button, the floor of this simple wooden box opened, dropping the corpse directly into the grave, but leaving the coffin free to be taken home again. Joseph II left the Viennese another curious legacy of his mere ten years of rule. A man of intellect and progress, he wanted his military doctors to have the best possible educational aids for their anatomical studies, before they were let loose on his soldiers. For this purpose he imported life-sized wax figures from Italy, plus the inner organs to be studied. The wax dummies and embryos can be seen in the **Josefinum**, the

sexton's house. In case of unexpected re-animation he would pull the string and get the bell in the house to sound the death knell. This curious alarm bell is one of the attractions of the **Bestattungsmuseum**. Another dates from the time of the economically minded Emperor Joseph II. He upset his funeral-loving Viennese with a very peculiar invention: the re-usable coffin. An alternative to opulent final resting places, this could be used repeatedly. On pressing a

Left, anatomical figure in the Josefinum. Above, the car in which the Archduke Ferdinand was assassinated, in the Heeresmuseum.

museum for the history of medicine.

His relatives Rudolph II and Archduke William had somewhat more sense of "higher" art, and their collections concentrated on masterpieces from Italy. They brought Tintorettos, Titians or pictures by Bernado Bellotto alias Canaletto to Vienna. A splendid setting for these imperial riches is the : **Kunsthisorisches Museum**. Built in 1891 in the style of the Italian Renaissance, the twelve departments of this temple of art—ranging from Egyptian mummys to enchanting porcelain and to masterpieces by Breughel, Rembrandt, Rubens, or Van Dyck in the picture gallery—provide an opulent feast for the eyes.

Imperial opulence is the keynote of the symbols of temporal and spiritual power sparkling in their modern glass cases in the **Schatzkammer** (Imperial Treasury) **of the Hofburg**. Imperial crowns and coronation regalia, scepters, the Orb of the Empire, the Golden Fleece, reliqueries set with jewels, ceremonial papal robes, small domestic altars, strictly segregated according to sacred or profane usage, they are evidence of the imperial splendor of past ages.

If you are interested in the 19th and 20th centuries, you will have to go on a treasure hunt through the museums. Museum directors, ministries, architects and other such experts may be busily projecting, planning and conceptualising a museum complex in the former imperial stables in the Lastenstraße, but whether the project of the century, which has already gained the cheeky name of "Vienna's Pompidou Center", will ever make it from nebulous dream to real museum, is a question which only an astrologer could answer with any degree of accuracy. At the moment, the exhibitions are scattered all over the city. Here is one suggested route for the Museum Rally: From the **Neue Galerie** in the Stallburg to the **Upper Belvedere** which was once the residence of Prince Eugene, today home mainly for the works of Austrian painters. Carry on to the **Museum des 20. Jahrhunderts** (Museum of the 20th century) with its sculpture garden opposite the Südbahnhof, filled with national and international works of art. Go back through the city to the 9. Bezirk, and you will find the **Museum für moderne Kunst** (Museum of Modern Art), specializing in American pop art, in the Baroque Palais Liechtenstein. On the way, make a diversion to the **Künstlerhaus**, with its architecturally arranged major exhibitions and to the **Secession**, which offers exciting works fresh from the studios. In the **Museum für Angewandte Kunst** in the Stubenring style and design are internationally mixed; everyday art, architecture and other art forms all make a colorful mixture.

Another colorful place is the most laughable museum in Vienna. The author Heino

Seitler may have had to give up his dream of earning his living as a clown, but he didn't want to do without a circus atmosphere entirely. He made his own Big Top. From 1927 on he has been collecting masks, costumes and tinselly knicknacks from the circus world. For visitors to his **Clown Museum** he will even expose some of the strictly guarded tricks of circus performers.

Pure science, not conjuring, was involved early this century when Sigmund Freud asked a paralysed patient to lie down on his couch, diagnosed her through psychoanaly-

sis as hysterical, and then let her go again. Today, the **Sigmund Freud Museum** occupies the house where the famous soul searcher lived and, ignoring the hostility of his "colleagues", hunted through the subconscious of his patients for childhood traumas and neuroses.

The Dokumentationsarchiv des Österreichischen Widerstandes (Archive of the Austrian Resistance) works on the collective and not the individual subconscious (or would-be unconscious) and reminds Austrians of what many would rather forget. Documents, letters and photographs give a moving picture of Austria under Hitler. At that time the Habsburg motto: "Let others make war: you, happy Austria, make marriages!" had long been out of date. However, even the Habsburg Emperors didn't always stick to it when they felt like adding some new territory. The collection of weapons in the **Waffensammlung** in the Heldenplatz and in the **Heeresgeschichtliche Museum** show their warlike aspect.

Austrian inventiveness, intended to further progress and the well-being of humanity, is preserved in the **Technisches Museum**. The production of tobacco, from leaf smoke. There's an atmosphere of sensual coziness in the only **Sex Museum** in Europe, too. Children aren't allowed in this domain of the erotic—whose goddess is supposed to be Venus, according to astrology. In Vienna, however, Venus isn't to be found in the Sex Museum but in the **Naturhistorisches Museum** (Natural History Museum), along with mammoths, small animals and exciting biological discoveries. As "Venus of Willensdorf", she is the oldest work of art in the Viennese region, dating from the Ice Age. The Venus of Willensdorf, actually a

to pipe, is portrayed in the Tabakmuseum: "Ohne Rauch geht's auch" (smoke isn't really necessary) is one of the slogans of the anti-smoking campaign, which really doesn't have much effect here. Not only is the Tabakmuseum the only museum in which smoking is permitted, but there are oil paintings showing Biedermeier idylls of cozy smoking rooms, while strange cigarette holders and almost architectural pipes conjure a bit of worldiness into the blue

Left, table laid for dinner in Franz Joseph's apartments. Above, crown of the Holy Roman Empire.

rather ugly figure, was created long before the Roman camp of Vindabona. However, the Romans did lay the basic ground plan for Vienna when they built their northern outpost against German barbarians around A.D. 40. This fact, and the subsequent eventful history of nearly 2,000 years, is excellently explained in the **Historisches Museum der Stadt Wien** (Historical Museum of the City of Vienna). Fluctuating between present and past, between serious and light-hearted— Vienna is not a museum city (not any longer), but is definitely a city of museums. For this reason alone, a visit to Vienna is a must.

THE VIENNESE

Viennese humor and Viennese grumpiness, Viennese Gemütlichkeit and the Viennese heart of gold—does any of it exist? Or is it perhaps just an illusion, like the little angels, who spend their holidays—where else?—in Vienna, at least according to a popular song. Dream and reality, caricature and original, the Viennese zigzag between these poles, constantly in danger of falling into sugarsweet pretense. Usually it's left to the last moment before they snap out of it and wink with self-directed irony: "It's all not true." If you believe it, it's your own fault.

Cliché city

Clichés are carefully guarded and polished up before each new surge of tourists arrives. "If we're not feeling cheerful, well then we're just a bit grumpy, if you please, your humble servant". Complaining in the style of the former film legend Hans Moser is part of the repertoire of every self-appointed one-man show between Grinzig and Kagran. And the Viennese undeniably like complaining about their city. But woe betide the "outsider" who dares to criticize us. Then we stick together like *The Third Man*. After all, we've nothing to be ashamed of, certainly not a few Nazi smears on our spotless past. The world's an ungrateful place, a sigh that's often heard in Vienna. After what we've done for the world: Maria Theresia and Bruno Kreisky, Johnny Strauss and Falco, Wiener sausages and Sachertorte. Tirelessly the Vienna Boys' Choir and the Lipizzaner horses travel the globe as special ambassadors of good will, in the New Year concert, the Philharmonic fiddles away on satellite TV, showing the world from Greenland to Timbuctoo what culture is all about. Major decisions in world politics may be made elsewhere today, but we only have to pop into the Kapuzinergruft where the Habsburgs are buried to remind ourselves

Preceding pages: Viennese housewives chatting. Left, a Fiaker.

that we are great. Or at least, we were once great. After all, we still live quite happily on the interest paid by the past. "Good day, Your Honours, would the longer city tour please you? From Schönbrunn to Mayerling, war and love, all included in the price".

The world has simply painted its own picture of Vienna and the Viennese, and we sigh and try to fit in. We're not interested in the invasion of the culture seekers. We'd rather invade our local round the corner and calmly watch events from a distance, through clouds of steam from the roast with

is Beautiful". Instead of slimming, a few seams are let out, it's that simple. Warning voices calling for restraint in this Land of Cockaigne are "not even ignored", which is why cholesterol levels are on the rise nationally. The so-called "Viennese cuisine" is rich and heavy. Nouvelle cuisine and healthy fiber is for ascetic weirdos.

The home-grown cuisine can claim to be a melting pot unique in the world. There may be no specific Paris, Berlin or London cuisine, but the collection of recipes and snacks innocently titled "Viennese cuisine" defi-

dumplings. Live and let live is our motto.

Food in Venice

People eat well in Vienna. For once that's no cliché but the obvious truth. "You're looking well" is one of the highest possible compliments among Viennese, and means that the person addressed is heavily overweight. The current ideal of beauty would probably make any figure-conscious American woman go on several months of severe diet. Vienna must be the only western capital in which a large fashion house has had several years of success with the slogan "Plump

nitely exists. It's a giant plagiarism of the most varied dishes of the multi-cultural Empire; Hungarian, Bohemian, Italian, Serbian, Croatian, Slovenian, Friaulian and Dalmatian national dishes, adapted to the Viennese palate.

The basic ingredient of most dishes is still the famous (or infamous) "einbrenn", a sauce made from butter and flour. From soup to vegetables to the paprika-flavoured stew à la goulash it's used in everything to "refine" it, thus neutralizing the taste. Meat is usually eaten "paniert", i.e. rolled in flour, egg and breadcrumbs and then fried swimming in lard or oil. It's claimed that the world famous Wiener Schnitzel was actually invented in Milan, a rumour which every housewife and cook considers a personal insult. At any rate, historical discoveries in the State Archives do show that Field Marshal Radetzky, returning from Italy in the year of revolution, 1848, not only reported to the Imperial government in Vienna on the defeat of the rebels but also mentioned a certain "costoletto alla Milanese" and gave the recipe to the Imperial kitchens—in the strictest confidence, of course.

The undeniable Viennese peculiarity,

man's Sunday dinner for many years. His satisfied inspection of this dish took up more time than half the meal. At first his eye caressed the delicate border of fat which surrounded the colossal piece of meat, then the individual little plates, on which the vegetables were served, the violet sheen of the beetroot, the rich green of the first spinach, the cheerful pale lettuce, the plain white of horseradish, the faultless ovals of the new potatoes, swimming in melting butter, which reminded him of dainty little toys... A fortunate fate allowed Trotta to unite the

however, is the cult of beef. Beef dishes have their fixed place on every menu, from the small pubs to the expensive restaurants. The dish of "Tafelspitz" isn't eaten, it's celebrated. In his novel, *Radetzkymarsch,* the author Joseph Roth describes the traditional Sunday meal of Tafelspitz in the family of a civil servant, Trotta. The meal acts as a symbol for the fading, quaintly pedantic Imperial world: "After the soup, the garnished "Tafelspitz" was brought in, the old

Right, outside the Demel. Above, at the sausage stall

satisfaction of his appetite with the demands of his duty. His was a Spartan nature. But he was an Austrian."

The famous restaurant in the Graben, Meissl & Schadn, which no longer exists, had 26 different kinds of boiled beef on its menu, from Tellerfleisch (a stew of cheaper cuts) to joint-sized Kruspelspitz. On October 26, 1916, after dining on one of these dishes, young Friedrich Adler, son of the legendary founder of the Austrian Social Democrats, Viktor Adler, carefully wiped his lips on his napkin, walked over to Graf Sturgkh, who was dining at the next table, introduced himself with a well-mannered bow—and shot the unloved Prime Minister dead. The world ends in style, at least it does in Vienna.

Today there isn't much in the way of shooting in Viennese restaurants, but the service tries too hard to please—particularly at tourist times. Then, the astonished Viennese sit staring at the menu thinking they're in Bielefeld or Omaha. Apricots instead of Marillen and Hawaiian style roast pork—it's enough to give you the horrors. Flight to the Konditorei (pastry shop) is a must.

Powidltatschlkerln, Guglhupf, Wuchteln,

The original Sachertorte

Sachertorte or Sacher Torte (depending which Konditorei you patronize) is perhaps the best-known Viennese cake. The original Sachertorte, a very rich chocolate cake iced with more chocolate, was invented in the kitchens of the Hotel Sacher about a hundred years ago. Several other Konditoreien also serve almost identical cakes—but the Hotel Sacher even went to court to establish its exclusive right to the name.

Now there is original Sachertorte, spelled

Millirahmstrudel, Palatschinken, Mohnbeugerl, Golatschn—Viennese cakes defy translation and description. The only answer is to eat them. The highest praise for a piece of the Viennese pastrycook's art is to say it's "like a poem".

Translations for foreign guests are often lengthy or unintentionally comic. "Besoffene Kapuziner", little cakes soaked in alcohol, turn into "drunk monks", "Topfengolatschn" become "puff pastry cottage cheese buns". So if you are faced with "Gebackene Mäuse" (literally: baked mice), don't panic. These are merely a form of Krapfen, a crispier, lighter relative of the doughnut.

as one word and sold in the Hotel Sacher, and there is Sacher Torte (two words, as sold everywhere else), the copy. The Konditorei Demel objects, however, and claims to possess the true original Sachertorte—their argument is based on the fact that the chef who invented it left the Sacher and came to work at the Demel, bringing the recipe with him.

Eating in Vienna is always combined with communication. If you want to test this statement, go to one of the two hundred or so Würstelstände (sausage stalls), which are

Above, Café Griensteidel.

THE BASSENA

A hundred thousand tenants in Vienna still live in so-called substandard flats, with no heating or proper sanitary arrangements. A fine front with a vile interior behind it was the rule for the gigantic tenements that were built around the turn of the century to absorb the constant stream of people from all parts of the Empire. One room, kitchen, cupboard was the description of an average flat for a large working class family. The center of events was the famous (or infamous) "Bassena", the communal standpipe. In 1910, there were still nearly 80,000 "hot-bedders" in Vienna, homeless

dries, nurseries and creches, libraries and lecture halls. A working class culture evolved. People learned Esperanto or joined the anti-clerical "Freidenkerbund" (Free Thinkers' Association), the pub round the corner was called "Zur Zukunft" (The Future).

Now preserved for posterity, the **Werkbundsiedlung** on the outskirts of Vienna is considered a jewel. Here Austrian and foreign architects, among them famous names such as Adolf Loos and Josef Hoffmann, realized their ideas of socialist lifestyle. The crown of these develop-

Above, dilapidated house of the Biedermeier.

people who rented a bed while its owner was out at work. Landlords reigned like absolute monarchs in their castles. Protection for tenants and restrictions on eviction were only achieved after a struggle after the First World War.

In the 20s, "Red Vienna" began its socialist administration with the building programs that still make up the townscape in many parts of the city. The so-called "Gemeindebauten" or community buildings were put up. These were blocks of flats with light, dry little apartments, garden courtyards and communal facilities such as laun-

ments, however, was and is the **Karl-Marx-Hof** in the green 19. Bezirk. It is exactly 0.621-mile (one-km) long and is built of 25 million bricks. During the confusions of the civil war of 1934, the "Reds" held out here against the "Black (i.e. Fascist) class society" and had to surrender after only a few days.

Today, young families compete for the flats, the old who fight for a better future, guard their memories like a long-sunken precious treasure. For every new community flat in the tower blocks on the other bank of the Danube, with a balcony on the sunny side of the street, there are tens of thousands of people on the waiting list. At the same time, there is a huge modernization program to improve the Bassena flats.

THE TYPICAL VIENNESE WOMAN
By Mayor Dr. Helmut Zilk

Only the dry statistical facts are definitely true: the women of Vienna will soon reach a life expectancy of 80 years and, and make up 55 percent of the population, definitely a stronger sex in the Austrian capital. All the rest is cliché, immortalized all over the world by literature (for centuries) and by films (over the last few decades). The range extends from the sweet laundry maid to the buxom Heuriger barmaid and the plump, comfortable Schnitzel cook to the dignified eldery court official's widow, who saw the

probably made it easier to connect Josefine Mutzenbacher and her reminiscences of life as a good-time girl with Vienna rather than indisputably great figures such as the Nobel Peace Prize winner Bertha von Suttner, the author Maria Ebner-Escherbach or the atomic physicist Lise Meitner.

It may sound like a paradox, but the typical Viennese woman often doesn't come from Vienna, or at least her ancestors aren't Viennese. In this you can still see Vienna's former role as

Emperor in person and spends the afternoons in the coffee house playing bridge with others of her sort. The legendary Donauweibchen (Danube woman) also belongs here—the Viennese version of the Lorelei and the ancient sirens who lures sailors to their doom in the river Danube. The motto that limits the Viennese male horizon to "Wine, Women and Song" fits into the cliché as well—and he usually greets the women (except for his wife) most humbly with "Kuß die Hand, gnädige Frau" (I kiss your hand, madame).

Who isn't familiar with all the different versions of these Viennese female stereotypes, portrayed by Johann Nestroy in his popular plays or by Arthur Schnitzler in *La Ronde*? Usually they have good bodies, lots of soul and strong characters, but not much intellect or education. This has

melting pot and magnet for the peoples of the Empire. The Viennese woman is also the result of this former multiplicity of peoples—Bohemian, Hungarian and Mediterranean blood has left undeniable traces, not only in physical features, but also in character.

We, the men, love our Viennese women and are convinced that they are the best and most beautiful in the world. As a good friend of mine recently said, thinking out loud over a glass of wine in my local pub: "There are more beautiful women in this city than anywhere else. A husband who stays faithful around here must be a bit of a fool!" That this remark probably referred to himself is neither here nor there. After all, he's married to a most attractive and intelligent Viennese woman who has him firmly under control.

found throughout Vienna in a strategically planned network. While eating a hot "Burenwurst" (order "einmal Heiße mit Senf"— a hot one with mustard) people reflect upon religion, the state of the world, politics and football. "The meat content of the "hot one" hardly bothers the Viennese. After all, they are world champions in repressing the unpleasant, an attitude that probably forced the development of psychoanalysis. They trust in the anti-toxic properties of the garnish, the hottest possible peppers." This is the ironic comment of the "alternative" guide *Dieses Wien—Klischee und Wirklicheit* (Vienna—Cliché and Reality).

At any rate, the Viennese are rightly pleased that a branch of an American hamburger chain had to close for lack of customers. Serves them right too.

Refuge for poets and revolutionaries

"Not at home and not out in the fresh air", that's a motto followed for centuries by the lovers of what is probably the most famous Viennese institution, the coffee house. In 1683, Franz Georg Kolschitzky received from the Emperor, as a reward for his services as a spy during the Turkish siege, permission to open a public coffee brewing house. It's claimed that he also baked the first Viennese Kipferl, a cake made of flaky pastry inspired by the Turkish crescent, which people like to dip furtively into their coffee. If it's not true, at least it's a good story, and that's the important thing.

If you go to a coffee house just to drink coffee, that's your own fault. You go to a coffee house to read, to write, to play chess or cards, to daydream, to flirt, to argue...It's a "place for people who want to be alone and need company to do so", the poet Alfred Polgar once wrote. Up until the time between the wars, the literary life of Vienna was mostly lived on red velour sofas at marble tables. When the legendary "Café Griensteidl" was knocked down at the turn

of the century, the era of the **Café Central** began. The guest list reads like a "Who's Who" of European intellectual history. Theodor Herzl and Viktor Adler, Peter Altenberg and Egon Friedell, Rainer Maria Rilke and Egon Erwin Kisch, Hugo Hofmannsthal and Arthur Schnitzler, Sigmund Freud and Alfred Adler, they all went to the Central in the Herrengasse. The guests were colleagues, friends or bitter enemies, they quarreled or ignored each other. Many a chess player was thoroughly underestimated by his contemporaries.

"Who's going to start a revolution in Russia? Herr Bronstein from the Café Central, perhaps?" That's what Graf Berchthold, the last foreign minister of the Empire, wrote in the margin of the despatch which reported the outbreak of revolution in Russia. "Herr Bronstein", alias Leon Trotsky, was well on his way home to the collapsing empire of the Tzars.

The talented chronicler of his times, Karl Kraus, sat in the **Imperial**. He was a one-man-band, who for 37 years published the magazine *Die Fackel* (The Torch), and worked on his monumental work *The Last Days of Mankind*. In the **Café Museum**,

Left, Mayor Dr. Zilk. Above, a Viennese woman—actress Julia Stemberger.

designed by Adolf Loos, there were tables reserved for famous artists. Alban Berg and Oscar Strauss came here, as did the artists Klimt, Schiele and Kokoschka. One or more scroungers were part of the decor in every good coffee house that had a reputation to keep up. They moved around from the "Central" to the "Herrenhof" or the "Museum" and provided the regulars with news and gossip—whose turn it was to be devastated by Karl Kraus' acidulous pen, for instance—and helped to start intrigues or smooth out misunderstandings. In between

lars emigrated—Sigmund Freud, aged 82, had to go into exile in London—or ended up in concentration camps.

With wit and dignity a whole generation of the Jewish intelligentsia went to their deaths. Shortly before his murder in Buchenwald, the Viennese cabaret artist Fritz Grünbaum asked for a piece of soap. He was told it was too expensive. Grünbaum calmly replied: "If you haven't got the money, you shouldn't run a concentration camp." In the postwar years, coffee houses rich in tradition were converted to banks or even had to

they quickly ate a small goulash on the house, and all of them nursed their daydreams of rising from the level of extras to the Olympian heights of the poets. The coffee house writer, Anton Kuh gave these uncounted wasted lives a memorial in one sentence: "Only a few people know that not writing is also the fruit of a long and difficult struggle."

The loss of a generation

The Viennese coffee house has never really recovered from the intellectual bloodletting of the Second World War. The regu-

accept the humiliating demotion to "Espresso" with gleaming Italian chrome coffee machines. It's only in the last few years that a Renaissance of these old Viennese institutions has begun.

Students and yuppies have rediscovered them as oasis in times of stress. The tourists sit amazed among the splendors of the renovated "Central" and are instructed by the "Herr Ober" in the complicated art of drinking coffee. The vast variety on offer is legendary. Only philistines and tourists ask for

Above, Friedensreich Hundertwasser.

CITY ARCHITECTURE TODAY

We are living in a time of change, in which old, inflexible values in architecture and in urban planning are being questioned more and more. The straight lines and the uniformity of the Bauhaus school are nearing their end, for they are without feeling, sterile, cold, heartless, aggressive and without emotion

The age of absolute rationalism is ending. The new values aim for a higher quality of life, not a higher standard of living. People long for the Romantic, for individuality, creativity, particularly creativity, and a life in harmony with nature.

dation, when the normal process would be for the adaptation of the environment to begin once people have moved in.

Architecture has become a farce and is no longer suitable for human beings. Over the centuries human beings have so maltreated their outer skins, namely clothing and architecture, that they no longer fit. Architects build prison cells in which the souls of human beings wither. Today we see the triumph of rational technology, but at the same time we face a great emptiness. Aesthetic emptiness, the desert of uniformity, mur-

Growing and changing

Human beings have three skins: their own, their clothes and their houses. All three of these skins have to be renewed, they have to keep growing and changing. However, if the third skin, the outer walls of the house, doesn't change and grow as well, it becomes rigid and dies.

Houses, like trees, are growing things. Houses grow like plants, they live and change continuously. Yet modern architecture is criminally sterile, because its fatal flaw is that all building comes to a stop when people move into their accommo-

Above, the Hundertwasser house.

derous sterility and creative impotence.

Friedensreich Hundertwasser, born Fritz Stowasser in 1928, is one of the best-known and most successful Viennese artists. Primarily a painter, he is perhaps best known for his realization of an "architectural dream"—the "Hundertwasser House" in the 3. Bezirk of Vienna. The design of the house—a colorful, romantic building—is deliberately asymmetrical and uneven. The building has aroused strong feelings among its supporters and opponents.

Supporters welcome the return of color and ornament, and point to its unique people-friendly features (one such example is the children's adventure playrooms) but detractors sneer at the "kitsch cathedral".

"einen Kaffee". Those in the know choose among a large or small "Brauner" (with little milk), a large or small "Schwarzer" (black), "Einspänner" (in a glass, with a blob of cream) "Verlängerter" or, simple and delicious, a "Melange" (half milk, half coffee). The obligatory glass of water is served as well on a silver tray, and renewed at regular intervals. You can sit for hours in the warm coffee house with a small Brauner for fifteen schilling, chat, read the paper, observe the other guests: "Aha, there's the editor with the Minister's secretary, well, well, well."

You're in the know.

Biting the wine

Only warm summer evenings can temporarily lure coffee house devotees away from their regular table by the window, right next to the cake counter. They swap it for a hard wooden bench, which should preferably be standing in a cool, shady courtyard in the area of Sievering, Nußdorf, Kahlenbergerdorf, Stammersdorf or Strebersdorf. Outside the gates a green bush is hanging on a long pole, a signal to the dehydrated traveler that the vintner's wine is ready to drink.

Here they sit, as they do every year, at the "Heuriger" to drink the "Heuriger", the new wine, or as they commonly say in Vienna, to "bite" it. This may all seem a bit complicated to foreigners, but after drinking several quarter liters, a comfortable comprehension is assured.

Vienna and wine, a combination famed in song, has many thousand years of history. Discoveries of grape seeds prove that the Celts were already using the mild climate of the region to grow vines. The legionaries of the little garrison town of Vindabona didn't despise the grape, either. They're commemorated by the Probusgasse, named after a Roman Emperor, in Heiligenstadt. The art of viniculture was passed on and refined from generation to generation, as was the art of drinking and "biting" the wine. During the reign of Leopold I, a priestly gentleman complained of the impious habits of the city: " On Sundays and holidays you hear a continual fiddling, lute playing, leaping and dancing in all the inns and drinking houses, from the afternoons till late at night." In the 19th century, the suburb of Neulerchenfeld was even described as "the largest inn in the Holy Roman Empire, where on a single fine Sunday 16,000 people sought refreshment."

Those in search of refreshment guard the address of their favorite Heuriger, now as then. Secret recommendations are passed on unofficially to a select few. A good Heuriger isn't crowded. Shuddering, the Viennese give the tourist traps of Grinzing, where the guests are served their roast chicken as if on a conveyor belt, while the next coachload is waiting outside, a wide berth. They prefer to drive out to **Nußdorf** or **Sievering** and turn into one of the twisting alleys, where they seem to be swallowed up without trace by the cobblestones. There you sit at a rough wooden table and fetch yourself a piece of bread and dripping with onion rings from the buffet, along with a few Brezeln. If you prefer to take the leftovers of Sunday's roast pork with you, you'll be given a plate and cutlery without any difficulty. With that you

Left: In the Café Landmann.

THE JEWS IN VIENNA

The Jewish element in the Vienna of the late 19th century and during the 20s and 30s was much stronger and more visible than in other western European capitals. Ten percent of the population were Jews, from the assimilated members of the upper middle class to the small traders who had come from the "Stadteln" of Galicia and Bukovina. The progressively minded Emperor Joseph II, son of the great Maria Theresia, had granted the Jews of the Empire substantial rights in his "Edict of Tolerance" in 1781. In the 2. Bezirk, in Leopoldstadt, the "Mazzesinsel"

book *The Jewish State*, which detailed his vision of an exodus to Palestine. Anti-Semitism was put on the back burner, it was simply bad manners. "In my eyes this city is a pearl! I will give it a setting worthy of such a pearl", enthused a corporal, who had failed miserably as an artist in Vienna. In 1938, Adolf Hitler put his threat into action. Austria was added to the German Reich. In the Viennese Kristallnacht of November 9, 1938 the windows of Jewish shops were smashed, and nearly all the synagogues were burned to the ground.

grew up, an orthodox community with Tora schools, synagogues and kosher shops.

The author, Arthur Schnitzler described, in minute detail, a quite different world in his novels and plays, namely that of the enlightened Jewish bourgeoisie. Jewish intellectuals shaped the development of art and science, literature and journalism. Of the 174 editorial posts in the Viennese daily papers, 123 were held by Jews.

The Berggasse in the 9. Bezirk was where Sigmund Freud had his practice in the treatment room with the red wallpaper. Opposite, in Berggasse no. 6, Theodor Herzl worked on his

Above, Freud's couch.

Before the Holocaust, more than 200,000 Jews lived in Vienna, today the number is barely 7,000. Coming to terms with the Nazi past is limited to private groups and individuals. The "Nazi-hunter" Simon Wiesenthal has set up his documentation center in the former Jewish textile quarter, the Jewish Welcome Service tries to keep in contact with emigrants all over the world. Recently, political developments have encouraged a cautious Renaissance of Jewish culture in Vienna. The Synagogue in the Seitenstettengasse has rising attendance figures. But the wounds have still not healed, and a young Viennese Jew has summed up the feelings of his generation: "You never know when you'll have to pack again."

drink a liter of white wine, for starters, in a wide-bellied glass carafe. You might have a Grüner Veltlinger or a Müller Thurgau, a Neuburger or a Riesling. The wine should be fruity and dry, pleasantly acid. You can sit contented like this hour after hour, swapping salt and pepper and a few profound pearls of wisdom with your neighbors, slapping in vain at the gnats.

Class and social barriers are torn down as twilight falls, a classless society toasts its members with big, beermug-style glasses: "Servus, du." The company director pats his secretary's knee. Next morning nobody remembers anything anyway.

You may be lucky and catch the the special Viennese Heuriger mood, a bit sad and a bit sentimental, Weltschmerz and the knowledge of the passing of the pleasures of the hour. "Whooping, cheerful, high-spirited and comfortable—that's merely the stereotype of the Viennese", according to an an essay on Vienna, in their heart of hearts the Viennese are melancholy. They may not manage tragedy, but philosophy is another matter. The Viennese song begins and ends in a minor key.

"The noblest nation of all the nations is resignation", said the talented but sharp-tongued 19th-century satirical playwright, Johann Nestroy. In Viennese song, the responsibility for personal failure is often attributed to supernatural powers: "If God doesn't will it so, it's all in vain". Visitors can hum along with these songs, but they'll hardly understand a thing, even if they speak German. These original Viennese texts are hard to understand for those who live outside Semmering. Here a "Hallodri" (womaniser) has yet another "Gspusi" (affair), for once we're "fidel" (happy), but only till the next "Pallawatsch" (catastrophe), as long as we don't indulge in "Spompanadeln" (daft ideas). The language is a cosmopolitan mixture of Czech and Hungarian, Italian and French, plus the Yiddish that is such an important element of Viennese dialect. You're usually preserved at the last moment from descent into deep depression after a lengthy Heuriger session by the classic Viennese diminutive, the syllable "erl". That really was quite a "Räuscherl" (I was really drunk) yesterday evening, but don't be cross, Schatzerl (darling), I'll give you a "Buschketterl"(kiss).

Schrammel music and death, who is a Viennese

A very specialized branch of Viennese song is the Schrammelmusik. The very first band was founded at the end of the last century by the brothers Johann and Joseph Schrammel. They played in the Heuriger on a concertina and a bass guitar—the combination produces an addictive sound, its followers claim. Good Schrammel music is never sweet or schmaltzy, but a bit on the bitter side, for some ears, a bit coarse. Like folk music everywhere, the Heuriger songs are in danger today of degenerating into inoffensive tootling and sing-songs. One musician who is trying to keep up the true Viennese musical tradition is Roland Neuwirth with his "extreme Schrammel". He loathes the fake Viennese coziness, and prefers to offer his enthusiastic audiences numbers like *Delirium-Tanz* or Every Rat loves its Sewer. In his song *Ein echtes Wienerlied* (A Genuine Viennese Song) sixteen different expressions for dying are introduced with feeling: "He made an exit, he stretched out his slippers, he laid himself down, he studied the potatoes from underneath, he put on wooden pyjamas..."

The Viennese don't find such a text tasteless or shocking. After all, Roland Neuwirth is only continuing an old and honorable tradition—the unafraid and easy-going attitude to death. Sometimes it seems as if it actually lives, personified, in this city. "Death must be a Viennese", the late Alfred Polgar discovered—and the Viennese are good friends with one of their own, it's an intimate relationship. Old grannies, silent drinkers, failed poets see the visit of the Grim Reaper as the last, possibly the only high point in an uneventful life. When they die, there ought to be a "lovely funeral",

Right, Leopold Hawelka in front of his café.

MY VIENNA

The **1. Bezirk** of Vienna is called the "Innere Stadt". Here, there's a cosy little undergound city with countless twisting little sewers, homely romantic catacombs and idyllic crypts. If you're lucky, you might meet the old Emperor Franz Joseph. Or Helmut Qualtinger. Then, you can watch them drink their coffee, read the paper and decompose. If you're lucky. But luck is fickle.

In the **2. Bezirk**, in Leopoldstadt, is the Prater. In the Prater there's a hill—the Laurenzerkogel. You can toboggan down it in winter. There's a lot

of yelling and yodelling when that happens. You don't know the Viennese could yell and yodel like elks in the forest. If one Viennese suddenly yells, another will yodel right back. Yelling to high heaven, yodelling from the abyss. Like elks.

The **3. Bezirk** is called "Landstraße" Sometime or other, you'll see, it'll be called "Beatrixstraße". In the Beatrixstraße there's the only video hire shop in Vienna that's open 24 hours. In this video shop, on February 25, 1989, shortly after midnight, a brutal murder will take place.

"Wieden" is the name of the **4. Bezirk**. Every hotel, every café, every restaurant, Beisel or gourmet, in Wieden is really a brothel. Every police station, every children's swimming pool, every park bench in Wieden is a brothel in disguise. Even the brothels in Wieden are brothels.

I've never been to the **5. Bezirk**. I don't know what it's called, either.

The **6. Bezirk** is called "Mariahilf". In the Mariahilferstraße is the Mariahilferkirche, dedicated to the Virgin Mary. Right next door is the Mariahilfer Cinema. Screen A is showing *Lust in the Dust*. Screen B: *Yodelling Under the Dirndl Skirts*. Screen C: *Johnny Longtale, the Cold Farmer* (original version, with subtitles). Screen D: *Yodelling Under the Dirndl Skirts Part 2*. I cross myself as hard as I can.

"Neubau" or new buildings is the name of the **7. Bezirk**. The New Building Song: "O horrible, terrible New Buildings. O sad and morbid New Buildings. Your dying breath smells of marzipan. Your cobwebs, spread from New Building to New Building, are of candy floss. Your children are full of tuberculosis. Your old folks of liver cirrhosis. O yes, soon, soon, in the next life, they will all be reborn as parasites in a vineyard. No need for tears. Cheers!"

In the **8. Bezirk**, in Josefstadt, is the famous theater of the Josefstadt. Here I worked for a few years as an actor. No, honestly. I played in the scintillating comedy *Indigestion*, by Axel von Ambeißer, starring Axel von Ambeißer. During his great show of emotion in the second act, Herr von Ambeißer, during the third performance, swallowed his false teeth and bit open his ulcer. No, honestly. I worship Axel von Ambeißer. Honestly.

Did you know that Adolf Hitler runs a sausage stall incognito in the **9. Bezirk**, in the Alsergrund? It's on the corner of Gürtelstraße and Nussdorferstraße and is called "Klein Sacher". The sausage stall, I mean.

I was born in the favored Favoriten, the **10. Bezirk**. And I'm buried in Simmering, in the **11. Bezirk** in the Zentralfriedhof. And I'm a bit chilly down there, six feet (1.8 meter) down under the ground. When you visit Vienna, please come to my grave in the Zentralfriedhof and weep a bit. Weep a few scalding tears, maybe they'll work their way down to me and warm me up a bit.

Thanks—Ludwig Hirsch

which should be something to talk about. With organ music and child choir, candles and wreaths, tears, pious fibs, sound and smoke. In Vienna people save up for such a spectacle, and the Sterbevereine (funeral associations) are highly respected institutions. All your life you can pay in little stages for the grand finale. Nothing upsets the true Viennese more than the prospect of being buried one day "like a dog", with only four Pompfüneberern (pallbearers, from "pompes funêbres").

Even the highly progressive social democrats of the years between the wars had their own funeral association, *Die Flamme* (The Flame), with 160,000 members. "A proletrian life, a proletarian death and a cremation in accordance with culture and progress" was the rather heretical slogan.

Children learn in school about "lieber Augustin", a singer and bagpipe player, who in the 17th century fell, totally drunk, into a plague pit, woke up and went on singing cheerfully among the stinking corpses. Right among the shoppers in the high-class pedestrian precinct, Graben in the 1. Bezirk is the splendid Baroque "Pestsäule" (Plague Pillar), a reminder of the "merciful removal of the divine chastisement of plague richly deserved by this city". All around the skilfully portrayed horrors, children are playing, Maronibrater (chestnut sellers) pour their hot wares into homemade paper bags, organ grinders turn their handles. Death and the joys of life are not mutually exclusive in this city. Even if those who suffer in and from Vienna are driven out to the furthest ends of the earth—to die in a foreign land, that really is a dreadful prospect, God preserve us.

There is the story of an elderly emigrant who during the 70s returned to Vienna three times to die. Frustrated twice, he had to leave again, he only achieved his end at the third attempt. At least the old gentleman thoroughly earned his grave in the Zentralfriedhof, near the third gate.

André Heller once called the Viennese cemeteries "stations of farewell". Yet they

are much more. They are not only, as in other cities, places of grief to be avoided if possible. In Viennese cemeteries, you can take a walk, chat a bit, get some fresh air, feed the squirrels and the sparrows, decode inscriptions on weathered tombstones. They're particularly lovely in autumn, when colorful leaves cover the narrow gravel paths, the last rays of the sun light up the statues and eternal flame lanterns on the graves. Near the exit, you can buy a sausage and hot tea.

The biggest cemetery in the city, the Zentralfriedhof, is more than 0.78 sq miles

(2 sq km). The giant park has its own bus service, and every autumn there's a hare hunt among the graves. "Long live the Zentralfriedhof, and all its dead," sang the Liedermacher Wolfgang Ambros, and his song became a hit in the Austrian charts. The magnificent state tombs provided by the city are all too often witnesses to a bitter truth: only once you're dead can you really make it in Vienna. Wolfgang Amadeus Mozart has his official last resting place here, a memorial stone in the state tombs, group 32a, no. 55. The life-loving composer was buried in 1791, quite impoverished, in a mass grave which can no longer be located in the Sankt

Left, the singer Ludwig Hirsch. Right, Waluliso.

Marxer Friedhof.

Children may be firmly shooed off the lawns, but the city has a big heart for the dead and for small animals. On the banks of the Danube, to the east of Vienna, lies the "Friedhof der Namenlosen" (Cemetery of the Nameless). Unknown corpses swept ashore by the river here found their last rest under simple wrought iron crosses. But dachshunds, pussycats and hamsters, much-loved companions in loneliness in Vienna, have for the last few years escaped compulsory delivery to the glue and fertilizer factories. Vienna's first mobile crematorium for pets will give dear "Waldi" dignified last rites. An employee of the company says a few deeply-felt words, the mourners noisily blow their noses, and Waldi's soul rises up to heaven. A little heap of white ash remains, which can be put in a dainty little urn and kept on the mantleshelf at home. God be gracious to him!

Curious characters

Strangers may shake their heads over customs like these, but in Vienna the times—and the hearts—are a bit different. Strange and wonderful characters thrive here. Eccentrics are lovingly cared for. Undeniably the most popular eccentric in Vienna is Waluliso (the acronym stands for Wald-Luft-Licht-Sonne, Forest-Air-Light-Sunshine). Dressed in a white toga and equipped with a nice red apple and a Biblical staff, Waluliso (a.k.a Wickerl Weinberger) strides through the city center, blessing astonished tourists, occasionally stopping to pose for the clicking cameras.

Waluliso's fight for peace and protection of the environment on this dunghill of a planet has already taken him to Moscow and Washington, where in Red Square and in front of the Capitol he told the powerful off in no uncertain terms. In summer Waluliso likes to wander through the nudist area of Lobau, where a laurel wreath on his head is his only apparel.

However, Waluliso's one man show shouldn't draw attention away from the fact that the so-called "genuine Viennese" are threatened with extinction. These are the characters, bad-tempered, devious, loyal and charming, commemorated by the unforgettable cabaret artist, author and actor Helmut Qualtlinger in his piece *Der Herr Karl* (Mr. Karl). The whole of Vienna was outraged at the exposure, I beg your pardon, the premiére. In enclaves you can still find them: in the markets of Vienna, for instance, in the Brunnemarkt in the suburb of Ottakring, the Viktor-Adler-Markt in the working class area Favoriten, or in the Naschmarkt, which stretches across the regulated river Wien starting at the Karlsplatz, flanked by gold-decorated Otto Wagner houses. Here the stallholders run their well-regulated businesses, usually rather well-built women with aprons and headscarves who stand out in all weathers praising their "Kronprinz" (a type of apple) potatoes and kohlrabi: "Well, what about it, madam, it's all fresh, want to try some?"

The Ringstraße coachman

A very picture of the "genuine" Viennese warm heart and kindly nature is presented by the Fiaker waiting for customers at the Stephansplatz. Well, it's one way of getting a tip out of the impressed tourists. Their name comes from the Rue Saint Fiacre, in which the Parisian cabbies used to park their traps. With whips and bowler hats, a good grip on the reins of their well-groomed horses, they drive "Amis" (Americans) and "Itaka" (Italians) round the Ring, and in broad Viennese interspersed with bits of other languages—"This is the Hofburg castle, you know"—they give a short embroidered account of Austrian history. The first coach hire license was given by Leopold I in 1693, the best time for the Fiaker was the economic upsurge of the so-called "Gründerjahre" in the second half of the 19th century. There were Fiaker balls, in which the guests danced waltzes and polkas till they dropped in the grey dawn. The personal coachman of Crown Prince Rudolf served his master as a discreet companion on nightly excursions, and was also a popular whistler and singer of "Heurigen" songs.

One of the most beautiful Viennese songs is about the melancholy farewell of a Fiaker leaving his "Zeugl" (team). Today there are only about 30 traps still driving in Vienna, and of course they leave behind certain traces, the so-called "Roßknödel" (horse dumplings). The perfectly serious suggestion made by the city adminstration in 1979, that given the fouling of the streets the horses should wear "diapers", aroused the vigorous protest of the coachmen. The cunning argument, " then you'd have to put panties on the pigeons," put the bureaucrats in the Town

There are 35 routes altogether traveling on nearly 156 miles (250 km) of track, moving about 250 million travelers a year. Vienna can boast the biggest tram network in the western world. The loved and hated "Schaffner" (conductors) turn every trip into an adventure safari. Their insignia are official caps and clippers, their domain is the coach, their word is law. "Come along there, move up, no pushing, ladies and gentlemen." Today, more and more routes are being converted to driver-only trams. A tram ride is now only half as much fun, Vienna is a little

Hall on the defensive and in the end they had to give in. After that, peace descended once more, and even the first female Fiaker in Vienna, a cheeky young lady, was stoically accepted by her male colleagues.

The Viennese of course never ride in a Fiaker (except in moon-in-June operettas), but in the tram. But visitors from all over the world love our trams: like the terrorists who in December 1975, attacked the conference of OPEC ministers meeting in a building on the Ring—and like good little commuters they took the tram to get there.

Above, stallholder at the Naschmarkt.

bit poorer.

Viennese humor—the Schmäh

A good Schmäh is quite a rarity nowadays. What is a Schmäh? "An untruth, joke, trick, but also skill, cunning, charm." That's how a current dictionary translates it, not without the parting shot: "A straight forward translation would basically be a Schmäh." A Schmäh can be made, told, acted or arranged. A Schmähtandler is someone who isn't schmähstad (has a sense of Schmäh). You still don't understand a word? Sorry, then we can't help you.

Speisen von Heute:

Gulaschsuppe 22.-
Leberknödelsuppe 20.-
Geb. Fisch 50.-
Čevapčiči   50.-
Gulasch 50.-
Rindsbraten 90.-
Schweinsbraten 70.-
Kalbsbraten 90.-
Rehbraten 90.-
Geb. Schweinsschnitzel 70.-
Zigeunerkotellettes 90.-
Ham and Eggs 45.-
Toast m. Schinken u. Käse 22.-
Klobasse   m. Senf 25.-
Frankfurter "   "   25.-
Preßkopf i. Essig u. Öl 27.-
Knackwurst   "   " " 27.-
Salzstangerl m. Schinken,
       Käse u. Gurkerl 23.-

A City on a Human Scale

Vienna is a city for pedestrians, for strollers and promenaders, for thinkers and dreamers. You don't need a car to see Vienna at its most beautiful. The heart of Vienna is in the Bezirk inside the Ring, in the "Innere Stadt".

You should take plenty of time to view Vienna, time and leisure, to let the city work on you like a piece of music, to rediscover the magic of the past: in the delicate, romantic charm of St. Ruprecht's Church, in the wide vaults of the Gothic nave of St. Stephen's Cathedral, in the twisting medieval alleys of the old city, in the aristocratic palaces around the Herrengasse, in the Imperial state rooms of the Hofburg and the upper middle class apartments on the Ringstraße.

The following pages show several routes through the city center. The first leads from the Opernkreuzung, the center of present-day Vienna, through the pedestrian precincts of the Kärntnerstraße and the Graben to the medieval squares of Am Hof and Freyung. From there, follow the Herrengasse to the Imperial Vienna of the Hofburg and back to the Opera House.

The second tour begins and ends at St. Stephen's Cathedral. It leads into old Vienna, the Vienna of narrow alleys, in which the medieval buildings of the once walled city have survived.

The Ringstraße is different. A keener wind blows here. The walls had been demolished, and at last the middle class could and would show what they could do: in the Viennese style, of course, historically, imitating the best buildings of the past. A necklace of impressive buildings surrounds the city center. Here too, there are two routes leading from the Opernkreuzung to help you discover the splendors of the Gründerzeit.

After the second siege by the Turks, the city threatened to burst at the seams. The court and the aristocracy built their pleasure palaces outside the city. Today, they are favorite destinations for Viennese outings. But you can find jewels of Baroque architecture even further out: the guide to the suburbs and surrounding countryside will point them out. One thing you shouldn't forget when walking through Vienna. The architectural scenery is only the background against which the life of the delightful Vienna of today is lived, in which visitors very quickly find their way about and feel at home. "The Art of Living" explains this aspect of a city so full of the love of life.

Preceding pages: in the park at Schönbrunn; façade of a Wagner house; Viennese menu; table laid for coffee in the Sperl. Left, Fiaker lamp.

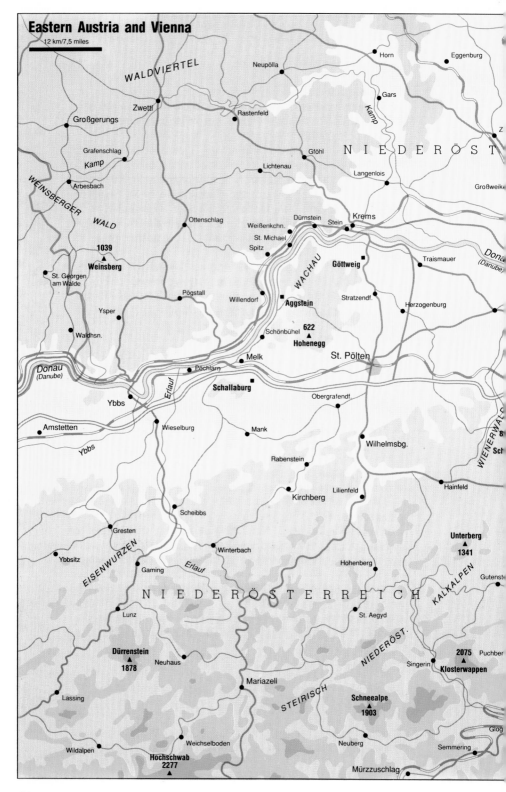

Eastern Austria and Vienna

12 km/7,5 miles

WALDVIERTEL

Horn

Eggenburg

Neupölla

Gars

Zwettl

Rastenfeld

Kamp

Großgerungs

Z

Grafenschlag

Gföhl

NIEDERÖST

Kamp

Lichtenau

Langenlois

Arbesbach

Großweike

WEINSBERGER

Ottenschlag

Dürnstein

Krems

Weißenkchn.

Stein

WALD

St. Michael

Traismauer

1039

Spitz

Donau

▲ Weinsberg

WACHAU

Göttweig ■

(Danube)

St. Georgen
am Walde

Pögstall

Willendorf

Stratzendf.

Herzogenburg

Ysper

Aggstein

Waldhsn.

Schönbühel

622

Donau

Pöchlarn

Melk

▲
Hohenegg

St. Pölten

(Danube)

Erlauf

Schallaburg ■

Ybbs

Obergrafendf.

Amstetten

Wieselburg

Mank

Wilhelmsbg.

WIENERWALD

Ybbs

Rabenstein

Sch

Kirchberg

Lilienfeld

Hainfeld

Scheibbs

Gresten

Unterberg

Ybbsitz

EISENWURZEN

Winterbach

▲
1341

Gaming

Erlauf

Hohenberg

KALKALPEN

NIEDERÖSTERREICH

Gutenst

Lunz

St. Aegyd

NIEDERÖST.

Dürrenstein

Neuhaus

2075

Puchbe

▲
1878

Singerin

▲
Klosterwappen

Mariazell

Lassing

STEIRISCH

Schneealpe

Glog

▲
1903

Weichselboden

Semmering

Wildalpen

Neuberg

Hochschwab

2277

Mürzzuschlag

▲

90

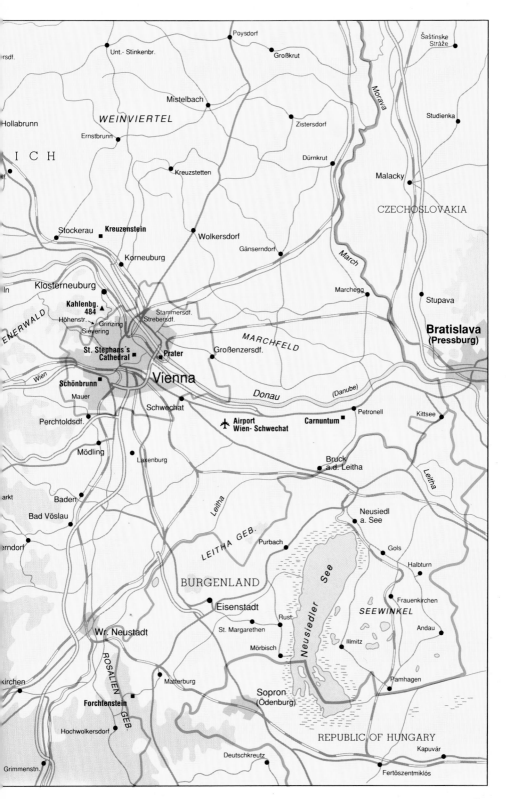

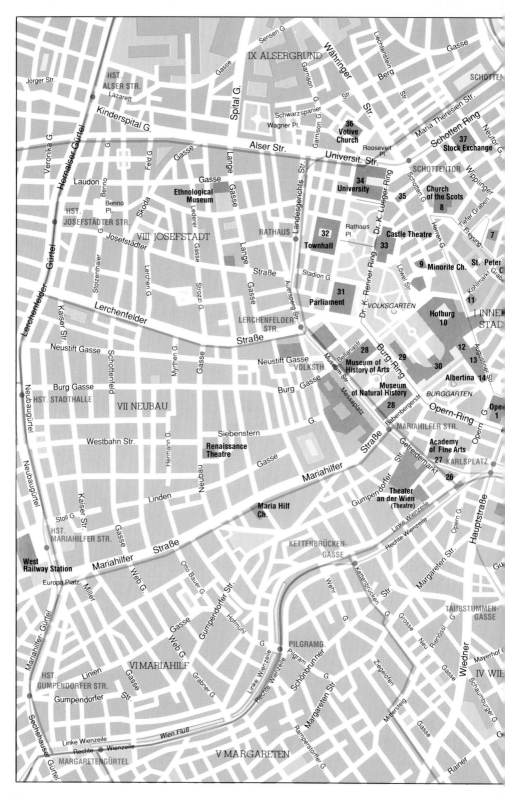

IX ALSERGRUND

SCHOTTEN

Jörger Str.

HST. ALSER STR.
Lazarett

Kinderspital G.

Sensen G.

Wahringer Str.

Gasse

Berg

Gasse

SCHOTTEN

Garnison

Schwarzspanier
Wagner Pl.

36
Votive
Church

Maria Theresien Str.

Schotten Ring

37
Stock Exchange

Neutor G.

Alser Str.

Universit. Str.

Roosevelt Pl.

SCHOTTENTOR

Wipplinger

Veronika G.

Hernalser Gürtel

Laudon

Benno

Benno Pl.

HST.
JOSEFSTÄDTER STR.

Josefstädter

VIII JOSEFSTADT

Skoda

Feld G.

Lederer Gasse

Gasse

Gasse

Lange

Ethnological
Museum

Gasse

Lange

RATHAUS

Landesgerichts Str.

34
University

35

D.-K.-Lueger-Ring

Schotten G.

Church
of the Scots
8

Tiefer Graben

Freyung

7

Herren G.

32
Townhall

Rathaus Pl.

Castle Theatre

33

9 Minorite Ch.

St. Peter
C

Kohlmarkt Graben

Straße

Stadion G.

Auersperg Str.

D.-K.-Renner-Ring

Löwel Str.

11

Lerchenfelder

Gürtel

Stolzenthaler

Lerchen G.

Strozzi G.

Gasse

LERCHENFELDER
STR.

31
Parliament

VOLKSGARTEN

Hofburg
10

I INNER
STAD

12

13

Lerchenfelder

Straße

Kaiser Str.

Schottenfeld

Neustift Gasse

Myrthen G.

Gasse

Neustift Gasse
VOLKSTH.

Burg Gasse

28

Museum
of History of Arts

29

Burg-Ring

30

Augustiner Str.

Albertina 14

Burg Gasse

VII NEUBAU

Neubaugürtel

HST. STADTHALLE

Hermann G.

Neubau

Burg Gasse

G.

Messeplatz

Museum
of Natural History
28

Babenbergerst.

BURGGARTEN

Opern-Ring

Oper
1

Neubaugürtel

Westbahn Str.

Siebenstern

Renaissance
Theatre

Gasse

Mariahilfer

Straße

MARIAHILFER STR.

Getreidemarkt

Academy
of Fine Arts
27

Opern

Opern

Hauptstraße

Linden

Kaiser Str.

Stoll G.

Gasse

HST.
MARIAHILFER STR.

Mariahilfer

Gumpendorfer

Theater
an der Wien
(Theatre)

26

KARLSPLATZ

Maria Hilf
Ch.

Linke Wienzeile

West
Railway Station

Europa Platz

Mariahilfer

Straße

Miller

Web G.

Otto Bauer G.

Gumpendorfer Str.

Hofmühl

Wehr

Kettenbrücken

Str.

KETTENBRÜCKEN-
GASSE

Rechte Wienzeile

Margareten Str.

TAUBSTUMMEN-
GASSE

Gu

VI MARIAHILF

HST.
GUMPENDORFER STR.

Linien

Str.

Gumpendorfer

Gasse

Web G.

Grabner G.

PILGRAMG.

Pilgram

Schönbrunner

Linke Wienzeile

Rechte Wienzeile

Grosse Neu Pienössi

Ziegelofen

Mitterstieg

Wiedner

Mayerhof

Gasse

Gasse

Schaumburger G.

IV WIE

Sechshauser Gürtel

Mariahilfer- Gürtel

MARGARETENGÜRTEL

Linke Wienzeile
Rechte Wienzeile

Wien Fluß

V MARGARETEN

Margareten Str.

Rampersdorfer G.

Rainer

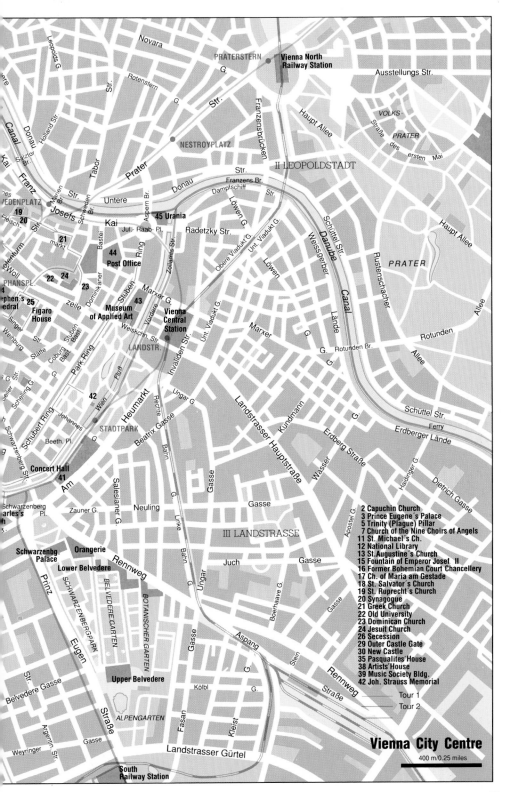

Novara

PRATERSTERN
G.
Vienna North
Railway Station
Ausstellungs Str.

Leopolds G.
Rotenstern
Str.

Holland Str.
Donau
Franzensbrücken
Haupt Allee

VOLKS-
Straße PRATER
des ersten Mai

Canal
Kai
Franz
Salztor
Tabor
Prater
NESTROYPLATZ
Str.
II LEOPOLDSTADT

Donau
Str.

VEDENPLATZ
Untere
Franzens Br.
Dampfschiff

19
20
Josefs
Kai
45 Urania
Löwen G.
Schüttel Str.
Haupt Allee

21
markt
Jul. Raab-Pl.
Radetzky Str.
Löwen
Weissgerber
Rustenschacher

44
Post Office
Ring
Obere Viadukt G.
Unt. Viadukt G.
Löwen
PRATER
Allee

22 24
23
Marxer G.
Danube
Canal
Lände

PHANSPL.
zelle
Dominikaner
43
Museum
of Applied Art
Vienna
Central
Station
Marxer
G.
Rotunden Br.
Rotunden
Allee

phen's
edral
25
Figaro
House
Stuben
Weiskchn. Str.
Marxer
Rotunden

Singer
Weinburg
Str.
Stäte
LANDSTR.
Unt. Viadukt G.
Invaliden Str.
G.
Schüttel Str.
Ferry

Coburg
Bast.
Park Ring
Wien
Fluß
Ungar G.
Landstrasser Haupstraße
Erdberger Lände

42
Heumarkt
Rechte
Beatrix Gasse
Bahn
Kundmann
Erdberg Straße
Wasser

STADTPARK
Johannes

Beeth. Pl.
G.

Concert Hall
41
Am

Salesianer G.
Gasse
Gasse
Dietrich Gasse

Schwarzenberg
arles's
h.
Pl.
Zauner G.
Neuling
Gasse
III LANDSTRASSE
Gasse
Apostel G.

Linke
Bahn
Gasse

Schwarzenbg.
Palace
Orangerie
Lower Belvedere
Rennweg

Juch
Gasse

Prinz
SCHWARZENBERGPARK
BOTANISCHER GARTEN
BELVEDERE GARTEN

Upper Belvedere
Kölbl
G.

Belvedere Gasse
Eugen
ALPENGARTEN

Str.
Fasan
Kleist
Rennweg
Straße

Weyringer
Argentin. Str.
Gasse
Landstrasser Gürtel

South
Railway Station

2 Capuchin Church
3 Prince Eugene´s Palace
5 Trinity (Plague) Pillar
7 Church of the Nine Choirs of Angels
11 St. Michael´s Ch.
12 National Library
13 St. Augustine´s Church
15 Fountain of Emperor Josef II
16 Former Bohemian Court Chancellery
17 Ch. of Maria am Gestade
18 St. Salvator´s Church
19 St. Ruprecht´s Church
20 Synagogue
21 Greek Church
22 Old University
23 Dominican Church
24 Jesuit Church
26 Secession
29 Outer Castle Gate
30 New Castle
35 Pasqualites´House
38 Artists´House
39 Music Society Bldg.
42 Joh. Strauss Memorial

_____ Tour 1
_____ Tour 2

Vienna City Centre

400 m/0.25 miles

TWO TOURS OF THE CITY CENTER

From the Opera House to Stephansplatz

For the starting point of your first walk, choose the crossroads of the Ringstraße and the Kärnter Straße at the State Opera House, and you will be standing at a historically interesting point in the city center. The Kärntner Straße leads to the Stephansplatz. Where it narrows, medieval Vienna begins. Nearby was the fortified Kärnter Turm, fought over fiercely during the first siege by the Turks. The Ringmauer, dating from the end of the 12th century, was then replaced by Renaissance fortifications with huge bastions, surrounded by a glacis free of buildings. The fortifications were demolished in 1857, except for some insignificant remnants. The State Opera House stands on the site of one of the projecting bastions. The Ringstraße, which stretches out to both sides, is like the whole Ringstraßenzone, on the site of the former glacis. Looking out of town, you can see the oldest suburb, the Wieden, today the 4. Bezirk. The first massive building on the Ringstraße to be completed was the **State Opera House** (1861-69) {1}, designed by August Sicard von Siccardsburg and Eduard van der Nüll, a notable example of the Historic style. Famous artists were employed for its decoration, among them the sculptor Julius Hähnel, who created the bronze statues in the Loggia and the Pegasus statues above the Opera House and Moritz von Schwind (who painted the Loggia and the Foyer). These are among the few parts of the Opera House that survived the devastating bomb attacks in March 1945. The fountains, one on either side of the Opera, display allegorical figures

State Opera House, Opernkreuzung.

by Hans Gasser. After the Opera had been restored in the old style (only the auditorium was modernized), it was reopened with a performance of Beethoven's *Fidelio*, when the occupation troops left in 1955. The State Opera is the leading opera house in Austria and the company is of international standing. It had always been able to attract the best conductors and singers and has made a considerable contribution to establishing Vienna's reputation as a musical city. The orchestra is provided by the Vienna Philharmonic. The annually held Opera Ball is a social event famous all over the world. The district around the Opera was the first on the Ringstraße to be built during the 60s of the last century. In the **Kärntner Straße**, before you get to the pedestrian precinct, you can see to your right the Palais Todesco (no. 51), built in the Renaissance style by Theophil Hansen and Ludwig Förster. In the 19th cen-

tury, the salon of the banker Eduard Todesco was a popular meeting place for VIPs from the world of politics and theater. If you look into the Walfischgasse, just past the Palais (to your right), you can still see the line of the old city wall in the way in which the houses (past the Moulin Rouge) bend back on the city side. To the left, in the Philharmonikerstraße, is the famous **Hotel Sacher**; part of the site used to be the Kärntnertortheater, demolished once the Opera House was completed. The Kärntner Straße has fundamentally changed its appearance several times. In the 18th century, the Gothic houses were replaced by Baroque buildings, in the second half of the 19th century, most of these buildings became victims of the widening of the street. In 1944/45 many Gründerzeit houses were destroyed by bombs and fire. Since 1974 the street has been a pedestrian precinct. Among the few historically im-

Hotel Sacher.

portant buildings left are the Baroque Palais Esterházy and the Malteserkirche. The Palais Esterházy (no. 47) dates from the middle of the 17th century, and is one of the few palaces in Vienna which go back to before the second Turkish siege (1683).

In the **Annagasse**, which leads off just past the Palais, a few steps will take you to the **Annakirche** (no. 3b). It was built as a Gothic church (14th century), but altered in Renaissance times and finally given a Baroque interior by the Jesuits in the 18th century. Above the entrance is a notable 17th-century sculpture of St. Anne and the Holy Family, and over the altar is a carved wooden sculpture of the same subject (c. 1510). Around the church are a number of other interesting old buildings which have survived.

The **Malteserkirche** (Kärntner Straße 37) has a façade in the French Empire style of Louis de Montoyer

(1806-08), but has kept its Gothic character within. The Knights of Malta were invited to Vienna in 1200. On the left in the church is a memorial (1806) to Jean de la Valette, defender of the capital of the island of Malta against the Turks.

After taking a look at the Johannesgasse (on the right); no. 5, Palais Questenberg-Kaunitz, was probably built around 1701 according to plans by Johann Lukas von Hildebrandt; no. 6a, Hofkammerarchiv, built around 1843-46, with a room commemorating the poet Franz Grillparzer, who was director of the court archives (1832-36)— continue along the Marco-d'Aviano-Gasse opposite the Johannesgasse to the **Neue Markt**. You are now right in front of the **Kapuzinerkirche** {2}, famous because of the **Kaisergruft** (Imperial Vault), also know as the Kapuzinergruft. In 1619, the Emperor Mathias and his wife Anna had it built as a tomb for Habsburg family mem- **Kärntner Straße.**

96

bers, underneath the monastery founded by Anna. Over the centuries the crypt has been extended several times. In the center of the building, which is open to the public, you can see the famous Rococo double sarcophagus made for Maria Theresia and her husband Francis Stephen (designed by Balthasar Moll, 1753). Once the Kapuzinergruft became well known and mentioned in works of literature, it turned into a synonym for the Habsburgs. The facade of the church was rebuilt in 1933-36 according to old drawings. The inside is a single barrel-vaulted nave. The high altar, decorated with inlay work, dates from the first half of the 18th century. On the left is the Kaiserkapelle (Imperial Chapel).

Going towards the city, on the same side as the church (past the Plankengasse), some Baroque houses have survived (nos. 13-16) which give an impression of the original appearance of the square. In the middle of the square is the **Providentiabrunnen**, the fountain for which the famous Baroque sculptor, Georg Raphael Donner created the models (1737-39). This is the first fountain put up by the city adminstration for the simple purpose of decorating a square. In the middle of the basin is the figure of Providentia (Providence); the sculptures around the edge of the basin symbolize tributaries of the Danube. Today, you can only see copies in bronze, the original lead figures are in the Baroque museum in the Lower Belvedere. Maria Theresia had them removed because of their "inadequate" clothing, but the sculptor Messerschmidt managed to save them from destruction.

Looking from the fountain to the Plankengasse, you can see the tower of the Protestant Church (built in 1783-84). The Emperor Joseph II's, Edict of Tolerance (1782) allowed non-Catho-

Donner's fountain.

lic denominations to build churches as well. Take a look at the Herrnhuterhaus (no. 17, built 1900-01) which has been connected with the textile industry since the end of the 18th century. Now go back to the Kärntner Straße via the Kupferschmiedgasse. In the **Himmelpfortgasse** opposite (no. 8) pay a visit to the former **Stadtpalais** of **Prince Eugene** {3}. This Baroque palais, begun in 1695-98 by Johann Bernhard Fischer von Erlach and completed by Hildebrandt in 1702-09, has a suberbly crafted façade and a most interesting interior (now the Ministry of Finance). Pass the Kärntner Durchgang (with a bar whose interior was designed by Adolf Loos in 1907) and the Weihburggasse (here you'll find the house by Kornhäusel, no. 3, "Zur Kaiserin Elisabeth"; no. 4 is the top class restaurant "Zu den drei Husaren", and past the bend along the road is the Franziskanerplatz with the **Franzis-**

kanerkirche) and you'll arrive at the **Stock-im-Eisen-Platz**.

The name comes from the "Stock in Eisen" (club in iron) on the corner of the Kärntner Straße, a tree trunk studded with nails, mentioned in 1533 and is the subject of a local legend. Ever since some houses were demolished in the 19th century this square leads straight into the Stephansplatz and the Graben (to the left), and offers an unobstructed view of the cathedral tower. The square is outside the Roman camp of Vindabona, and the oldest church of St. Stephen was also built outside the Roman walls of the city center in 1137.

St. Stephen's Cathedral {4} (see chapter on St. Stephen's Cathedral) should be seen from the outside and from the inside. The main parts of the Cathedral are Gothic. The west front of the Romanesque basilica, one of the last built in the German speaking countries, remains: the two Heidentürme mark the

Franzis-kanerkirche

breadth of the cathedral at that time. The high roof with its glazed tiles (renewed after the fire of 1945) has considerable influence on the appearance of the cathedral and harmoniously combines the various architectural styles of different periods. In the center of the west front is the "Riesentor" (Giant's Doorway), a late Romanesque (c.1230-40) portal richly ornamented with sculptures, the work of a company of masons working in and around Vienna. Around 1500, it received the projecting pointed arch. There are doors leading into the cathedral on the two sides, as well. On the north side is the Bischofstor (1380-90), opposite the Bischofshof (Bishop's palace—today the Archbishop's palace, Rotenturmstraße 2), on the south side the Singertor by Hans Puchsbaum (1440-50), both late Gothic. You can also enter the cathedral at the foot of the two Gothic towers (the northern one was never completed). Notice the statues of wordly founders (Habsburgs and their wives) in some of the doorways—this was a rarity in the Middle Ages.

Going into the **Interior of the Cathedral**, you'll see a Gothic three-aisled nave of impressive dimensions: height of the central aisle is 92 feet (28 meters), width of the nave is 118 feet (36 meters). The fan vaulting rests on pillars almost nine feet (three metres) thick, each with six niches for statues. The three-aisled choir, the oldest part of the Gothic cathedral (1304-40), has cruciform vaulting. Here the series of Gothic statues on the pillars wasn't completed till the end of the 19th century. The symbol of the cathedral (and also of Vienna) is the South Tower dating from the high Gothic period (almost 450 feet or 137 metres-high, the highest in central Europe after Ulm and Cologne) begun in the reign of Duke Rudolf IV in 1359, completed by Hans

Roof of St. Stephen's Cathedral.

Prachatitz. The northern tower (Adler-turm or Eagle Tower) was begun in 1467, but building stopped in 1511. Kaspar and Hans Saphoy built an octagonal top for the tower in 1556-78. On a platform high up the tower (take the lift!) you can see the new "Pummerin" (Boomer), the biggest bell in Austria. Going round inside the church, you can limit yourself to the most important works of art: the high altar with the picture of the *Stoning of St. Stephen* by Tobias Pock, behind, in the choir, remains of Gothic stained glass (c. 1340-60); in the left aisle of the choir is a Gothic altar with triptych ("Wiener Neustädter Altar", 1447), with 72 saints painted on the gold background of the panels; to the left of the altar is the (empty) tomb of Rudolf IV and his wife with reclining figures (Rudolf began the building of the naves and the tower); in the right aisle of the choir is the tomb of Emperor Frederick III (1452-93), designed by Niclas Gerhaert van Leyden (1467-1513), a sarcophagus of red marble with reclining figure and intricate carving; in the central aisle the late Gothic pulpit by Anton Pilgram (c. 1500), the most notable work of art in the nave, with the self-portrait of the artist at the pulpit's foot (*Fenster-gucker*, showing Pilgram looking out of a window); in front of the pulpit is the *Dienstbotenmadonna* (Madonna of the Servants, 1340); in the left aisle, near the exit to the tower, is the late Gothic organ base with the portrait bust of Pilgram (1513). The chapels, built onto the outside of the Romanesque towers, can be reached from the aisles: to the left the Kreuzkapelle with the Prince Eugene's tomb and a 15-century crucifix, plus the tomb of the humanist Johannes Cuspinian, to the right the Herzogskapelle with its late Gothic carved triptych altar and its stone statue of the Virgin carved sometime in the middle of the 14th century).

Tour around the cathedral (clock-wise): On the left façade of the main body of the church is a relief of the Mount of Olives (c. 1440); near the Adlerturm a Renaissance epitaph for the humanist Conrad Celtis (1459-1508); on the choir an epitaph with a sandstone relief of the *Day of Judgment*, next to it the funeral chapel (funeral of Wolfgang Amadeus Mozart, 1791) and the Capistran pulpit (c. 1430), surmounted by a Baroque group showing St. Capistran with banner above a fallen Turk, after designs by Francois de Roettiers, a reminder of the Crusade sermons of Johann von Capistran in the 15th century; six late Gothic frescos of the *Passion* (c. 1500); to the right of the Singertor, *The Man of Sorrows* (c.1435). Immediately to the right of the Riesentor you can see the scratched sign "0 5" of the Austrian resistance movement of World War II. A separate tour will take you on a visit of the buildings surrounding the square

St. Stephen's Cathedral.

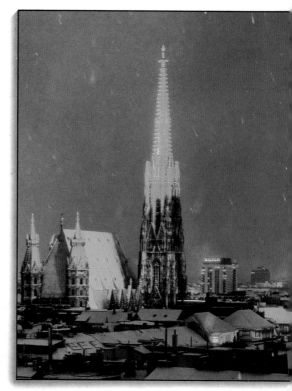

(see chapter on Through the Oldest Part of the City). On the **Stephansplatz**, next to the cathedral, you can see the outline of the Chapel of St. Mary Magdalene, the old cemetery church which burned down in 1782, outlined in red stones. Passing the house Zur Weltkugel (no. 2), which had its façade restored around 1900 by the Sparkasse savings bank which had its headquarters in the house, you arrive back in the **Stock-im-Eisen-Platz**. Here you will find the richly ornamented Equitablehaus (no. 3), built in 1890-91 for a New York insurance company (note the US eagle on the roof). The bronze doors were created by Rudolf Weyr (reliefs illustrate the Stock-im-Eisen legend).

The **Graben** gets its name from the ditch surrounding the Roman camp, which was leveled around 1200. In the Middle Ages the Graben was an important market, in the 18th century a popular meeting place for high society, and today it's a busy pedestrian shopping center. Up until the middle of the 19th century both ends were bounded by blocks of houses. Of those Baroque houses, only the **Palais Bartolotti-Partenfeld** (no. 11) survives. It may have been built by Hildebrandt (c. 1720). Today, except for the neo-classical Sparkasse building (no. 21), the buildings along the Graben almost all have Historicist or Secessionist façades. Noteworthy are no. 10 (built in 1894 by Otto Wagner, the only surviving office block by this architect), no. 13 (Generalihof, gate of the company Knize by Adolf Loos), nos. 14-15 (Grabenhof, built 1874-76 by Otto Wagner and Otto Thienemann), no. 16 (built 1909-11, with Secessionist mosaics in the 5th storey), no. 20 (built 1855-58 by Ferdinand Fellner, with striking caryatids) and, at the beginning, on the right nos. 29-29a (Trattnerhof, built 1911). In the middle of the

Fiaker in the Stephansplatz.

road is the **Dreifältigkeitssäule** (Trinity Pillar) {5}, better known as the **Pestsäule** (Plague Pillar), as it was commissioned by Emperor Leopold I in 1679 to commemorate an outbreak of plague. It is an excellent example of the architectural sculpture of Viennese high Baroque, designed by Johann Bernhard Fischer von Erlach and Ludovido Burnacini, who created the pyramid of clouds together with Paul Strudel. It is crowned by a group portraying the Trinity. At either end of the Graben there are fountains, which originally stood in front of the houses bounding the square. They bear statues of St. Leopold and St. Joseph by Johann Martin Fischer (1804). Near the fountain in front of no. 21 is another special attraction—an underground toilet in pure Art Nouveau style.

From the Graben, streets lead off like ribs to the south, which were laid out by the Babenbergs (c. 1200) and quickly built up. As they have to a large extent kept their appearance over the centuries, it's worth taking a look. The district up as far as the Stallburg is a center of the Viennese antique trade. The auction house **Dorotheum** can be found here too (Dorotheergasse). Between Graben no. 25 and 21 you can see the Baroque **St. Peter's Church** {6}, one of Hildbrandt's works. For centuries a Romanesque church stood on this site. The church, built in 1702-33 (portal by Andrea Altomonte, 1751-53) derives its characteristic appearance from the diagonally placed towers (1730-33) and the cupola. The cylindrical central space is raised above an elliptical ground plan. The fresco in the cupola, *The Assumption of the Virgin Mary*, was painted by Johann Michael Rottmayr (1713-14). Of special note, inside is the high altar by Antonio Galli-Bibena (altar panel by Martino Altomonte), the pulpit by Mathias Steinl (c. 1716) and the gilded wood sculpture opposite, the *Fall of St. John Nepomuk*

into the Moldau by Lorenzo Mattielli (c. 1729). Mattielli was also responsible for the statues on the outside of the choir. The aisles are decorated with paintings by famous artists. In the Middle Ages the **Kohlmarkt** was the city's connection to the long-distance trade route leading west (now Mariahilfer Straße). The name comes from *Holzkohle*, charcoal, which was sold here. From the 14th century on, the street moved upmarket due to the nearness of the Hofburg, and it developed into an expensive shopping street. No. 7 dates from the Vormärz (1840), the office block no. 9 was built by Max Fabiani for the Artaria company (1901-02). In the Middle Ages, the **Tuchlauben** were the homes of wealthy cloth merchants. In the pedestrian precinct you can see a very remarkable Baroque building, the Hochholzerhof (no. 5). Built in 1719, it has an impressive, richly ornamented façade, which fol-

The Fenstergucker.

lows the curve of the street. The pharmacy "Zum weißen Storch" has been at no. 9 since the 17th century. In no. 19, a medieval house with a Baroque facade built in 1716, the oldest secular frescos in Vienna were discovered—they date from c. 1400, and can be seen in the museum. Via the **Steindelgasse** (no. 4, Zum goldenen Drachen, dates from the 16th and 17th centuries, note the house sign and the late Gothic Madonna), which offers a good view of the Gothic choir of the church Am Hof, and the Seitzergasse you arrive in the **Bognergasse** (no. 9, pharmacy "Zum weißen Engel", Art Nouveau decorated shop façade) and back at the Graben. Following the **Naglergasse** you arrive at the square Am Hof. On the southern side of the Naglergasse (on your left) is a well-preserved line of burgess' houses from the late Middle Ages and early Renaissance, which lay along the Roman camp wall (later the city wall);

at Haarhof you can still see the dip of the ditch, and the curve of the walls can be followed as far as Heidenschuß.

Leave the Naglergasse via the Irisgasse (to the right) and move on into the square **Am Hof**. Here Henry II Jasomirgott had his castle built in 1155. Today the older buildings in the square are Baroque in style. The church **Zu den neun Chören der Engel** (The Nine Choirs of Angels) {7}, of which you have already seen the Gothic choir, has an early Baroque facade which dominates the square. From its mighty balcony Pope Pius VI gave his blessing *urbi et orbi* in 1782. It is a strong reminder of its models in Rome. Originally this was where the core of the castle stood; then the Carmelites built a Gothic church here in 1386-1403, and in the early 17th century, the Jesuits gave it a Baroque appearance. The side chapels and the white stucco hide all trace of the Gothic style. The most

The Plague Pillar in Graben.

famous preachers in Vienna have preached in the pulpit with its neoclassical reliefs. The church is the oldest Jesuit church in Vienna, the only one in the style of Jesuit churches in Rome, and marks the climax of early Baroque. The **Palais Collalto** (no. 13), connected to the church by an arch, received its Baroque façade in 1720 (note the portal and the wrought iron balcony railings). This was where Wolfgang Amadeus Mozart first appeared in public, at the age of six. During the French occupation of Vienna in 1809 Napoleon's General Lefébvre lived in the Palais. The **Urban-Haus** (no. 12) next door was given its Baroque façade in the style of Hildebrandt around 1730. The relief of the Virgin dates from the 16th century, the inn sign "Urbanikeller" from the 18th.

Also in Am Hof is the former **Bürgerliches Zeughaus** (City Armoury, no. 10), now the headquarters of the Fire Brigade. The fine gabled façade was created by Anton Ospel after French and Spanish models (1731-32).The sculptures (allegorical figures, symbolizing a favorite quotation of Charles VI and bearing a terrestrial globe) are by Mattielli. The Zeughaus played an important part during the two sieges by the Turks, and also during the 1848 revolution. The Minister of War at that time, Latour, was murdered by the enraged crowd in Am Hof. Up until the 19th century no. 9 was the home of the Mayor (note at first floor height, the angel with the shield showing the Viennese double eagle with imperial crown). House no. 7, one of the most beautiful Baroque houses of the city center, was built from 1727-30 by Hildebrandt. The proportions of the façade are similar to those of palaces of the nobility dating from this period, but the ground floor has been altered (garage doors for the Fire Brigade have replaced the portal). In the middle of the square is the **Mariensäule** (Pillar of the Virgin); it replaces an older pillar set up by Ferdinand III in 1644 to mark the end of the danger from the Swedish army during the Thirty Year's War. Going towards the Freyung, you leave Roman and medieval Vienna behind in the low ground, but before you go you can see the curve of the camp boundary, mentioned above, in the Naglergasse (on the left). To the right, a stream flowing in the **Tiefer Graben** once afforded additional protection.

The **Freyung** is surrounded by impressive buildings, but is dominated by the Schottenkirche (Scottish Church—though the monks it was built for were actually Irish). To the left of the square, start with the **Palais Hardegg** (no. 1), a palais-style apartment block in the Romantic Historicist style, built by Romano and Schwendenwein in 1847. Next door (no. 2) is the **Palais Ferstel**, built from 1856-60 by Heinrich Ferstel (who designed the University) in His-

Detail of the Plague Pillar.

104

toricist style; it was built for the Austro-Hungarian Bank. A lane through to the Herrengasse widens into a square with a fountain, the **Donaunixen-Brunnen** (Fountain of the Danube Nymphs) by Fernkorn. No. 3 is the **Palais Herrach**, built at the end of the 17th century. The main façade, dating from 1845, gives it its present-day appearance. In the extension of the Herrengasse is a jewel among Vienna Baroque palaces—the **Palais Daun-Kinsky** (no. 4), built from 1713-16 by Hildebrandt for Reichsgraf Daun, father of Maria Theresia's victorious general. In 1784, the Palais came into the ownership of the Kinsky family—the salon of Rosa Kinksy was famous in Vienna. The well-proportioned portal, the statues and the splendid staircase all bear witness to the decorative gifts of the architect. Next to the Schottenkirche is the **Schottenhof** (no. 6), built from 1826-1832 in the Neo-classical style by Joseph

Kornhäusel, the great architect of the Biedermeier period. It was one of the earliest big apartment houses in Vienna (the composer Franz Liszt lived here from 1869-96). In the gallery of the monastery you can see the famous Altar of the Scottish Master (c. 1470), which shows two of the oldest views of Vienna. In the monastery's high school, the **Schottengymnasium**, a number of famous men have studied, among them the Nobel Prize winner Wagner-Jauregg, and also Johann Nestroy, Johann Strauss and Victor Adler. The **Schottenkirche** {8} was founded by the Babenberg Henry II Jasomirgott in 1155, outside the walls of the 12th-century city. Today it appears as a Baroque church (1638-48), with towers that rise only slightly above the central portion of the building. We know that among the architects were members of the Carlone and d'Allio families. The interior was altered by Ferstel in 1883-

Am Hof

89 (especially the high altar, pulpit and painted ceiling). Seventeenth-century paintings have survived on the partially renovated side altars, and above the tabernacle of the altar in the left transept the oldest statue of the Virgin in Vienna (c. 1250) is venerated.

The route from the Freyung to the Hofburg follows the Herrengasse. This street follows the line of the old Roman road along the Limes. Many noble families built their palaces here in the 16th century, because of the nearness of the Hofburg, and the name "Herrengasse" (Lords' Street) became current. Palaces dating from the 16th to the early 19th century have survived, particularly on the right-hand side of the street. Start with the **Palais Porcia** (no. 23), with its almost unchanged façade in the Italian style (mid-16th century), the **Palais Trauttmansdorff** (no. 21) dating from the mid-17th century and the Palais Trauttmansdorff (no. 19, on the corner of the Bankgasse) dating from the early 18th century (note the interesting portal). Further palaces of the nobility can be seen in the **Bankgasse** (no. 3, Austro-Hungarian Bank building, built in 1873-75 by Friedrich Schmidt, who designed the Town Hall). On the opposite side of the Herrengasse you can see the backs of the Palais Harrach and the Palais Ferstel. On the corner of the Strauchgasse is the legendary **Café Central**, a meeting place for the intellectuals of Vienna from the turn of the century to 1938 (now re-opened). Its only rival was the Café Herrenhof. Opposite the junction with the Strauchgasse is the **Landhaus** (no. 13), seat of the Lower Austrian government. It is a free-standing, late neo-classical block of buildings with an impressive row of pillars and an interior which goes back in parts to Renaissance and Baroque times. During the 1848 revolution there were dramatic scenes in **Café Central**

front of the Landhaus. If you walk around the Landhaus, you will come to the **Minoritenplatz**, which you definitely ought to see. The square is surrounded by impressive palaces. Particularly notable are the **Palais Dietrichstein** with its delicately proportioned Rococo façade (no. 3), the **Stadtpalais Liechtenstein** (no. 4, main façade with its impressive portal Bankgasse no. 9), which has another noteworthy portal in the Minoritenplatz (the sculptures are by Giuliani), and the **Palais Starhemberg** (no. 5) which dominates part of the square and was built around 1650 by an unknown architect. In the middle of the square is the **Minoritenkirche "Maria Schnee"** (St. Mary of the Snows) {**9**}, the Italian national church in Vienna. The Minorite order was invited to Vienna in 1224, and church and monastery were built from 1340-1400. You enter the three-aisled church through the impressive central portal (c. 1350) with its three-part relief, which shows French influence, on the tympanum. The interior is 18th century. In the center of the left side wall is a remarkable mosaic copy of Leonardo da Vinci's *Last Supper*, commissioned by Napoleon in 1806. The monastery was demolished in the early 20th century to make room for the Haus-, Hof- und Staatsarchiv (Household, Court and State Archives - no. 1). Next door is the Bundeskanzleramt (Federal Chancellery) on the Ballhausplatz.

Go back to the Herrengasse and turn right towards the Michaelerplatz. You'll see the offices of the Lower Austrian State Government (no. 11), built in 1846-47 by Paul Sprenger, and the **Palais Mollard Clary** (no. 9, Lower Austrian State Museum); its present appearance dates from 1760. The neo-classical façades of the **Palais Modena** (no. 7) conceal parts of the

Emperor Joseph II's memorial.

building dating from the 16th century. Nearby are the **Palais Wilczek** (no. 5) with its noteworthy façade dating from the post 1719 period (the poets Grillparzer and Eichendorff both lived here for a time) and the **Palais Herberstein** (nos. 1-3), built by Carl König in 1897 as part of the alterations to the Michaelerplatz.

The Hofburg

The **Michaelertrakt** is the most recent part of the Hofburg, built in 1889-93 by Ferdinand Kirschner according to old plans by Joseph Emanuel Fischer von Erlach. The characteristic concave wall with its portals forms an impressive front onto the **Michaelerplatz** and the city center. On both sides of the main portal there are four statues of Hercules, and at the side are two monumental wall fountains, (to the left *Power on the Seas* by Rudolf Weyr,

1895; to the right *Power on Land* by Edmund Hellmer, 1897). The development of the area in front of the Reichskanzlei was delayed because the old Hofburgtheater couldn't be demolished until the new theater on the Ring had been opened (1888). Behind the left part of the Michaelertrakt lies the Winter Riding School, which was connected to the Burgtheater. You go through a magnificent wrought iron gate and enter a circular hall, surmounted by a huge dome, with pairs of statues symbolizing mottos of the Habsburgs. To the left is the **entrance to the Imperial Apartments** (Schausammlung). If you go through a further gate you come to the **Platz in der Burg {10}**, in the center of which is a memorial to the Emperor Francis I of Austria (1792-1835) by Pompeo Marchesi (1842-46).

If you look around you'll be able to read the history of the building of the **The National Library.**

Hofburg like a book. To your left is the oldest part of the Hofburg, the **Schweizerhof**, Gothic in origin, which was begun in the late 13th century. The **Hofburgkapelle** was first mentioned in 1296; it was rebuilt in 1447-49 and the interior redesigned in the Baroque style in the 17th and 18th centuries. You enter the courtyard through a splendid Renaissance gate (1552). Here are the entrances to the Hofburgkapelle (you can see the Gothic choir from a neighboring courtyard) and the world-famous **Geistliche und Weltliche Schatzkammer** (Imperial Treasury) with the Imperial crown jewels. To the right the Platz in der Burg is bordered by the **Amalienburg** (originally a separate building). A Renaissance building (1575-77), its present appearance dates from 1600-1611.

The connecting building is the **Leopoldinische Trakt**, built in 1660-66 in the Early Baroque style according to plans by Philiberto Lucchese. Today it's the official seat of the Federal President. The six sets of windows to the left date from the 16th century and were the residence of Archduke Ferdinand. The fourth side of the square is the High Baroque **Reichskanzleitrakt** by Joseph Emanuel Fischer von Erlach (1723-30). Until 1806 (when the Habsburgs relinquished the crown of the Holy Roman Empire) this was the home of the imperial government departments. Three portals form the focal points of the façade, and the sculptures at the side (by Mattielli) again refer to the Hercules myth. Go through the living apartments of Ferdinand and you come to the Heldenplatz with its neo-classical Zeremoniensaal (Ceremonial Hall), to the left, built from 1802-06 by Louis de Montoyer, and the Neue Hofburg (1881-1913; see chapter on The Ringstraße). If you leave the Platz in der Burg between the Leopoldinis-

Public rooms in the Hofburg.

che Trakt and the Amalienburg, you come to the **Ballhausplatz**. Sticking out to your left is the Leopoldinische Trakt, further over is the Volksgarten, and straight ahead the **Bundeskanzleramt** (Federal Chancellery). The building was put up in 1717-19, according to plans by Hildebrandt, as the Geheime Hofskanzlei (Court Privy Chancellery), altered by Nikolaus Pacassi in 1766 and extended into the Löwelstraße in 1881-82. The main façade still follows Hildebrandt's design. The building, in which the Congress of Vienna met in 1814-15, is the seat of the Federal Chancellor and the Federal Government. During a National Socialist coup in 1934 the Federal Chancellor, Dr. Dollfuß was shot in this building.

Return via the Schauflergasse (right) to the Michaelerplatz. The building at the start of the **Schauflergasse** (left) is modern, with a historic style facade. In the 16th century a building for ball games stood here, which gave its name to the Ballhausplatz.

The first **Michaelerkirche {11}** was built around 1100. Towards the end of the 12th century it was included in the Babenbergs' expansion of the city and at the end of the 13th century it was improved during the building of the Hofburg (Schweizerhof section). The oldest parts of the present church date from the second quarter of the 13th century (choir and transept), the nave followed during the third quarter. You can still see Romanesque carved arches and Gothic elements (choir) if you go into the Habsburgergasse. The porch (sandstone sculpture *Fall of the Angels* by Mattielli) is still Baroque (1724-25), but the façade is neo-classical (1792). Inside is a three-nave pillared basilica with cruciform vaulting. The Baroque high altar, set forward like a stage, contrasts with the central nave with its late Romanesque arches and capitals. The wall painting (*Last Judgment*) on the triumphal arch is 14th century, the

stucco relief *Fall of the Angels* on the choir wall above the high altar is by Karl Georg Melville (1782).

Looking around the Michaelerplatz you will see a variety of building styles. The Große Michaelerhaus (no. 4, corner of Kohlmarkt 11) was built in 1720, the Kleine Michaelerhaus (no. 6) in 1735. In a passage along the outer wall of the church there is a massive relief of the Mount of Olives, framed in color (1494). If you take a look into the Reitschulgasse, you will see the **Stallburg**, an important Renaissance building. The **Reitschultrakt** of the Hofburg opposite is Baroque, the Michaelertrakt Historicist. The most recent building (no. 3), was built in 1910-11 by Adolf Loos, and the unaccustomed simplicity of its Secessionist façade caused considerable excitement and criticism.

An arcaded passage leads through the Stallburg, part of the Hofburg that was

Portal of the Minoritenkirche.

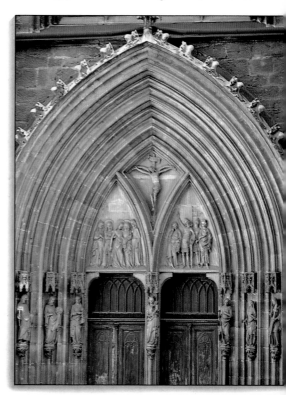

110

built from 1558-65 as a residence for Archduke Maximilian, later Emperor Maximilian II (1564-76).

The Lipizzaner stables

The four-winged building with its almost square design was once an independent complex and is now joined on to the **Winter-Reitschule** (Winter Riding School). The magnificent three-storeyed arcaded courtyard is the most important Renaissance building in Vienna. The Stallburg contains the **stables of the Spanish Riding School** (the Lipizzaner horses), the **Neue Galerie** and the **Alte Hofapotheke** (Old Court Pharmacy). The performances by the Spanish Riding School take place in the Winter Riding School, commissioned by the Emperor Charles VI and built from 1729-35 by Joseph Emanuel Fischer von Erlach.

Leaving the arcaded passage you

The Schweizertor.

come to the **Josefsplatz**, architecturally the most uniform square in the city center. In the middle is the **Horfbibliothek** {12} (once the Court, now the National Library), begun by Johann Bernhard Fischer von Erlach in 1723 and completed by his son in 1726. The main façade of the Baroque building is dominated by the central section with its cupola-like mansard roof, behind which is the world-famous Prunksaal with its oval cupola space, decorated with a grandiose painted ceiling by Daniel Gran in 1730. The architectural shape of the square was finalized in 1767-73, when the two side buildings were built, with façades that were stylistically in keeping with the library building. To the right are the two **Redoutensäle**. The left-hand building was erected in front of the the façade of the Augustinerkirche, whose Gothic style can now only be seen from the side of the church on the Augustinerstraße. Opposite the library are two buildings: the **Palais Pallavicini** (no. 5), with a neo-classical facade, built after the demolition of the Königinkloster (Queen's Monastery) in 1783-84 by Johann Ferdinand Hetzendorf von Hohenberg, and the **Palais Pálffy** (no. 6) , built in a plain style by an unknown architect in 1575 (but note the neo-classical portal). In the center of the square is the **memorial to the Emperor Joseph II** (1780-90) by Franz Anton Zauner (1795-1807). The bronze equestrian statue, portraying the Emperor as a Roman imperator, is modeled on the statue of Marcus Aurelius in Rome. Joseph II, son of Maria Theresia, was one of the most important imperial reformers of the House of Habsburg.

The **Augustinerkirche** {13} was built from 1330-39 by Dietrich Ladtner of Pirn, a Bavarian. It stood beside an Augustinian monastery founded in 1327 by Frederick the Fair. In 1630, influenced by the Counter-Reformation, Frederick II transferred the monastery to a stricter branch of the Augustinian order, and raised the church to Court Church status. The tower was not built until 1652. Alterations to the Josefsplatz robbed the church of its façade, but the Gothic side façade and interior (three aisles, very long and high with slender pillars) remained. In 1784-85, the interior of the church was given a new "Gothic" appearance by Hetzendorf von Hohenberg. In the right-hand aisle of the church is the neo-classical tomb of Marie-Christine (daughter of Maria Theresia and wife of Albert von Saxe-Teschen) by Antonio Canova. Here you will also find the Lorettokapelle and the Georgs-Kapelle, and behind them lies the "Herzgruft" (Heart Vault) with the urns containing the hearts of the Imperial family from 1637-1878).

In 1683, Jan Sobieski's Service of Thanksgiving for the liberation of Vienna from the Turks was held in the Augustinerkirche. In 1810 the wedding of Napoleon and Marie Louise was held here, and in 1854 that of Franz Joseph to Elisabeth.

From the Augustinerstraße, go and take a look in the Dorotheergasse. Here you will find two Protestant churches and, on the site of the former convent of St. Dorothy, the auction house "Dorotheum", built in the early 20th century. Then, passing the **Lobkowitzpalais**, turn towards the **Albertina** {**14**}. You follow a ramp leading up to a surviving part of the city fortifications, at the foot of which is the sculpture, Reclining Youth by Fritz Wotruba, and arrive at the palace of Duke Albert of Saxe-Teschen. In 1801-04 he had parts of the Palais Taroucca (1742-45) rebuilt by Louis de Montoyer, incorporating parts of the Augustinian monastery.

The interior was re-designed in the neo-classical style by Joseph Körnhausel. Albert was the founder of the "Graphische Sammlung Al-bertina", the largest collection of graphic works, drawings and woodcuts in the world. In front of the Palais is the equestrian statue of Archduke Albrecht, victor of Custozza (1866), by Caspar Zumbusch (1899). Albrecht was the son of Archduke Charles, who was the first to defeat Napoleon in 1809 at Aspern. You can look back at the Palais Lobkowitz from the platform of the **Augustinerbastei**. Its façade was still built in the style of palaces predating the second Turkish siege, although it was not built until 1685-87, probably by Giovanni Pietro Tencala. Johann Bernhard Fischer von Erlach gave the facade its present form. Ludwig van Beethoven's *Eroica* was first heard in 1803 during a private concert in the palace. The **Danubiusbrunnen** (Danube Fountain) (1869) decorates the fortifications at the Albertinaplatz. It was designed by Moritz Lohr and the sculptures are by Johann Meixner.

View from the Albertina ramp. Right, the Spanish Riding School

Through The Oldest Part Of The City

The second tour through the oldest parts of the city starts at **Stephansplatz**. The cathedral in the middle of this square was built in the 12th century, but not until the 18th century did it begin to look as it looks today. In 1732 the cemetery was opened up, in 1792, a row of houses in front of the big gates was demolished, and in 1803, access was built to "Stock-im-Eisen-Platz". In April 1945, not only the cathedral, but many of the neighboring houses went up in flames.

Walking (anti-clockwise) round the cathedral, your first building is the **Haus zur Weltkugel** (No. 2) which stands close to the (protruding) **Churhaus** (No. 3). The Churhaus was erected in 1738-40 to replace the old grammar school and the work-place of the stone-masons employed by the church, and it was rebuilt in 1806 by Louis de Montoyer. At the corner you come to that part of the **Deutschordenshaus** (No. 4) which extends to Stephansplatz, where the tour will finally end. Next to it is the **Domherrenhof** (No. 5), built in 1837-42, which has a striking façade. On the north side of the square you pass the **Zwettler Hof** (No. 6), built in 1844 and housing the famous **Dom- und Diozesanmuseum** (ecclesiastical museum). Continue to the **Erzbischofliche** Palais. Its entrance faces **Rotenturmstraße**, but the chapel choir (1638) overlooks the square. The Palais is the seat of the Archbishop of Vienna (archbishopric since 1732) and was built in 1632-41.

You now approach Lichtensteg, leaving till much later your visit to Sonnenfelsgasse and **Bäckerstraße** (on the right), both beautifully preserved. Turn

Preceding pages: Griechengasse. Below left, view of the altar in the church "Maria am Gestade". Right, Ruprechtskirche.

left instead, and you will shortly be at **Hohe Markt**, the oldest square of the town. This was severely damaged in World War II and was never restored.

Medieval Vienna

Vienna is built on the Roman encampment called Vindobona (entrance to the **Roman ruins** at No. 3) where the palace of the commanding officer once stood. In the middle ages, Hohe Markt was the center of the old town (comprising the market, courts of justice, guildhalls and the houses of the patricians) until the new market was built in the expanding suburb created by the Babenbergers. House No. 5 (1855) and No. 10/11 (1913/14, the Ankerhaus) survived the last war. They are connected by a flying buttress on which is to be found a Jugendstil **anchor clock** (Franz Matsch, 1913)—its parade of historical figures attracts spectators at midday. The **Josefsbrunnen 15** (the fountain for the "bridal pair") was built by Joseph Emanuel Fischer v. Erlach. When in 1702, Archduke Josef was laying siege to the fortress Landau, his father, Emperor Leopold I, promised to donate a column if he was victorious. This column was later replaced by the fountain. The "bridal pair" (Joseph and Mary) and the high priest by Antonio Corradini stand on a massive round base, arched by a bronze canopy and crowned by the Holy Trinity.

Leaving the square behind, you now turn down **Wipplingerstraße**. Here, at its narrowest point, two historically and architecturally important buildings face each other: On the left is the **Ehemalige Böhmische Hofkanzlei** (the former court chancellery) **16** (No. 7). It was originally built by Johann Bernhard Fischer v. Erlach (1708-14) and enlarged by Matthias Gerl (1751-54) with such skill that it is impossible to tell where the old part ends and the addition begins (only the front that

looks out over Judenplatz is Gerl's own design). It is the first building in Austria with a façade designed in the neo-classical Palladian style, although French and Italian motifs, taken from the High Baroque, are also blended in. Opposite (No. 8, on the right) is the **Alte Rathaus** (the old town hall), with its main part (in Salvatorgasse) dating back to the 14th century. The **Salvatorkapelle** (chapel) belongs to the same century. The town hall was enlarged several times during the centuries. Then, after the second siege by the Turks (1683), the court, the nobility and the bourgeoisie suddenly found themselves gripped by a fever called Baroque. At the turn of the century, the municipal government instructed an architect (whose name is not known) to replace the existing façade of the town-hall by a Baroque façade. Its lavish style is reminiscent of Johann Bernhard Fischer v. Erlach's. The two imposing main entrances are embellished with sculptures of an extraordinary quality (at the east entrance, closer to the square, the sculptures were added by Johann Martin Fischer as late as 1781). The rebuilding and refurbishing was completed in 1713/14, when all the rooms were painted and decorated. (The coats of arms painted on the ceiling in a hall on the first floor represent all members of the senate in office in 1713/14.) The **Dokumentationsarchiv des österreichischen Widerstands** (archive of Austrian resistance) is housed in the old townhall. The fountain in the courtyard was built by Georg Raphael Donner (1741) and has a famous lead relief, "Perseus and Andromeda", and a heraldic angel built in the 18th century.

You pass through a narrow, small street ("Stoß im Himmel"). Here, at the corner to Wipplingerstraße, you encounter a Gothic angel (bearing the coat of arms of Austria and Vienna). You then arrive at "Salvatorgasse", which houses a gem of the Gothic period; the church **Maria am Gestade 17**. In the middle of the 12th century, you would have seen a Romanesque church (built partly on the walls of the Roman fortress) on this hill which then looked down into the "Tiefe Graben" and a tributary of the Danube (Salzgries). The Gothic church dates back to the 13th and 14th centuries. The choir was built between 1330 and 1369, the main aisle by Michael Knab, the dome of the spire between 1394 and 1414.

The ground plan of the church had to be adapted to the site (a break between choir and nave). The narrow west front is notable because of its height (over 100 ft) and its main entrance (relief ca. 1410). The side entrance dates back to 1500. The dome of the spire is one of the most beautiful examples of Gothic art in Vienna. Inside, one is struck by the contrasting narrow and dark main aisle and the spacious, light choir. The organ-loft (1515) looks as if it were floating high above angels and corbels (also impressive is the delicate tracery of the balustrades). The interior design mainly dates back to the 19th century, with the exception of four windows in the choir (14th/15th century), a Renaissance altar, Gothic and Baroque statues under canopies and the Baroque cross on the main altar (finished in 1730).

Looking down into the "Tiefe Graben", you will notice a row of houses going back to the late 15th century. Walking back through **Salvatorgasse**, you now find yourself (just having passed the rear entrance to the old townhall) at the main entrance (Renaissance) of the church called **Salvatorkirche 18** (No. 5). It was originally the chapel belonging to a patrician's home, then became the town hall. It was enlarged after 1520, when the charming main entrance was built. Passing along opposite of the Fischerstiege, you enter **Sterngasse** (on the right) and then Marc-Aurel-Straße (statue, No. 6, of the Roman emperor). Here you cross the road in order to get to that part of the city where, after the Romans had departed, the first suburban houses sprang up (hardly discernable today), a settlement called "Berghof", with the Ruprechtskirche and a market square. The squared stones which were found nearby once formed part of the Roman baths. No. 3 is the **Wiener Neustädter Hof** with an impressive façade and a very pretty inner courtyard (built 1735-37). The "Turkish cannon ball", embedded in a wall, dates from 1683. At the end of Sterngasse is **Ruprechtsplatz**, with the Ruprechtskirche on your left and Judengasse (the 'Jews' Alley') on your right. Judengasse did not, however, form part of the medieval ghetto around the Judenplatz (the 'Jews' Square). The houses No. 7, 9, 11 and 16 were built between 1796 and 1838. During the day, this area is the home of second-hand clothes shops and second-hand dealers. In the evening, its small and cosy inns and pubs attract locals and visitors alike.

The **Ruprechtskirche 19**, is probably the oldest church in Vienna, founded, so it is said, in 740. More likely, however, the main aisle and the spire were built during the 11th century. The plain Romanesque style church also shows on the outside traces of Romanesque and the Gothic period.

Its interior was greatly altered in 1934-36 (the wooden ceiling was replaced by a barrel-vault), but still has the oldest stained glass (on the window in the middle of the choir) dating back to the 13th century. In front of the church is a statue of St. Ruprecht (with a salt-cellar). Where the steps leading up to the church are today, there was a small harbor during the Roman occupation which was important for the salt trade. Turning into **Seitenstettengasse**, you come to the home of the Jewish Community (No. 2, built in 1824-26 by Joseph Kornhäusel) with the **Synagogue 20** in its courtyard (built in 1825/

26, also by Kornhäusel) which is the oldest Jewish place of worship in the city since the Jews were driven out in 1421. It is the only synagogue in Vienna that survived the notorious "Kristallnacht"violence of the Nazi regime in 1938. All the others were burnt down. It was saved by the fact that it had been erected in what had become a densely populated area. No. 5 is the Seitenstettner Hof with its ornamental relief on the front, probably also built by Kornhäusel. Walking past the **Kornhäuselturm** (No.2, at the corner of Judengasse and Fleischmarkt), which the famous "Biedermeier" (early 19th century) architect had built for himself (1825-27), you will now find yourself in **Fleischmarkt**.

Fleischmarkt is probably one of the oldest streets in the suburb created by the Babenbergers (documented as early as 1220, oldest seat of the butchers' guild). In the 18th century, Greek trad-

ers settled here. Whereas the first part of the street is dominated by Jugendstil architecture (Nos. 1-7, and 14), the latter has many buildings which are considerably older. Looking at No. 9, for example, with its curved façade, the Gothic oriel, the Renaissance relief depicting the Virgin Mary and the arcades in the courtyard, it becomes clear that in essence it dates back to the 15th/ 16th century. It is connected to No.11 by a flying buttress, arching the whole wide span of Griechengasse. No. 11 has late Gothic baywindows and a Baroque façade and is the home of the **Griechenbeisel**, a name which points to the Greek ("Griecheon") traders. During the time of the Black Death, the folk singer Augustin (very popular in Vienna under the name "Lieber Augustin") was a frequent visitor to this inn. In the 19th century, it was the meeting point for such eminent personalities of the city's cultural and political

he Greek
hurch.

life as Richard Wagner, Johannes Strauss, Johann Brahms and writer Franz Grillparzer. In **Griechengasse**, you will notice a number of old-fashioned kerb-stones, placed there to prevent the fronts of the houses from being damaged by carts passing through.

In the Greek Quarter

Next to the "Griechenbeisel" stands the **Greek Church 21** (No. 13), built during the reign of Joseph II. It was originally built by Peter Mollner (1782-87) and extended when a Byzantine front was added by Theophil Hansen in 1858-61. There are two houses in the vicinity which are connected with the church: On the third floor of No. 18 there is a plaque commemorating the "Edict of Tolerance" issued by Joseph II in 1781 granting religious freedom and thus enabling the Greek community to have the church built. No. 20-22 was built (1823-1825) as the home for banker, Simon George Baron of Sina, the Royal Greek Ambassador, who paid for the extension built by Theophil Hansen. The birth place of the painter Moritz Schwind (No. 15) is not to be missed. It has a beautiful façade, lavishly decorated in the Baroque style of the early 18th century. At the end of the street, there is the main post office on the left, once a monastery and dissolved in 1782 as a consequence of Joseph II's monasterial reforms. Next, you come to the building that once housed the customs offices in **Postgasse** (No. 8, built in 1773, façade in 1852).

Then, turning right, where the street broadens out like a square, you come face to face with Kornhäusel's part of the library of the **Old University 22** (1827-29). Turning right would lead into Schönlaterngasse (but you will come to this street later). Bearing left brings you to the **Barbarakirche** (No. 10), the second Greek church (building: 1652-54, interior: second half of the

18th century), and a little further on to the **Dominikanerkirche 23** . The Order of the Black Friars ("Dominikaner") was called to Vienna in 1226 by Duke Leopold VI and later built this church (1631-34, dome and façade 1666-74). It originally stood high up on a bastion, the outer fortification walls of which can still be seen.

The façade of the church (without a spire), looking out into Postgasse, corresponds to the Roman style of early Baroque. The interior is dominated by lavish stucco decorations (1666-75) and frescos by Matthias Rauchmiller (nave) on the ceilings and (by Carpoforo Tencala) on the choir stalls. Opposite the church, are the buildings of the Old University founded by Duke Rudolf IV in 1365; building began in 1385. The Jesuits undertook extensive alterations (1623-27) having been entrusted with the philosophical and theological faculties by Ferdinand II. (The

A typical Viennese organ-grinder.

Jesuits were suppressed in 1773.)

A passage through the building right at the end leads to **Dr. Ignaz-Seipel-Platz** which has a somewhat cozy look about it and borders on two sides onto the old university. Facing you now is the old auditorium, and on your right is the **Jesuitenkirche [24]**, built in 1623-27 by an unknown architect. It was given its present-day look in 1703-07 when Andrea Pozzo made slight alterations to the (early) Baroque facade and added the spires with their massive (late) Baroque domes. The Jesuitenkirche is a classical example of the way façades were built in the early period of the Baroque. Inside, however, a successful experiment was carried out in order to make the long aisle into a wider central hall, specially favored in the early years of the 18th century (four side chapels, juxtaposed, thematically and in pairs were added). Andrea Pozzo broke the barrel-vault down into sec-

tions and furbished it with trompe d' oeil fresco paintings and an illusary dome.

The **Auditorium of the University** is the only monumental Rococo building in Vienna, built by Jean Nicolas Jadot de Ville-Issey (1753-55). Today, it is occupied by the Austrian Academy of Sciences. The building stands on its own, the main front with two in-built fountains facing the square. Allegorical figures protrude from the pediments at the two sides of the building, representing the medical and legal faculties.

Churches, Pubs and Inns

Between the auditorium and the church you now enter Sonnenfelsgasse (No. 19, the porter's lodge, 17th century; No. 17, also 17th century, with oriel windows on all floors; No. 15 with a Renaissance gate), and instantly turn right again into **Schönlaterngasse**. At the corner, where it curves to the right, you have a superb view over one of the oldest quarters of the city. No. 7 is the Basiliskenhaus, so called according to a legend about a "Basilisk" (apparently a cross between a cockerel and a toad) whose poisonous breath presented a great danger to the workmen digging a well. The house is immediately recognizable by a block of sandstones shaped like an animal. The foundations date from the 13th century, the façade was built in 1740. Opposite (No. 6) stands the house called **Zur schönen Laterne** ("The Beautiful Lantern", made obvious by its sign). Its front is a typical example of the prevailing style at the time of building (1680). The adjacent building, No. 4 (second half of the 17th century), is one of only very few buildings in this particular style still to be seen in Vienna. Through a gate (covered by a turret which greatly enhances the overall impression of the small passage behind the gate) you enter **Heiligenkreuzer Hof**. The building of

In front of the "Figarohaus" (Domgasse).

the monastery Heiligenkreuz was begun in the first half of the 13th century. It had developed into an impressive complex by the 16th century and was completed round about the middle of the 18th century. The Bernhardskapelle (on the left in the courtyard) dates back to 1730 and is of great artistic value. The painter Martino Altomonte, who had worked in the monastery, died in this courtyard in 1745.

Cross this peaceful yard and leave it through an entrance on the opposite side. Then walk back to **Sonnenfelsgasse** via Köllnerhofgasse (No. 2, the Kölner Hof with its neo-classical façade, was built in 1792/93 by Peter Mollner). Looking down Sonnenfelsgasse, you will notice a row of old houses with partial Baroque façades. On the left, these are notably No. 3 (Hildebrandthaus, lavish Baroque façade in the style of Johann Lukas v. Hildebrandt, with traces of Rococo, 1721), No. 5 (neo-classicism) and No. 11 (Baroque entrance door, ca. 1710). The row of houses on the right extends as far as Bäckerstraße, your next stop.

First, cross **Lugeck** Square, which has a few old buildings (No. 7, at the corner of Rotenturmstraße, the Große Federlhof, built in 1846/47; No. 5, façade early 19th century). Between Sonnenfelsgasse and Bäckerstraße stands the former department store Orendi (1897), on the medieval site of the court of the merchants of Regensburg—who, could even boast of entertaining the Emperor Frederick III (there is a statue of him at the side of the house in Bäckerstraße). The home of the merchants of Cologne was close by (Köllnerhofgasse). It is easier to understand the historical importance of this part of the city once you know that for centuries there was broad green a linking Sonnenfelsgasse and Bäckerstraße which formed the center of this 'merchant suburb', called "Behind the Hungarian Gate".

One of the very few remaining patrician houses from the 16th century in Bäckerstraße (which has a number of very beautiful old houses), has the only existing Renaissance courtyard (No. 7, built before 1587). The wrought-iron works in the yard once belonged to the collection of the Biedermeier painter Friedrich Amerling. At No. 12, a house dating from the 15th/16th century (façade 18th century), a Renaissance window and a fresco from the 16th century were discovered. The fresco depicts a cow and a wolf (symbolizing Protestantism and Catholicism) playing backgammon. By going along Essiggasse (between Nos. 8 and 10), you reach **Wollzeile**, leading to the medieval Stubentor in which only a few old houses have been preserved. Walk along Strobelgasse, and turn into **Schulerstraße** ("Schule" = school) which took its name from the resident School of Law (Juristenschule, 1389), or perhaps from the St. Stephen Bürgerschule (1237). Other buildings of interest in Schulerstraße are the Mädelspergerhof (No. 7), and the house called **Zum König von Ungarn** (The King of Hungary) (No. 10, façade 18th century), one of the oldest inns of Vienna (today a hotel).

The birth place of the *"Marriage of Figaro"*

The **Figarohaus 25** (No. 5) brought world fame to **Domgasse**. Wolfgang Amadeus Mozart lived in this house in 1784-87 where, among other works, he composed the opera *The Marriage of Figaro*. It is the only remaining home of Mozart in Vienna, today a museum. No. 4 is the Trienter Hof, commissioned by the episcopate in 1755. No. 6, with an impressive façade representative of its time, and an image of the Virgin Mary, which is framed by Rococo ornaments, dates back to 1761.

To finish off this round trip, you visit

Blutgasse (entering it at No. 5, Fähnrichhof), first documented in the 14th century and situated in a very old part of the city. Although the main façades of a number of important buildings look out onto other streets (No. 1, Trienter Hof, Domgasse; No. 2, Domherrenhof, Stephansplatz; No. 4, Deutschordenshaus, Singerstraße), the charm of Blutgasse lies in its many courtyards offering peace and tranquillity. The whole complex provides an interesting insight into the way the Viennese lived in the 17th and 18th centuries. It is also a perfect example of how old places and buildings can best be preserved and restored by keeping most of the old foundations.

Leaving the courtyards, you will find yourself in Singerstraße. No. 7 is the enormous **Deutschordenshaus** building (extending to Stephansplatz), a medieval complex rebuilt into one building in the 17th century with two courtyards at its center. Mozart lived here in 1781. In the Deutschordenshaus is the **Schatzkammer des Deutschen Ordens** (the Treasury of the Teutonic Order, called to Vienna at about 1200, where it later became permanently established). Next to it is the **Deutschordenskirche**, erected on the site of a chapel built in the 13th century. It was redesigned in 1720-22 and 1864-68 respectively (neo-Gothic alterations).

Inside, the most impressive sight is the high altar, a Dutch altar with side wings from the Marienkirche in Danzig (ca. 1520) and with an altar-piece by Tobias Pock (1668). The walls are hung with the coat-of-arms of the knights of the Teutonic Order (ca. 1720) and a Renaissance epitaph for the classical scholar, Johannes Cuspinian. This church is an example of the Baroque post-Gothic period of the early 18th century. By returning to the Stephansdom, your tour is completed.

lutgasse.

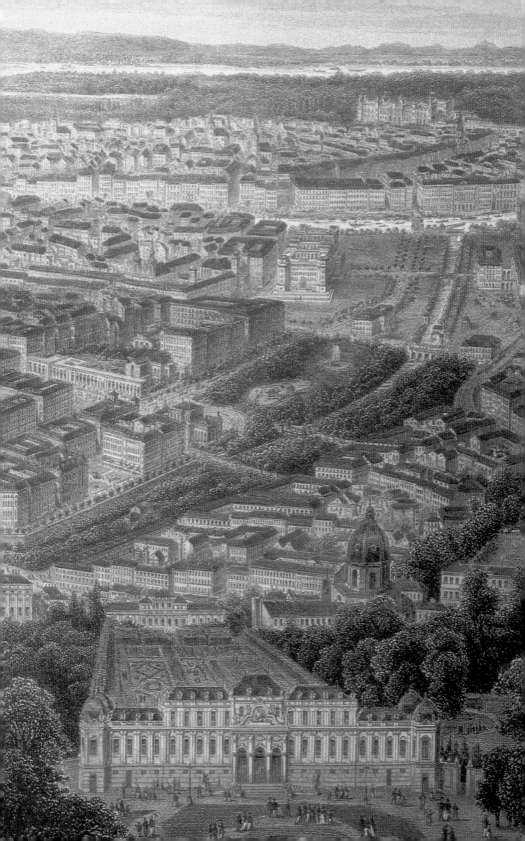

THE RINGSTRASSE

After the Emperor Franz Joseph I had ordered the Renaissance fortifications (bastions) to be demolished and houses to be built on the woodland surrounding the town, an international competition was established in order to have the Ringstraße redesigned. Eighty-five architects from all over Europe entered the competition. The emperor demanded the capital to be "made bigger and more beautiful". A jury then decided on the "final design" which was approved by the monarch in 1859. The first public and representative building to go up was the opera (Hofoper). To the present day, this period in the building of the Ringstraße is still referred to as the "Ringstraßenära" ("era of the Ringstraße"), whose almost mythically nostalgic fascination still remains. It coincides with the periods of classical and late Historicism.

Only at Stubenring, where barracks were left standing after the revolution in 1848, were the building erected as late as the 20th century. Here you will find the only buildings of Ringstraße representing the style of the "Secession" artists (see chapter on A Lively and Living City). This new Ringstraße soon became the domain of the upper classes and the aristocracy, intent on imprinting their stamp forever on this part of town. The court was represented by several official buildings, the church, however, was not.

It was a happy coincidence that the greatest skills in the fields of art and architecture were combined to present to the world such an impressive example of artistic individuality. Today, no-one can fail to be impressed by this "complete work of art" which has no parallel in the town planning of the late

Preceding pages: Vienna 1871; arcades at the university. Below, The "Secession".

19th-century Europe. This magnificent boulevard is about 2.5 miles (four km) long and 62 yards (56 meters) wide. It was officially opened on May 1, 1865, although it was not completed until just before the outbreak of World War I.

From the National Opera to the Stock Exchange

Once again the sightseeing tour starts at the National Opera (see chapter on Two Tours of the City Center) which was built in 1861-69 and based on a design by Siccard v. Siccardsburg and Eduard van der Null. Walking along Operngasse (leaving town), you come to the building of the **Secession 26** which Otto Wagner's disciple, Joseph Maria Olbrich, built in 1897/98 for those artists who shunned the company of their contemporaries, and admirers of the highly acclaimed painter, Hans Makart. A strictly cubic building, it is immediately recognizable from afar by its gilded dome formed by its iron laurel twigs. At the **Opernring** Square, there is a row of houses (Nos. 7-23), almost wholly representative of the early days (1861-63) of the construction of Ringstraße. No. 23 is the house in which the famous operetta composer, Franz von Suppé, passed away. On the right, between the Palais Schey (No. 10) and the Burggarten, is the **Goethe Memorial** by Edmund Hellmer (1895-1900). The Palais Schey, by the way, became quite famous when it was featured in a popular television series about the rebuilding of the Ringstraße. Opposite the Goethe Memorial, facing Robert-Stolz-Platz (with a monument commemorating the famous composer who lived nearby), towards Schillerplatz, is the **Academy of Arts 27** (Akademie der bildenden Künste). It was built by Theophil Hansen in 1872-76 in the Italian Renaissance style. The massive main entrance is impressive. The 24 figures carved into the niches between the windows are copies of original antique terracotta sculptures. Inside, the painting on the ceiling—*Titanensturz* (The fall of the Titans)—by Anselm Feuerbach is impressive, and the collection of paintings includes the most magnificent German, Dutch, Italian and Spanish masters. In the academy's park, you will find a rare collection of statues of writers (e.g. Friedrich von Schiller, Nikolaus Lenau, Anastasius Grün).

At the **Goethe Memorial** you can enter the **Burggarten** which provides a beautiful view of the "Neue Burg". In it are such fine sculptures and relics as (at the back, on the right) a Jugendstil conservatory by Friedrich Ohmann (1901-05). Leave the park at the **Mozart Memorial** (by Viktor Tilgner) and proceed to the outer gate of the castle, passing by the "Corps-de-Logis" part of the castle, which was built (1821-14) in the Neo-classical style by Luigi Cagnola and Pietro Nobile. Here is the center of a complex designed by Gottfried Semper, which was never completed. His idea was to design a "forum for the Emperor" which was to consist of two new wings of a new Hofburg (only one was built). His design also included the middle section of the Leopoldian part of the old Hofburg and some gigantic triumphal arches spanning Ringstraße from the wings of the castle to the castle museums. What remains, however, is impressive. There is perhaps also an advantage in the unfinished work, in that the view from Heldenplatz to another splendid architectural ensemble of Ringstraße, consisting of the parliament, the town hall, the university and the (Burgtheater).

Carl Hasenauer was commissioned in 1866 to design **The Museum of the History of Art** (Kunsthistorische Museum) **28** (Burgring 5) and the **Natural History Museum** (Naturhistorische Museum) (No. 7). The façades were later redesigned by Gottfried

Semper, but most of the interior design has remained as Hasenauer originally intended it. The two four-story buildings are symmetrically juxtaposed and bear the signs of the Italian Renaissance (1872-81).

In the middle stand octagonal domes with four side domes attached to each. At the main entrances, (Maria-Theresien-Platz) you pass allegorical seated figures. The most important sculptors of the time (Hellmer, Kundmann, Tilgner, Zumbusch) were responsible for the design. Inside, what catches one's eye is the spaciousness in the design of the hall and the staircase, with the paintings, *Apotheose der Kunst*, (The Deification of Art) by Michael Munkaczy, and *Kreislauf des Lebens* (The cycle of Life) by Hans Canon, on the ceiling. On the landing of the main staircase in the Museum of Art stands the marble sculpture, *Theseus Conquers the Centaur* (by Antonio Canova), in the Natural History Museum hangs the painting, *Emperor Franz I* surrounded by his governors (1760). The art collections in both (now nationalized) museums are among the largest and finest in Europe. The Museum of Art houses the fourth largest collection in the world (amongst others, a master collection of Brueghel's work). The monument of **Maria Theresia** was created by Caspar Zumbusch (1874-88). It covers an area of about 756 sq yds (604 sq meters) and is nearly 66 sq ft (604 sq meters) high. Four equestrian statues (Laudon, Daun, Khevenhüller, Abensberg-Traun) are grouped around the bottom, the center is occupied by four statues of diplomats (Kaunitz, Haugwitz, Liechtenstein, van Swieten). The arches depict 16 famous people (including the composers Mozart, Haydn and Gluck).

The mews for the emperor's horses (at Messeplatz, at the other end of the street) were built in 1719-23 by Johann Bernhard and Joseph Emanuel Fischer v. Erlach. They have been the home of the Vienna International Trade Fair since the end of World War I. You now leave by the **Äußere Burgtor** (the outer gate) and enter **Heldenplatz 29**, where once the Burgbastei (bastion) stood, heavily besieged in 1683. After Napoleon had it blown up, the ground was flattened and a park (Volksgarten) built. There is a rather famous coffeehouse there.

In 1933/34, the main gate of the castle ("Burgtor") was redesigned as a cenotaph, and after World War II, a memorial for the victims of the Austrian freedom fighters was erected. Most people know that in March 1938, Hitler, standing on the balcony of the Neue Burg, accepted the ovations of a large crowd of followers. One should, however, also remember that the memorial, so close by, commemorates the 35,000 Austrian members of the resistance who were condemned to death or died in Nazi prisons and concentration camps, and also more than 65,000 Jews who also died at the hands of the Nazis. Another 100,000 Austrians were imprisoned for political reasons.

On the south east side of Heldenplatz stands the **Neue Burg 30**, which was designed by Semper and Hasenauer. Building began in 1881 and finished in 1913. Emil Förster, Friedrich Ohmann and Ludwig Baumann (in that order), who made some alterations to the garden façade, supervised the building during those years. Towards Heldenplatz, the building curves inwards, and the middle is dominated by the balcony mentioned above. The Neue Burg is, amongst others, the home of the National Library and the **Museum of Mankind** (Museum für Völkerkunde). There are two monuments erected in memory of two great generals at Heldenplatz: **Prince Eugene** (near the Neue Burg), who conquered the Turks and was a great patron of the arts, and **Archduke Carl** (one of the wings of the castle was dedicated to him) who defeated Napoleon at Aspern in 1809. Both monuments were created by Anton Dominik Fernkorn in 1853-1865.

Walking through the **Volksgarten** (built 1819-23) which is famous for its rose gardens and its coffee-house (originally, the famous Corti'sche Kaffeehaus, built by Pietro Nobile, where Strauss and Lanner used to give concerts), you come, at the other end, to the **Temple of Theseus** (by Nobile, 1820-23, based on the original in Athens), the monument commemorating Grillparzer (Franz Grillparzer, who died in 1872 at the age of 80, was one of Austria's most important dramatists.) The monument was built by Kundmann and Hasenauer (with reliefs depicting scenes from the writer's most famous plays). Go on to the memorial of the Empress Elizabeth, by Ohmann and Bitterlich (1907). The sculpture on the fountain, *Faun und Nymphe* (The Satyr and the Nymph), is by Tilgner, and the fountain by Fernkorn. You will now find yourself in Ringstraße once again, with the **Palais Epstein** directly opposite (occupied now by the education authority). This was designed in the style of the Italian Renaissance (Theophil Hansen, 1870-73) for the banker Gustav Ritter v. Epstein. A plaque is dedicated to the Social Democrat Otto Glöckel, who successfully fought for revolutionary school reforms in the years following World War I. From 1945 to 1955, the Allied military leadership took up residence in the Palais Epstein. Further on, in the direction of the parliament, is the **Denkmal der Republik** (memorial for the republic), erected in 1928 with bronze busts of Dr. Viktor Adler, the founder of the united Social Democratic Party (by Anton Hanak), Jakob Reumann, the first Social Democratic mayor of Vienna (by Franz Seifert) and Ferdinand Hanusch,

Theseus Conquers the Centaur (Museum of Art).

the founder of modern social policies (by Mario Petrucci). Looking across Schmerlingplatz (behind the memorial), you can see the **Justizpalast** (Central Law Courts), a monumental building, built in 1875-81 in the style of the Italian Renaissance by Alexander Wielemans. The main hall is more than 66 ft (20 meters) high, with a glass ceiling and a staircase with the statue of justice on the landing (by Emanuel Pendl), and is very impressive indeed. In 1927, during the Civil war, rebels set the Justizpalast on fire, and between 1945-55 it served as the headquarters of the Allied military leadership. The ceremonial changing of the guards took place outside. Towards the end of World War II, this area had become the centre of the military Austrian resistance movement "05", with their headquarters in the nearby Palais Auersperg. If you now walk along **Dr. Karl-Renner-Ring** (as far as the Burgtheater, on the right), you once again find yourself confronted by another group of impressive buildings (parliament, town hall, university, Burgtheater), all linked together. This part of Ringstraße owes its existence to the mayor Dr. Cajetan Felder (1868-78) who managed to convince Emperor Franz Joseph that even in this part of the street, which had until then been reserved for military parades, houses should be built. Each architect involved in the construction of this particular ensemble of buildings had his own reasons for his design and the style favored. Friedrich Schmidt, formerly master-builder at the cathedral of St. Stephen, chose neo-Gothic for the town hall because he wanted to remind people of the golden days of the bourgeoisie in the Gothic period. Theophil Hansen, the Dane who had come to Vienna from Athens, decided upon the Hellenic style for the home of the Fed-

The "Neue Burg".

eral Council (the seat of parliament since 1918) because he wanted to establish a connection between the Ancient Greek city-state and the constitutional monarchy (ignoring the fact that there was no general right to vote in the Austrian-Hungarian empire in those days). Heinrich Ferstel, who at the age of 26, had started to build the Votivkirche, preferred the style of the Italian Renaissance because that period stood for the golden age of European universities.

Monuments

The **Parliament 31**, today the seat of the representative assembly and the Federal Council, was built between 1872 and 1883. It is two storys high and has two side wings. There is a monumental ramp leading up to the entrance, accentuated by an eight-column portico with an allegorical relief in the pediment (in the middle the "Investiture of the Constitution by Emperor Franz Joseph"). The ramp is lined on each side by seated figures carved out of marble and representing ancient historians (the Greeks on the left, Romans on the right) with two bronze horse-breakers at the bottom. There are also eight bronze quadriga, and on the balustrades are 60 marble figures of famous Greeks and Romans. In front of the parliament, the **Pallas-Athene-Brunnen** was erected in 1898-1902 (designed by Hansen in 1870). The goddess of wisdom, on top of the fountain, is in the company of water-nymphs and such, also of various ladies symbolizing the executive and legislative powers. The **Rathaus 32** (town hall), built in 1872-83 by Friedrich Schmidt, should originally have stood opposite the Stadtpark. The massive front is dominated by the main tower, over 300 ft (90 meters) high (with the Rathausmann statue on top, a copy of which can be more closely inspected in the park), flanked by two side towers, almost 200 ft (60 meters) high. The Arkadenhof, open to the public, is one of the most important courtyards in Austria (concerts are held here during the summer). The main representative rooms are on the first floor (banqueting hall, committee-rooms for the national and municipal councils) and open to the public. Guided tours start in the Schmidthalle (with an information center) at the rear of the building. The ornaments on the building itself are lavish—in the middle of the front façade a Vindobona, flanked by standard-bearers carrying the coat of arms of Vienna and the monarchy and 18 soldiers, also bearing their coat of arms. There are also various statues representing the white-collar professions. The **Rathauskeller** is one of Vienna's most popular inns.

Walking through the **Rathauspark**, you come to the Burgtheater. The park, designed and landscaped by Rudolf

Emperor Franz Joseph.

FRANZ JOSEPH I.

Sieböck (director of the municipal parks) in 1872/73, is one of the most beautiful and historic parks in Vienna. It is divided into two parts, the border lines being formed by four statues of famous personalities on each side. Vienna's "Christkindlmarkt" (Christmas fair) is held here every year. There are two fountains and numerous monuments: for the chancellor Dr. Renner in Ringstraße near the parliament (by Alfred Hrdlicka), for the mayors Seitz (1923-24) and Körner (1945-51) opposite the Burgtheater, plus the Strauss-Lanner memorial in the southern corner and the Waldmüller memorial in the northern corner, to name only a few.

The **Burgtheater 33** was built in 1874-88 (Italian Renaissance style) based on the design by Semper (outside) and Hasenauer (interior). It replaced the Burgtheater at Michaelerplatz, which had been given the status of "Nationaltheater" by the Emperor Joseph II in 1776. The most impressive feature of the theater is the arched, protruding front with its almost 60 ft (18 meters) long relief—*Bacchantenzug* (Worshippers of Bacchus)—by Rudolf Weyr. Above the relief is the massive statue, *Apollo mit den Musen Melpomene und Thalia* (Apollo and the Muses Melpomene and Thalia). Hunched above the windows on the first floor are a number of busts (by Tilgner) of famous playwrights, each allocated a character from his play right beneath him (by Weyr). On the ceiling, in the foyer, the original paintings (some by Gustav and Ernst Klimt) have been preserved. The Burgtheater is one of the most important stages in the German-speaking world. The list of the actresses/actors and directors reads like a 'Who's Who' of the most famous artists of every age.

The **University 34**, founded in 1365 by Duke Rudolf IV, was redesigned by Heinrich Ferstel in 1873-83. This university is the oldest German language university. In 1848, it regained its autonomous status which it had lost in the middle of the 16th century. An outside staircase and a ramp lead up to a portico with a balcony crowned by a pediment. Another striking feature of the building are the 38 statues representing important men of letters who greatly influenced Western culture. The rear of the building (the library in Reichsratsstraße) is decorated with sgraffito. The buildings are grouped round a big courtyard, with arcades sheltering statues of former directors and professors of the university. The Kastaliabrunnen (fountain for the guardian of the spring) was built by Edmund Hellmer in 1904.

Opposite the university are the ruins of the bastion Mölkerbastei, dating back to the 17th century. It was demolished in 1861-72. There, at No. 8, is the **Pasqualatihaus 35**, where Beethoven lodged several times between 1804 and 1815 and where he composed the opera

The statue of Athena in front of the parliament.

Fidelio (1805), the piano concerto No. 4, the symphony No. 7 and the violin concerto in D-major. The apartment where he lived is now a museum. Another room in the house is dedicated to the writer Adalbert Stifter, the most important representative of German Realism in Austria. Further on (Schreyvogelgasse 10), you come to the so-called **Dreimäderlhaus** (House of the Three Girls). The story that connects Franz Schubert with this building is pure fiction. You now walk past the **Ephrussipalais** (Dr.-Karl-Lueger-Ring 14), built by Theophil Hansen (1872/73) and easily recogniszable because of its yellow-reddish front, and come to the **Schottentor**. Although the gate that once provided entry into the town in Schottengasse is no longer there, this gate at least took over the name.

Schottengasse is a very narrow street, like so many in this part of the town, and famous for its cloisters. On the left is **Schottenhof**, built by Joseph Kornhäusel (1826-32), on the right **Melker Hof**, which dates back to the 15th century, was rebuilt by Josef Gerl (1770-74). The cellars underneath these cloisters have been converted into restaurants. A little off Ringstraße is the imposing neo-Gothic **Votivkirche 36** with two 33 ft (10 meters) high spires. It was built by Heinrich Ferstel in 1856-79 (before the demolition of the fortifications) and opened for the silver wedding jubilee of Emperor Franz Joseph and Elizabeth. It is also a reminder of the assassination attempt on the emperor's life in 1853.

The only building of importance between **Schottenring** and **Franz-Josefs-Kai** is the **Stock Exchange**, built in 1874-77 (designed by Hansen).

You now walk back to the Opera where your next round trip is about to begin.

The town hall.

FROM THE STAATSOPER TO URANIA

Starting from the Staatsoper, the last stroll along the Ringstraße takes you first to Schwarzenbergplatz (via Karlsplatz).

The upper classes used to parade round this square on Sunday mornings, exchanging pleasantries and indulging in a little flirting. Later, they would retire to one of the famous coffeehouses (Demel at Kohlmarkt, or Gerstner in Kärntner Straße) or perhaps have a meal at the restaurants of the Sacher or the Bristol. The outbreak of World War I put an end to this. But first, let's stop at **Karlsplatz**. Many designs were drawn up for the reconstruction of this square, many an architect despaired.

The uneven Baroque Karlskirche was one problem. And, before the turn of the century, a tributary (the river Wien) flowed past the church. The church had to be integrated, as it could not be changed. The river was straightened and other obstacles were eventually overcome. Today, the square is surrounded by many beautiful buildings: for example, the **Handelsakademie** (commercial college), built in 1860-62 by Ferdinand Fellner the elder, instantly recognizable by its Gothic façade and the statues of Christopher Columbus and Adam Smith.

Others include the Künstlerhaus, the Musikvereinsgebäude, the Museum of History, the Karlskirche, and the polytechnical college (with a new library). The most striking feature of Karlsplatz is perhaps the underground station (U 4), built in 1894-1900. The "suburban" side of the square (today the 4th District) contains (from left to right) the Historische Museum, the Karlskirche, the Technical University, the Protestant School and the new buildings of the Technical University library.

The **Künstlerhaus 38** (Italian Renaissance) was designed by a team of architects and built by August Weber in 1865-68. The Society of Viennese Artists was founded in 1861, and the Museum Of History use the building for exhibitions and conferences. The marble statues were carved by well-known sculptors.

Hellenic style

The **Musikvereinsgebäude 39** (Dumbastraße 3) was built by Theophil Hansen (1867-69) as a home for the Society of the Friends of Music (founded 1812). Hansen chose the Hellenic style (as he would later for the parliament), although not always strictly adhering to it. The Society of the Friends of Music, organizes national and international concerts. The main front of the building faces the Künstlerhaus. Inside, the "Golden Hall" is the

Preceding pages: the "Johann Strauss" monument in the Stadtpark. Below, Karlskirche.

most striking feature. It is beautifully decorated. Along two walls, 16 gold-plated caryatids on each side face each other across the floor. The fresco on the ceiling (*Apollo and the Nine Muses*) is by August Eisenmenger. The house next to it used to be the palace of Duke Philipp of Württemberg (Kärntner Ring 16). It was built by Arnold Zanetti and Heinrich Adam in 1862-65. It was rebuilt into a hotel in 1872/73 to accommodate the rich and famous who were expected to come to the World Exhibition (1897). The **Hotel Imperial** is still a hotel favored by very much the same clientele. Richard Wagner stayed here most of the time in 1875/76 while rehearsing his operas *Tannhäuser* and *Lohengrin* at the Hofoper.

The exhibits in the **Historische Museum** (Museum of History), built by Oswald Haerdtl in 1954-59, tell the history of Vienna in great detail. There are two rooms dedicated to the writer Franz Grillparzer and the architect Adolf Loos respectively.

Only a few steps away is the **Karlskirche 40**, which is the most important Baroque church in Vienna. During an outbreak of the plague in 1713, the emperor Karl VI vowed to have a church erected on this spot if the realm was spared further deaths. The building was begun by Johann Bernhard Fischer v. Erlach (1716-23) and finished by his son, Joseph Emanuel, in 1723-37. It was erected near the river Wien and was surrounded by vineyards; the church had been erected in a way that would make it stand out from a distance and make it look like an extension of Augustinerstraße. It was this particular construction that make the rebuilding of the Karlsplatz (trying to incorporate the church in its original design as a vital part of the square) such a nightmarish task for the architects and designers.

Designed by many

The Karlplatz still dominates the square as much as it must have done in those days. The most striking features are the Greek portico entrance, the massive dome, the two columns with their spiral reliefs and the two oriental bell-towers. Many famous and gifted sculptors had a hand in decorating the church's façade with beautiful reliefs. Inside, the fresco on the dome (by Johann Michael Rottmayr) immediately catches one's eye. It depicts the Virgin Mary begging the Holy Trinity to deliver the population from the Black Death. There are two notable altar-pieces, one by Daniel Gran (the aisle on the right) and one by Martino Altomonte (oval chapel, to the right of the main entrance). The Fischers, father and son, masterfully combined various styles—Roman, Greek and Byzantine—in this remarkable building. The aim behind this masterful blending of

The underground station at Karlsplatz.

styles was to point out that the ruler of the realm was endowed with both imperial and ecclesiastical powers. The church is intended to impress the visitor with the universal Divine Right to rule both the Catholic church and the Imperial power. In front of the church is Henry Moore's sculpture *Hill Arches*, a present from the artist to Vienna.

The **Technische Universität** (No. 13) was built (1816-18) by Joseph Schemerl v. Leytenbach. It became the permanent home of the Polytechnical Institute (founded in 1815 by Johann Joseph Prechtl). The main front, with its Ionic columns, faces **Resselpark**. Most of the statues in this park are dedicated to the memory of Austrian inventors: for example Siegfried Marcus (petrol engine), Josef Madersperger (sewing machine), Joseph Ressel (ship's screw-propeller). There is also a statue of Johannes Brahms (by Rudolf Weyr).

Brahms left Hamburg in 1862 and came to Vienna, where he passed away in 1897, in a house close to the park (Karlsgasse 4). The fountain was built in memory of the sculptor Viktor Tilgner. At the corner of Wiedner Hauptstraße, is located the Protestant school, built in 1860-62 by Theophil Hansen. It has quite a remarkable collection of statues of evangelists (by Vinzenz Pilz).

The next stop is **Schwarzenbergplatz**, named after Field Marshal Carl Philipp Duke of Schwarzenberg. He commanded the allied armies in the battle of Leipzig (1813) in the Napoleonic Wars. The square was built round the monument erected in his honor (1867, Julius Hähnel)—the **Schwarzenbergdenkmal**. Near the Ring are the former palace of Archduke Ludwig Viktor (No. 1, built 1886-89 by Ferstel, on the right) and the former Palace of Wertheim (No. 17, built 1864-68, also

One of the idyllic ponds in the Stadtpark.

by Ferstel, on the left), both Italian Renaissance. The opposite side is dominated by two neo-Baroque buildings facing each other. The House of Industry (No. 4) was built in 1907-09 by Karl König. It was the headquarters of the Allied Commission in 1945-55. In 1955, conditions of the Austrian Stahe Constituition were negotiated here.

Stay on the road

The "House of the Trade Board" has an equally impressive and flamboyantly designed façade and was built in 1905. A little further on is the **Hochstrahlbrunnen**, a fountain erected in 1873 to commemorate the mountainous source that has been providing Vienna with its pure drinking water ever since. Behind it is the **Befreiungsdenkmal der Roten Armee** (1945), a monument celebrating the liberation by the Red Army. If you carried on walking in this direction, you would come to the impressive ensemble of Schloß Belvedere, the Schwarzenberg-Palace and the two churches Gardekirche and Salesianerinnenkirche.

Stay on the outer ring road (called Lothringerstraße here), however, and proceed to the concert hall (Konzerthaus), the **Hochschule für Musik und darstellende Kunst** (Academy of Music and Interpretative Art) and the **Akademietheater**. This complex was built in 1910-13 by the famous duo of architects who specialized in theaters (Fellner and Helmer) and Ludwig Baumann. The **Konzerthaus 41** is the second most important concert hall in Vienna. Walk across **Beethovenplatz** and look at the Akademische Gymnasium (Academic Grammar School), a neo-Gothic building with its strict lines only relieved by elaborate central section (Friedrich Schmidt, 1863-66) and

Peaceful scene in the Stadtpark.

the **Beethovendenkmal** by Caspar Zumbusch (1880). You are now back in Ringstraße, at the point where it was named after the composer Franz Schubert (Schubertring).

Once the home for aristocary; now a historical landmark

The historical buildings along the Ringstraße between Schwarzenbergplatz and Wollzeile used to be the homes of the aristocracy and the upper classes. In **Parkring** (the next stretch of Ringstraße), alongside the Stadtpark, are some fine examples of these palatial homes: the Palais Leitenberger (No. 16, 1871), the Palais Henckel v. Donnersmarck (No. 14, 1871/72, today a hotel), the Palais Erzherzog Wilhelm (No. 8, also called "Deutschmeisterpalais", 1864-67, by Theophil Hansen) and the Palais Dumba (No. 4; Dumba was one of the most influential patrons of the

"Ringstraßenära"). From here, you get a glimpse of the **Coburgpalais** with its neo-classical façade. It was erected on the ruins of a bastion in 1843-47.

The **Stadtpark** is the largest historical park in the vicinity of Ringstraße. Like the Rathauspark, it was landscaped by Rudolf Sieböck, based on a design by the landscape painter Josef Selleny (1862). The town hall should originally have been erected on a site in Parkring. It is said that the architect, Friedrich Schmidt, was quite pleased that the Stadtpark should form the background for his splendid building—and not so pleased, when it was decided that the town hall was to be built on "Paradeplatz", a bleak and empty square in those days.

Long before it was decided to have the Stadtpark built (early 19th century), people came here to take the waters (mineral springs). In a way, this led to the erection of the **Kursalon** in 1865-

The national savings bank (with a bust of Coch).

142

67 (Johann Garben). It had been designed in the style of the Italian Renaissance and provided a splendid setting for social events. Concerts were performed in the pavilion.

Serene Stadtpark

Eduard Strauss and his orchestra played here many times. At one side, the park borders onto the river Wien. The embankment is beautifully designed and landscaped (pavilions, stairs, terraces). The gate, Wienflußportal is Jugendstil (Friedrich Ohmann and Josef Hackhofer, 1903-06). Large areas in the Stadtpark are covered by woodland, there are ponds and lakes, and statues of composers (Bruckner, Schubert, Léhar and Stolz) and painters (Amerling, Canon, Markart and Schindler). Outshining them all at the park, however, is the impressive **Johann-Strauss-Denkmal**

Jugendstil sculpture on top of the national savings bank.

42, built by Edmund Hellmer in 1921.

Leave the park at the entrance of Weiskirchnerstraße. To your left is another monument, the **Luegerdenkmal** , erected in 1926 in honor of the mayor Dr. Karl Lueger (1897-1910). Mayor Lueger is remembered for his social achievements (gas, electricity and water supplies, electrification of the tramlines, etc.).

You now enter the part of Ringstraße between Wollzeile and the Danube Canal, called **Stubenring**. On your right are the Academy (Museum) of Applied Art and various government offices. On your left (once the site of the former barracks, "Kaiser-Franz-Josephs-Kaserne"), you will see many buildings which were designed in the style of the Secession (notably the Post Office Saving Bank). The **Museum für angewandte Kunst 43**, was built in the Italian Renaissance style by Johann Ferstel between 1906-08. It was later enlarged by Ludwig Baumann. It houses some splendid collections of art—for example, antique furniture, porcelain, carpets, glass objects, ceramics and textiles. On the wall connecting the academy (No. 3) with the museum is a fountain with a mosaic of the goddess Athena (or Minerva) on a gold background.

The **Postsparkassenamt 44,** a strictly cubic building, was built in 1904-06 by Otto Wagner. It is one of the finest examples in Vienna of the style of the rebellious Secession. This area reflects the contrasting styles of the two dominant architects of the time—Ludwig Baumann and Otto Wagner. Baumann was much favored at court. The rebellious Wagner was finally banned from court by Archduke Franz Ferdinand, the successor to the throne, who was assassinated in 1914.

At the very end of this tour, you come to the Jugendstil building called **Urania [45]** (1909/10, Max Fabiani). Its dome houses a planetarium.

Haupt Ansicht der Residenzstadt Wien, und des größten Theils ihrer Vorstädte, von Belvedere anzusehen.

1. Maria Hilf.   2. St Ulrich.   3. Koblkirche.
   Bilcherr auf der Wieden.   Pfarrkirche in der Josephstadt.   Pfarrkirche in der Alstergasse.   4. Augustiner Hofkirche.

Vüe de la Capitale de Vienne, et d'une grande partie de ses Fauxbourgs, prise du coté du Belvedere.

St. Stephan Domkirche.   die Universität.   Salesianerinnen auf dem Rennweg.   Pfalzlsthenerinnen.

die Leopoldstadt.   Offertkirche an Solbrig.   Augustiner auf der Landstraß.

DISTRICTS AND SUBURBS

One of the many paradoxes that add to rather than diminish the charm of the Austrian capital is the fact that the town of Vienna consists of the district called "town" (Stadt) and a further 22 districts. The "town" is the inner city area, the 1st district, but you will have difficulty finding anyone who refers to it as that. The "Stadt" is the old part of the town, once ringed by fortifications and today still surrounded by the ring road ("Ringstraße"), and thus in a way still something of an enclave. The remaining districts surround the center in concentric circles. Vienna has grown— the higher the number of a district, the later the date of its integration into "Greater Vienna". But growth was not immoderate, and once the realization had dawned that Vienna had exceeded a reasonable size, something quite remarkable and previously unheard-of occurs. This city of millions shrank, de-incorporated some incorporated districts, limited itself to a smaller, more easily administrated area.

Vienna is still a great city, but not a particularly large city. It has not thrown out cancerous excretions that eat away at the surrounding countryside. Vienna has kept itself to itself, and has remained a city on a human scale. Over the last 75 years, Vienna has been the first city with a population of over a million which has lost and not gained inhabitants—its population has decreased by a good 30 per cent. Outside the walls of the city there has always been a wide belt of settlements, some of them documented much earlier than Vienna itself.

These settlements (farmers and vintners) were often also fortified with earthworks and ditches, formed the

Preceding pages: view from Belvedere, 1784; Schloß Schönbrunn in winter.

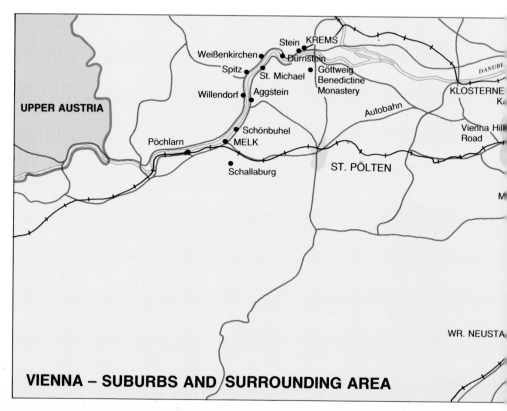

VIENNA – SUBURBS AND SURROUNDING AREA

natural hinterland of Vienna, and their natural growth over the centuries was, in all those years, only twice rudely interrupted, both times by the Turks (in 1529 and 1683) laying siege to Vienna. In the process, they ruthlessly burnt down every farmhouse and every vineyard that lay outside the town's fortifications. This explains why in the suburbs you will hardly find a building that is older than 300 years.

When the Turks were finally beaten back in 1683 and Austria was on its way to becoming one of the super-powers of Europe, construction fever broke out. The surrounding villages and the suburbs were rebuilt. The aristocracy had their summer palaces built just outside the town, quite a few of which have been preserved. The most beautiful of these is without doubt the palace "Belvedere" (Schloß Belvedere), former residence of Prince Eugene of Savoy.

With the economy booming, more and more tradesmen and artisans began to settle in the suburbs. Since 1703, these have also been fortified by a wall. This "Linienwall" served as a kind of customs-barrier; the roads to and from Vienna were guarded by customs officials. A tax was levied on all victuals to be taken into Vienna and had to be paid at the check-points. This law was enforced until the 19th century. Already in those days the inner suburbs were incorporated into Vienna for tax purposes, if not as an administrative unit.

In compliance with the tradition of their respective guilds, the tradesmen had established themselves in certain areas—the 7th district, for example, was once the domain of the silk-spinners. In those days, people referred to it as the "Diamond Mine", an indication of the incredible wealth amassed by the silk-spinners who dominated the European market for decades.

The tanners and dyers had settled

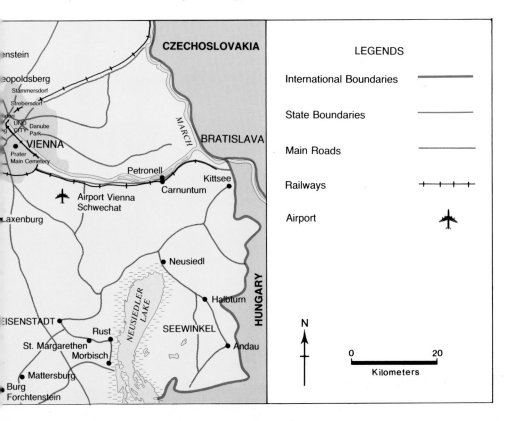

along the river Wien (District 14), not all together to the delight of the people who already lived there. They did not take kindly to the foul smell of the waste water from the tanners' and dyers' works. The district was literally "in bad odor". Even in the 19th century there were already environmental problems.

Like everywhere else, the Jewish people had their own quarter in those days on the other side of what is now the Danube Canal in Leopoldstadt (District 2). They were forced to settle there in the 17th century, only to be driven out again 50 years later. During the latter part of the 19th century, Leopoldstadt became the home of the poor Jewish immigrants having fled the Eastern provinces of the kingdom. Over 50,000 Jews lived here until 1938.

This is what Vienna and its surrounding suburbs would have looked like around the middle of the 19th century: right in the center was Vienna, tightly corseted by its walls, not having grown since the middle ages. This inner core was ringed by the suburbs, which were growing ever closer together. Outside the wall that held these together lay the loose ring of small towns and villages where the factories and mass housing were being built and where the new working-class was beginning to settle.

This large but compact economic unit, however, had no central government, but was still divided into dozens of administrative bodies—as much an anachronism as the two fortification walls in the age of industrialization. In 1850, things began to change. The suburbs, sandwiched between the wall round Vienna and the "Linienwall", were finally incorporated into Vienna.

At the turn of the century another burst of development hit Vienna. The bastions were demolished, signalling the beginning of the "Ringstraßenära" (1857), the splendid construction of the

Vienna, with the fortification walls still intact.

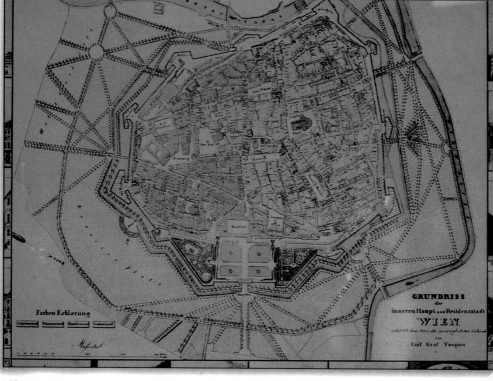

ring road. The outer suburbs also benefitted from this building boom. The Danube was tamed, the canal built, and two mountain springs provided Vienna with the purest drinking water of all major cities in the world.

The next boost for developers came at the turn of the century. In 1890, the suburbs outside the "Linienwall" were incorporated (Districts 10-19). In 1910, the town reached across the Danube and Floridsorf became the 21st district.

During the term of office of mayor Lueger (1897 - 1910), Vienna became a cosmopolitan city. The inner city area, the "Stadt", had been beautified during the "Ringstraßenära", during the "Lueger-Ära" it was now the turn of the outer districts. Vienna had over 2 million inhabitants at the turn of the century and was one of the six largest cities in the world. The "General Construction Plan" of Lueger's administration connected the inner city with its districts and suburbs. Tramways were built, the river Wien (a tributary of the Danube) and the Canal straightened. Mayor Lueger also saw to it that up to 4 million inhabitants would be able to enjoy the benefits of proper gas, electricity and water supplies.

The last monarch having abdicated, the Social Democrats took over the administration of Vienna. Although Lueger must without any doubt be remembered for his revolutionary social achievements, he had, nevertheless, completely ignored the housing sector. It is here that the Social Democrats deserve all the praise for their pioneering work. The monuments left by "Red Vienna" are the massive public housing blocks in the outer districts, built 50 years ago during the Social Democrats' term of office.

After the enforced "Anschluß", the union with Germany in 1938, yet more suburbs were incorporated into

Left, a typical 'Biedermeier" washerwoman. Right, waitress at the restaurant "KrahKrah".

"Greater Vienna" (it reached 26 districts), but were partly de-incorporated again after the end of World War II.

During the past decades, Vienna's population has steadily shrunk. At present, it has fallen below 1.5 million. This, however, has not stopped the town expanding—higher standards of living demand more housing.

Schloß Belvedere

When he was still a young Field Marshal in the army, Prince Eugene of Savoy acquired (1693) a building site outside the city gates where he planned to have his summer residence. Twenty years later, at the height of his career as general and diplomat, he started building his palace. Johann Lukas von Hildebrandt designed one of the most magnificent palaces not only in Austria but in the world for him, a masterpiece of the Baroque style. Strictly speaking, the name "Belvedere" (beautiful view) originally only applied to that part of the building that was used for official functions—the **Obere (upper) Belvedere**, built in 1721/22. The name is justified—here, on top of the hill, you probably get the best and most beautiful view of Vienna and the distant hills of the "Wienerwald" (Vienna Woods).

The main building of the palace, the **Untere (lower) Belvedere**, was built in 1714-16 and served as the prince's residence and also housed his most splendid art collection. The two main buildings of the palace are connected by the park with its ornamental fountains, statues and terraces. Unfortunately only parts of its original splendor remain.

The Belvedere has been called a "paraphrase in stone" of the pleasant, slightly Mediterranean aspect of the landscape around Vienna.

As much as anything else, the Belvedere complex is a homage to the prince

The "Untere Belvedere". Right, a baroque facade of the Belvedere.

himself who in his day was glorified as Hercules and Apollo all in one — the man of action and the god of the arts. After Prince Eugene's death, the Emperor bought castle Belvedere. Before World War I, it was the home of the heir to the throne, Franz Ferdinand. Today, it is the home of several museums: the **Österreichische Galerie** (Obere Belvedere), the **Barockmuseum** (Untere Belvedere) and the **Museum mittelalterlicher Kunst** (medieval art, Orangery). In the Obere Belvedere, the Austrian State Constitution was signed in 1955.

Schloß Schönbrunn

The palace of Schönbrunn (the beautiful fountain) is much more of an embodiment of the power and wealth of the monarchy than the "Hofburg", and it is no accident that it was designed to resemble the palace of Versailles. In Vienna, Schloß Schönbrunn is closely connected with the reign of the "old" Emperor Franz Joseph and, of course, the Empress Maria Theresia who made it her summer residence, although the palce itself is much older. It was destroyed during the Turkish siege of 1683. Emperor Leopold I then decided he wanted an official residence built here. The design drawn up by Johann Bernhard Fischer von Erlach would have made Versailles look ordinary—if it had been realized. He had designed the main building to be erected high up on the hill where now only the lonely ornamental temple remains.

In 1695, the construction of the palace began, after Fischer's second draft had been approved, and finally became, more or less, what you can see today. It is still an impressive building, with its wide ceremonial courtyard and its two massive staircases, one on either side of the façade of the building. The sur-

The avenue in Schloß Schönbrunn. Right, the ornamental temple (Gloriette).

rounding gardens were landscaped in the tradition of French gardens (geometrically arranged flower beds, hedges trimmed into shapes and perfectly straight lines of trees) and are quiet and quite beautiful. The circular menagerie, built in 1752, is the oldest zoological garden in Europe still open to the public.

Empress Maria Thersia commissioned Nicolaus Pacassi to redesign and enlarge the castle, and his most important and splendid contribution is the well-preserved, magnificient interior. High above the castle stands the ornamental temple with its airy colonades, the **Gloriette**, built in 1765. Another interesting part of the castle is the **Wagenburg** which houses a collection of state coaches and the delightfully small-scale "Schloßtheater".

The Viennese are notorious for their lack of desire to move house once they have settled down. It is, nevertheless, quite astonishing to discover that today they still live in very much the same districts where once their ancestors had settled.

Until 1918, the districts of Vienna were strictly divided into social classes: There were the "aristocratic districts", the "bourgeois" and the "working-class districts"—just like today.

The "bourgeois" and the "working-class" districts

Artisans and merchants, and to some extent civil servants, used to live in the former suburbs between the old city fortifications and the Linienwall, now Districts 3-9.

Most buildings in these districts went up at the turn of the last century, although there are (mainly in districts 7and 8) a few which date back to the early 19th century, the so-called "Biedermeier" era. These "Biedermeier"

Public housing-the Karl-Marx-Hof.

houses (once all of them had gardens) are very typical of their time: small and no more than two storeys high, the living area limited to what was thought to be reasonable and necessary, no unnecessary ornamentations either. Some of these houses have become museums—like the house in which Haydn died, or the houses in which Schubert was born and passed away. An example of the grander lifestyle of the upper middle class is the Geymüller-Schlössel (Schlössel = "little palace") in Distirct 19.

All the former suburbs were, and still are, the domain of the working classes, with the exception of the "Nobel- districts" in Hietzing, Währing and Döbling, and the vineyard communities at the foot of the Wienerwald. It was here, at the edge of town, that the factories were built during the age of industrialization and the thousands who came to work in them settled down.

Thus, they not only lived close to their working places, but also avoided having to pay the tax levied on victuals being taken into the town. In many cases this meant that the cost of living was reduced by as much as one third. The housing conditions, however, were deplorable.

"Beautiful" buildings were the privilege of the inner city area. Out in the suburbs, houses only had to serve the purpose of providing people with a roof over their heads — and pack as many as possible into one building. It was almost the norm for a family of ten to be living in a one-bedroom flat.

The flats were damp, dark and overlooked dreary streets with no trees. Parks simply did not exist. In fairness it must be added, however, that Vienna never developed the kind of appalling slums that were so characteristic, for example, of the industrial north of England in those days.

Left, Jugendstil the interior of church am Steinhof. Right, the first Wagner villa.

There was no tap water in the flats, of course, the water supplies being fetched at the **Bassena**, the tap installed on each floor, which also served as the only meeting point for the women.

Slowly but gradually, these tenement blocks were replaced by more pleasant housing, but only some of them. Even today, the grey and depressing façades are still prominent in these working-class districts.

The "Nobel- districts"

The landed and monied gentry, as well as the upper classes with real estate, had settled in the elegant flats in the inner city district, in the "diplomatic districts" (Districts 3 and 4), and in the suburban villas in Hietzing and Währinger and Döblinger Cottage — and, once again, nothing much has changed ever since. Houses in these areas fetch the highest prices and are the most sought after in Vienna.

Some of the distircts have lost a little of their appeal, others have only recently acquired the status of being "nobel", Grinzing being one of them. The traditional home of the "Heurigen" inns has also become an exclusive residential address.

Vienna and the Danube

It is not all that easy to assess whether Vienna actually lies on the Danube or not—it certainly was not so until way into the 19th century. In those days, the Danube and its many tributaries wound its way through meadows and farmland, and only one tributary actually flowed directly past the town.

In 1875, great efforts were undertaken to stop the devastations caused by heavy and frequent flooding. The bed of the Danube was straightened, the tributary flowing past Vienna made

The UNO-City complex.

into a canal. But this meant that the navigable stream was now many miles off the town. On the left bank of the Danube a broad space was left free of buildings. This formed a flood plain that could be deliberatly inundated when the river was high, removing the danger of flooding from Vienna itself. One part of the Danube, cut off when its bed was straightened, became known as the **Alte Donau** (the Old Danube). It still remains, fed by underground springs. It is now a haven for water sports lovers. The first open-air swimming pool, the **Gänsehäufel**, was built there in 1907. It can accommodate as many as 33,000 people.

Between the two world wars, the Viennese discovered another beauty spot with broad meadows along this part of the Old Danube, the **Lobau**, and made it into a nudist colony. In 1981, another river bed was cut into the flood plain, running parallel to the main river.

It was intended to carry excess water. This development formed the Donauinsel (Danube island), which is about 13 miles (21 km) long and 220 yards (200 meters) wide.

The island, which can be reached in less than 10 minutes by underground from the center of Vienna, has become another favorite recreation area. There is a 25-mile- (40-km) long beach, also mooring places and marinas, training centers for diving and surfing and many other water sports facilities. The island is also covered by a net of cycling tracks, and even in winter the Viennese flock to the island and practice cross-country skiing.

Other cities envy Vienna with its leisure parks along the river. When hundreds and thousand of city dwellers, starved of fresh air and sunshine, take over this El Dorado of leisure seekers, then you really could say that Vienna lies on the Danube.

The Danube Canal.

Tales from the Wienerwald

Ever since Strauss and his waltzes, Vienna and the Vienna Woods have been thought of as one entity. The Vienna Woods ("Wienerwald") are the very last foothills of the Alps, which reach the borders of the city. They make a perfet setting for the beauty of Vienna. The city lies in the curve of the hills like a pearl in an oyster, and the trees make a picturesque backdrop and a boundary to the sea of houses.

It is mainly due to the idealism and stubbornness of the first of Vienna's "greens", the former member of parliament, Josef Schöffel, that this green belt survived. For years he fought a lonely but successful battle to prevent the clearing of the woodland intended by a consortium of stock-exchange operators. When at last he succeeded in drawing public attention to his campaign, the permission (already granted) to cut down the trees was withdrawn in 1873. Schöffel was later elected mayor of Mödling and given the nickname "Saviour of the Wienerwald".

Thirty years later, during the office of mayor Lueger, the benefits of this green belt were fully realized at last and every step was taken to preserve this nature resort and to extend it into a belt of woods and meadows around the city. There are strict laws against building houses, and most of the time they are adhered to.

At one point, the Wienerwald almost touches the banks of the Danube. This beautiful spot — vineyards, lush meadows and tranquil beech groves—is much favored by the Viennese when they want to leave the hustle and bustle of the town behind. Standing on top of the **Kahlenberg** hill, you get a breathtaking view of Vienna. From here, you can walk or drive to the other favorite hill of the Vinnese, **Leopoldsberg**, via

View across to the "Kahlenberg" hill.

the **Höhenstraße** that runs between Hütteldorf and Klosterneuburg.

Vienna and wine

One cannot be separated from the other: Vienna and wine is like Tom and Jerry or Laurel and Hardy. There are hundreds of Viennese songs which tell of this partnership. Every tourist wants to visit a Heuriger inn, and a well-oiled tourist machine ensures that they all get something to drink. The "Heurigen" goes back to a very old tradition. Vintners would announce the arrival of their new wines by hanging a wreath of fir twigs over the door of the inn.

From these modest beginnings a vast industry has arisen. All too often, the quiet enjoyment of a glass of new wine has turned into a noisy affair, where Viennese songs are bawled in an atmosphere of fake bonhomie.

Vienna was, until very recently, sur- rounded by vineyards. The "Karls- kirche" and the "Belvedere", for ex- ample, were erected right in their midst. Gumpendorf (District 6), once famous for its wine, is today a densely built-up area, and it is only at the foot-hills of the "Wienerwald" and on the other side of the Danube ("Bisamberg") that wine is still grown these days.

The fact that wine is still being culti- vated within the borders of Vienna is another achievement of mayor Lueger who, you will remember, also pre- served Vienna's green belt. Vienna is still one of the largest vine-growing areas in the whole of Austria. Today, just as in the early 19th century, the view from the Kahlenberg shows the city bordered by vineyards.

Many of the suburbs—like **Grinzing, Sievering**, **Neustift am Walde**, **Nußdorf**, **Heiligenstadt** as well as **Stammersdorf** on 'the other side'—which were and still are the

Ghost train in the "Prater".

AUSGAN

domain of the vintners who have kept their village character. This is the true home of the Viennese Heurigen—one of the oldest traditions of this city, but still full of life. Even today you can find the plain inns with their shady gardens, green-painted tables and rough wooden benches. These places are symbols of the joyful aspects of Viennese life: pleasant company and thoughtful enjoyment, laughter and celebration and a melancholy awareness of the transitory nature of life.

Even many, many years ago, the wine industry played an important economical role, and although Viennese wine is not exported any longer, it is still an industry that brings in substantial sums of money. Instead of exporting the wine, the consumer is imported. It is as simple and lucrative as that!

Unfortunately, many of the traditional "Heuriger" inns, where you brought along your own picnic (bread, sausage and cheese)—and only these are the genuine ones—are disappearing. In their place, restaurant owners have set up their "Heurigen", providing the picnic in exchange for money and also offering other than "Heurigen" wine, something which makes a mockery of the whole "Heurigen" tradition.

If you want to find one of the last true "Heurigen", it is advisable to avoid going on an organized "Heurigen" crawl but set out on your own and find an inn where no coaches are parked anywhere nearby. It will be well worth your while. You might also find the true spirit of the "Heurigen" which is much more introvert and less noisy, often melancholy and pondering on the transcience of life. This leads directly to the Viennese attitude to death.

"Depositories of mourning"

—that's what André Heller called the

Entrance to a "Heurigen" inn.

Viennese cemeteries. A "schöne Leich", a beautiful funeral, is taken very seriously in Vienna. Most Viennese see to it that everything is done beforehand to give themselves a great send-off once the time has come. For many Viennese, death is the only chance they have of making a grand display. Many pay into special savings accounts in order to leave enough money behind for a grand funeral.

These days, the main cemetery in Vienna (the "Wiener Zentralfriedhof") is an important item on the sightseeing program of every Japanese tourist group. The "St. Marxer" cemetery (District 3) is also worth a visit, as its "Biedermeier" look has been very well preserved. The Jewish cemetery at the Währinger Gürtel is closed now, but still evokes shameful memories. The graves and the cemeteries in the "Nobel-districts"—for example in Hietzing, Plötzleinsdorf, Döbling or Grinzing—are beautifully situated.

Most Viennese, however, are buried in the main cemetery which was built in 1874, and later nicknamed "Europe's most lively graveyard". It is a vast place, covering an area of a good 500 acres (200 ha), where almost 2 1/2 million Viennese lie buried (considerably more than the city's live inhabitants). There are separate sections for the Protestants, Greek Orthodox Christians and Jews. The two Jewish sections occupy almost a third of the total area. There are also **state tombs** for the great sons and daughters of the city—though a tombstone may be the only generosity the city ever showed them.

There are two quite remarkable buildings in the "Zentralfriedhof": the church erected in memory of Dr. Lueger (1911) and the crematorium (Clemens Holzmeister, 1923) on the site of the former Renaissance palace of Emperor Maximilian II.

Avenue in the main cemetery.

AROUND VIENNA

Vienna is not only a beautiful city, it is also beautifully located. There are not many European cities of comparable size which can combine surrounding landscape of such beauty with a wealth of art treasures.

One of the favorite spots, the Vienna Woods, has already been mentioned. Others are the Danube valley and the "Burgenland" (land of castles) to the south east of the town.

The Danube valley

Following the Danube upstream, you will presently come to the monastery **Klosterneuburg**, the largest and most eastern of the many monasteries dotted along the Danube throughout Austria. Klosterneuburg, an Augustinian estab-

lishment, was founded by the margrave of Babenberg, Saint Leopold III. At around 1100, Leopold had his residential palace built here which became known as the "new castle" (Neue Burg) and next to it a monastery (Kloster)—hence the name "Klosterneuburg". Leopold was buried in the chapel of the monastery. The enamel Verdun altar (12th century) in the chapel is one of Austria's most precious pieces of art.

Klosterneuburg did not remain the capital of the kingdom for very long. In 1156, and Vienna became the capital—for good.

During the Baroque epoch (17th and 18th century), lavish designs were drawn up to rebuild the monastery. The initiator was Charles VI, Maria Theresia's father, who wanted to build a monumental burial place for the Austrian kings, which was to be modeled on the Escorial Palace in Spain (built by Philip II, 1563-86). The building was

Aggestein; the library in the monastery Melk Klosterneuburg. Below, skiing on the "Rax".

started, yet never completed, but even the remaining rump conveys enough of the intended flamboyant Baroque grandeur of the place. The two impressive domes are decorated with the imperial crown and the "duke's hat", symbol of the Austrian dukes.

Saint Leopold III, the patron saint of Lower Austria, is still very much a part of Klosterneuburg life today. Every year in November, the Austrians remember their saint with lively celebrations. These reach a climax on the feast day of the saint, every November 15, when the Austrians flock to Klosterneuburg in their thousands to slide down the gigantic barrel (with a capacity of 56,000 liters) that stands on the site. This barrel is a reminder that the monastery is still one of the largest vineyards in the country.

A little further upstream, on the opposite bank, stands the almost gigantic castle **Burg Kreuzstein**, built in the 19th century. It was pieced together from hundreds of bits and pieces taken from other castles and monuments, and still looks like a knight's castle out of a fairy tale—or one constructed by crazy history freaks, as some say.

The "Wachau"

"Wachau" is the name of that part of the Danube valley between Melk and Krems. It is said that these 22 miles (35 km) cover "the most beautiful region of Austria". The Wachau is indeed one of the most romantic and almost magic river landscapes in the world.

Both man and nature had a hand in creating this beauty spot. The hills, bordering the broad stream, keep out unfavorable winds. Man used the fertile soil (loess) to his advantage and planted vine terraces and orchards. The area is perhaps, at its most enchanting in spring when the many apricot trees

(called "Marillen" in Austria) blossom.

Many mythological, legendary and some historical facts are connected with the Wachau and add to its romantic charm. Armies of crusaders must have passed this spot on their way down the Danube and into the Holy Land. The Burgundy knights heroes of the medieval German epic, the Nibelungenlied must also have passed through on their way to the kingdom of the Huns. **Pöchlarn** (once called Bechelaren), not very far from Melk, is said to have been the residence of the margrave Rüdiger, one of the most noble figures of the German heroic legends.

Krems (and its twin-town **Stein**) has one of the best preserved old town centers in middle Europe. Krems survived the drastic changes that came in the wake of the industrial revolution during the 19th century. Its role as an important trading center ceased with the coming of the railways (that took the business away from shipping), and this was a blessing in disguise. Fortunately, this was recognized in time and the old town was carefully preserved and restored. The city walls, (with an impressive entrance gate, the "Wiener Tor", and the even more impressive tower—the "Pupverturm"—where once gun powder was stored) are more or less still intact, enclosing houses from five different centuries. The dominant features of the town are its arcades and courtyards, gables, turrets and gates, ornamented façades and wrought-iron window balconies.

The most notable buildings include the "Gozzoburg" (13th century), one of the oldest 'private residences' in Austria, a Gothic church (Bürgerspitalkirche), as well as two other beautifully restored churches—the Dominikanerkirche in Krems and the "Minoritenkirche" in Stein. (Both are used as exhibition halls today.)

The monastery of Melk.

If you cross over the old bridge connecting Stein with a place called Mautern and climb up the hill you come to another impressive Benedictine monastery called **Göttweig**, founded in 1803. It is one of the most splendid examples of Baroque monasteries in Austria, together with those of Florian and Melk.

The building was erected in 1719-24. Its front is over 650 feet (196 meters) long, and the whole complex looks more like a palace. This is not all together that surprising once you know that it was designed by Lukas von Hildebrandt, the architect who created the palace of Belvedere in Vienna. His original and grandiose design, however, which had spread out the monasterial buildings all across the top of the hill, was never completed. The so-called "imperial staircase" ("kaiserstiege") is one of the most striking staircases built in the Baroque style in Austria. Göttweig houses the second most important collection of copper engravings in Austria (first: Albertina Museum, Vienna).

Picturesque Wachau: The Dürnstein village

A few miles further upstream, on the 'Krems side' of the Danube (the communities in the Wachau are almost exclusively situated on the northern banks of the river), lies the "pearl" of the Wachau, the village Dürnstein. There is no doubt that it really is the most beautiful and picturesque place in the Wachau. On a rock jutting out into the Danube sits a chapel which once belonged to an Augustinian monastery. The most striking feature of the former monastery is the Baroque spire overlooking the Danube, which can be seen from far away. When, not so long ago, the façade of the building was restored,

Left, national costumes of the Wachau. Right, Dürnstein.

an outcry of indignation was heard in the country. The restorers had decided it should be painted blue ("An ugly blue," said the opponents) because the original coat of paint, they insisted, had in fact been blue. The traditionalists would have much preferred the customary white coat for ancient buildings, or the yellow of the Schönbrunn palace.

The legend of Richard the Lionheart and the minstrel Blondel

About 800 years ago, the hero of Christendom, King Richard the Lionheart, was captured and incarcerated in the stronghold of Dürnstein ("Kuenringer-Veste"). He was the prisoner of Leopold V of Babenberg, and he had been recognized and was captured on Christmas day, 1192, at Erdberg, near Vienna, on his return from the third crusade. Leopold V wanted to settle an old score with the king of England: Two

years before, at Acre in the Holy Land, Richard had insulted Duke Leopold and the country.

And now the legend really takes over: When the king did not return from his crusade, his loyal servant, Blondel, set forth to seek his master. He took his harp with him and played his familiar tunes in all the distant lands, wandering from castle to citadel and fortress in the hope of finding the King of England. When he reached the dungeon of Dürnstein, his tunes were at last answered. Blondel speedily returned to England, raised the king's ransom and freed his master.

Alas, only two things are true about this touching story: Richard the Lionheart was a prisoner in Dürnstein, and the ransom money was paid. (This operation was nothing less than a blatant kidnapping.) The introduction of the fictitious minstrel Blondel only serves to highlight Richard's reputation as the

Richard the Lionheart is captured (1192).

greatest "minnesingers" (amatory lyric poets, mostly of noble birth, popular during the 12th and 13th century) of his time in England.

There are also considerable doubts whether Leopold captured the king of England because he wanted to settle an old score. It is much more likely that the whole incident represents nothing more or less than a struggle for power and influence. Richard owned vast acres in the south of France that posed a threat to the French crown.

The German Emperor was of the house of Hohenstaufen, had pledged allegiance to France. The Babenberg duke of Austria was an ally of the Emperor's. Richard had to be removed as a danger to the French throne, and one thing led to another.

Richard's imprisonment in Dürnstein only lasted for three months. He was handed over to the German emperor who released him a year later.

From Dürnstein to Melk

The fortified churches in **Weißenkirchen** and St. Michael are a reminder that the people in the Wachau had to reckon with enemy invasions (Turks and Swedes, among others) at any time. The monumental Gothic church in **Weißenkirchen** consists of three churches built into one. The "Wachau-Museum", housed in a splendid Renaissance building, is well worth a visit.

St. Michael, first documented in the 10th century, is the oldest parish in this region. The strange "Seven Hares", carved out of stone and placed on top of the church, have puzzled people for centuries. The most plausible explanation seems to be that they were put there in order to ward off evil powers.

A little further upstream we find **Spitz**, which throughout the centuries has always been a well known market town. Have a look at the beautiful late

175

Gothic church with its wonderful stucco figures in the choir loft and the unusual choir stalls in the nave.

Willendorf, the next stop, is the home of the oldest Austrian lady, the famous "Venus of Willendorf". The statue (approximately 22,000 B.C.) is only about four inches (10 cm)high and is thought to have been a symbol of fertility. It can be seen in the Natural History Museum in Vienna.

On the other side of the Danube, towers **Castle Aggstein** which was once the safest stronghold along the Danube. The ruins are still impressive, defiant and almost awe-inspiring. More stories and legends surround this castle than any other, but hardly any of them are based on facts. The knights of the castle and the clergy, who controlled the media in those days, never really saw eye to eye, and the clergy made sure the world believed their versions about the goings-on at the castle.

Castle Aggstein was the main stronghold of the "Kuenringer", one of the most powerful families in the Danube regions in the middle ages. They are still accused of having been thieves and, although nothing has come to light to prove this.

"The terror in the woods"

Later, Georg Schreck (Schreck = terror) took over the castle. He ruled with an iron rod, but was a just man. The opposition grotesquely exaggerated his efforts to make his subordinates abide by the rules of law and order. They nicknamed him "Schrec-kimwald" (terror in the woods). Amongst others, there is the story about him "locking" the Danube with a chain and demanding toll from everyone wanting to ship their goods along the river—something he was legally entitled to do. Another tale tells of the "rose garden", a ridge of rocks jutting out over the rapid stream, where prisoners were put and given the choice of either starving to death or jumping to their deaths.

All these stories and legends add, of course, to the attraction of this castle. Of course, the most popular tales are those which dwell on the supposed horrors inflicted by its cruel owner, sending welcome shivers down the visitor's spine. And who knows, perhaps even hitherto "unknown" tales will one day be revealed...

On the south side of the Danube is yet another castle, **Schloß Schönbühel**, an impressive rectangular building with a tower reaching into the sky. It is, however, far less awe-inspiring than the "castle of terror".

The highlight of a trip through the Wachau must be the monastery in Melk (**Stift Melk**), one of Jacob Prandtauer's masterpieces and one of the loveliest of all Baroque buildings (1702-1739). The building is over 1000 ft (320 meters) long and towers high above the

One of the many picturesque streets in the Wachau. Right, a vineyard in Spitz.

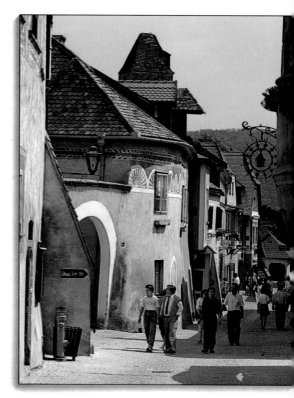

Danube on a protruding rock. The west front is turned towards the river like the bow of a ship. The library and the splendid marble hall deserve a visit. The Imperial rooms are now a museum. The lawn in front of the garden pavilion serves as an open-air theater during the summer months.

Melk was a Roman outpost along the *limes*, the boundary wall, and later became the residence of the Dukes of Babenberg who built the Benedictine monastery (1089).

Castle **Schallaburg** is one of the most striking Renaissance buildings in Austria. Some parts of the castle date back to the middle ages (the fortification walls, for example). The courtyard is littered with terracotta objects: busts, masks, escutcheons and others. The buildings have lovingly been restored in the past few years and today provide a splendid setting for art exhibitions.

The tiny village of Mauer, near Melk,

possesses one of the most remarkable carved altars (1515) in Austria.

The "Burgenland", Joseph Haydn and Eisenstadt

The town of Eisenstadt was formed by the merging of three separate autonomous (up till 1938) settlements. All three have retained their individuality and are still separated by invisible borders. The so-called "free town" has kept a lot of its Baroque and rural charm. "Oberberg" grew around the churches and the monastery which had been built by the Esterházys. "Unterberg" became the official district of the Jews in 1671. The first Jews had arrived in this area in the 13th century.

The history of Eisenstadt, like the history of the whole of the "land of castles" (Burgenland), is inextricably interwoven with the history of the princes and dukes of Esterházy. Their

A farmer in the village Podersdorf.

main residence, castle Esterházy, still dominates the center of Eisenstadt (a town, by the way, that looks much more like a village). Originally a rather clumsy looking but gigantic fortress, it was rebuilt into a Baroque castle in 1663. Today, it houses the offices of the federal government of the Burgenland. There is a splendid English garden, in which the first Austrian steam engine was put on display in 1803. The park surrounding the castle is so vast (approximately 120 acres), it would easily accommodate a football stadium.

The (unfinished) building complex of Kalvarienberg and the Bergkirche (church on the mountain) in the district of Oberberg are two truly remarkable and original constructions. The Kalvarienberg (mountain of Calvary) is quite an architectural achievement. This artificial mountain was built around 1700 and pays homage to Christ's sufferings along the Way of the Cross. The path, partly built through the mountain, is lined with pictorial representations of the stages of Christ's progress to Calvary. It leads past niches, fantastic grottos and chapels and is a marvelous example of romantically idealized popular Christianity. The "church on the mountain" is the last resting-place of the composer Joseph Haydn, and is usually referred to as "Haydn's church". The composer and the town are almost inseparable. Haydn was born in Rohrau (1732) in Lower Austria, on the border to Burgenland. From 1761-1790 he was the conductor of the orchestra at the court of Prince Nikolaus Esterházy, performing both at the castle in Eisenstadt and the prince's castle, Esterháza in modern Hungary. The house he lived in during those years is a small museum today. The street was renamed in honor of him and is now called Haydngasse. The summerhouse, where he preferred to work, has

Street selling in Neusiedl.

also been preserved.

The beautiful Baroque "Wertheimer-haus" in Unterberg, the former Jewish district, once housed the synagogue is and now a museum. A few steps away is the former home of the Austrian merchant and amateur folklorist Sandor Wolf. Its modern addition houses the Burgenland's regional museum.

The "Seven Communes"

Burgenland was the domain of Jewish people until the persecution of the Jews in 1938. The expression "shewa kehillot", or the "Seven Communes", was familiar to every Jew living outside of Israel.

According to tradition, the first Jewish settlements in this most western part of the kingdom of Hungary date back to the 13th century. Jewish immigrants were first documented just before 1500, after they had been driven out of Steier-

mark (Styria) and Kärnten (Carinthia) in 1496.

In this region that lay just outside the Austrian border, the Jews experienced great religious and economic tolerance. Their individual feudal Lords issued them with charters of rights.

It was under the sovereignty of the Esterházys, who owned (and still own) most of the northern part of Burgenland, that the seven communities were founded: Eisenstadt, Mattersdorf (later renamed Mattersburg), Kobersdorf, Lackenbach, Deutschkreuz (Zelem in Hebrew), Frauenkirchen and Kittsee. (Further south, where the Hungarian princes of Batthyány reigned, a further three Jewish communities were established, in Güsing, Rechnitz and Stadtschlaining.)

These "chartered Jews", most of them craftsmen and tradesmen, enjoyed the sovereign's protection and had the right of self-government in their

Left, Haydn's tomb. Below, the "church on the mountain" in Eisenstadt.

own communities.

The excellent teaching at the school of Talmud (the fundamental code of Jewish law) in Eisenstadt had become renowned beyond the Austrian borders as early as the 18th century. Many an eminent scholar came to study here.

In 1848, the Jewish communities became autonomous municipalities with a governing body consisting of a mayor and a bailiff. They were also allowed their own school and even their own fire-brigade. These autonomous governments were dissolved again in the course of the 19th century. Only Mattersdorf retained its self-governing body until 1903, Eisenstadt-Unterberg until 1938.

Obeying an old tradition, the Jewish community of Unterberg was "secured" every day at nightfall, when a chain was put right across the main street. Then, in 1938, the holocaust started. The only reminder today of the prosperous and peaceful times the Jews who lived here enjoyed, are a few forgotten graves and tombstones.

The Esterházy dynasty still owns most of the land and many of the castles and former strongholds in Burgenland.

Forchtenstein is one of their most impressive strongholds. It was erected (about 1300) high up on a limestone rock of the Rosalien mountain range. In the middle of the 17th century it came into the hands of the Esterházys. The rock and the castle were secured by almost impenetrable fortifications and bastions. Its main features are the two very different towers: a round tower (middle ages) on the western side, and a Baroque tower with a bulbous spire on the eastern side. There is a well which is more than 470 ft (142 meters) deep and was dug by Turkish prisoners of war during 30 years of slave labor. Castle Forchtenstein houses a remarkable collection of Turkish art and an equally

The countryside surrounding the Neusiedler Lake.

splendid collection of weapons. **Schloß Kittsee**, in the most north-eastern part of the state, is another of the Esterházy castles. The Baroque building, which was designed in the shape of a horseshoe, houses one of the departments of the "Volkskundemuseum" in Vienna.

Schloß Halbturn, situated in the "Seewinkel", is also used as a museum today. It was built around 1710 by Lukas von Hildebrandt. It had been designed as an elegant manor house and is without doubt a splendid example of Baroque architecture.

The castle was badly damaged during World War II, as well as by a devastating fire in 1949. The extensive restoration works lasted until 1964. Luckily, the fresco on the ceiling of the so-called garden hall (1765, Franz Anton Maulpertsch), an important Rococo painting, was not destroyed by the fire.

The center of Burgenland is the shallow Neusiedler Lake, called the "Viennese Sea", in a region where the land is level, with treeless grassland.

Many riddles surround the **Neusiedler See**. The most puzzling one is the question where all the water comes from, and where it gets its vital oxygen from as it has only one influx (the river Wulka) and no outflow whatsoever. The normal water level is around three feet (one meter), but differs greatly according to the rain falls.

Usually, one can wade across the lake (at its narrowest point, between Mörbisch and Illmitz, an annual 'lake-crossing' party is held), but very often heavy storms, which are not unusual in this area, literally just push the water aside and reveal the mud at the bottom of the lake. Several times, the lake disappeared all together—once, in 1866, for as long as 10 years! During those years, farmers used the lake as farmland. As suddenly as it had disappeared, the lake came back again in 1876.

Harvesting the reeds outside the village of Rust.

The Neusiedler See, dotted with sailing boats maneuvering past the numerous islands of reeds, usually presents a peaceful picture. This can change very suddenly with the approach of a storm. Within minutes, the sailors will have to battle with incredibly high waves, despite the low water level.

This lake is without doubt Burgenland's biggest attraction. It is also its most endangered enviroment.

It was first discovered by natural scientists who were fascinated by its extraordinary and rare vegetation and animal life. It is one of the three or four large bird sanctuaries in Europe. The heron colony is unique.

No-one and nothing endangered the wildlife and vegetation until fairly recently. The natural environment provided by the reeds formed an ideal habitat for plants and animals alike and was only disturbed once a year, when the reeds were harvested in winter.

After World War II, the lake became a tourist attraction. At the same time, the surrounding farms were modernized and many were converted into vineyards. Now, the lake is being polluted by insecticides and pesticides, as well as by the garbage which thousands of tourists leave behind. It will need a lot of re-thinking and environmental planning to save this environment unique in Europe.

The tiny town of **Rust am Neusiedler See** (some well preserved houses, 16th to 18th century) is famous for its storks. They have lived and bred there for centuries and have always been lovingly looked after by the inhabitants there.

The chimneys, on which they build their nests, are constructed in a way that takes account of their nest building habits (the nests can weigh up to 100 kg). The alarming decline in the stork population, despite all these efforts, is

Horses grazing on the "Puszta".

184

due to the disappearance of the marshes, which are the natural feeding grounds of these birds, and the pollution through modern farming. The enormous nests high up on the chimneys remain, but more and more of them also remain empty.

In **Mörbisch**, a stage was built into the lake. Each summer, operetta festivals are held here, which are not only attended by the regular fans, but also by millions of mosquitoes! But the operetta enthusiasts don't seem to mind. For them, the stage and the closeness of the Hungarian "Puszta" provide the perfect setting for such popular "Puszta-operettas" as the *Czardasfürstin* and *Gräfin Mariza*.

Where the lake gently curves is the region called **Seewinkel**, one of the most deserted areas in the whole of Austria. This almost classical "Puszta" landscape gives one the impression of actually being in Hungary. Here, you

can still see a number of old and rusty draw-wells. The villages are spread far apart. Some just consist of a row of houses on each side of the main road, often for a stretch of several miles. The houses are limewashed, with wide entrance gates, and only the former reed-thatched roofs have disappeared.

The many shallow lakes (with no outflows), some small, some large, are also characteristic for this area. They are called "Lacken". Some are protected areas. The World Wildlife Fund created a nature reserve at the "Lange Lacke" which has become a haven for many rare plants and animals.

A peaceful paradise—until you come to the signpost "Andau, 6 km" and are reminded of the bridge of Andau... How long ago did it happen? The Hungarian uprising—when was it? O yes, in 1956. The iron curtain, the ominous watchtowers along the border—they are still there.

Left, a watchtower at the border of Hungary. Right, leaving the town of the "storks" (Rust).

DANKE AUF-WIEDERSEHEN

THE ART OF LIVING

It must have happened around the middle of the 1970s, although no-one can remember the exact date or year. Vienna had been quietly ill, under a canopy of cobwebs, stuck in a corset of cliché and tradition. A thousand years of history weighed down the former capital of the Austro-Hungarian Empire, the present didn't exist. And then, suddenly and unexpectedly, the town woke up. It started, of all places, in the oldest part of Vienna, in the small and narrow streets with their cobblestones and wrought-iron street lamps. To be precise, the "explosion" happened between the Ruprechtskirche and the Rabensteig. Curious new bars and Beiseln—a cross between a pub and a plain restaurant—opened. Loud music filled the streets, neon lights flickered over Baroque façades. A whole city rubbed its sleepy eyes.

The "joy of living" proved to be a fever that spread as rapidly as the plague had in former years. Elderly ladies of good family fled to the safe twilight interiors of dusty pastry shops. Chrome instead of velour, punk instead of pomp—the smell of decay was replaced by the aura of modernity. Some local prophets were heard to say "it would pass". They were very wrong. The new found life was here to stay, obviously proof against the efforts of spoilsports. It even had an effect on potential suicide candidates.

Not so long ago Vienna had one of the highest suicide rates in the world, but today it is down to an "acceptable" rate: only 28 Viennese in every 100,000 take their own lives. Most of the others prefer to seek a solution to their problems in the famous (and infamous) "Bermuda Triangle", as the small district—

Preceding pages: A Heuriger inn; live music in a pub; the Opera Ball. Below, the Griechenbeisel.

formerly the Jewish textile quarter—around the Ruprechtskirche has been nicknamed. Here, the Viennese in-crowd rules, a mixture of amateur performance artists, jokers, heavy drinkers, top-class hairdressers and honorary gurus. Each has his or her own personal program of evening entertainment.

A lot of paths cross at **Oswald und Kalb**, the center for the latest hot gossip. Most tourists ignore the old, unassuming exterior in the Backerstraße, while inside the media people and their victims communicate over a glass of wine at the wooden counter in front of the mirrored bar. The wine is poured by expert Yugoslav waiters. The main choice is between an extremely palatable dry white wine and the famous Schilcher Rose cultivated in Styria. The salads, dressed with dark pumpkin seed oil, are quite delicious, and if you are lucky you can order fresh Slovak goose liver. Having dined, quenched your

The stage in the Red Angel.

thirst a little and gathered the information you sought, the journey continues. Cross the road and enter **Alt Wien**, only a few steps away. During the day, the Alt Wien is a quiet, rather shabby café with a few snooker tables. At night, it reminds you of a vision of Dante's Inferno. One guide book to Vienna warns the outsider: "If you enter a bar in this city, you must be prepared to be stared at, critically assessed, have the mickey taken and be generally tested. But you will also be accepted once you have passed these tests".

The less daring never make it past the billowing tobacco fumes and babble of voices at the entrance. The braver ones are rewarded by a good though alcoholic live show. There is always at least one love-sick figure, huddled in a corner, drowning his sorrows. An intoxicated unrecognized genius recites his poetry, and there's a small but harmless squabble at the bar. It's not surprising

that the Alt Wien was the favorite of Helmut Qualtinger, the late actor and cabaret artist, who used to celebrate here nightly and throw out anyone who didn't "look right", i.e. people whose clothes suggested middle-class aspirations. These normally took refuge in the **Weincomptoir** across the street. Here you can enjoy some of the best wines available in "civilized" company. Top quality bottles are stacked in the wooden racks. The handwritten menu offers snacks, or a beautifully fattening meal such as spinach dumplings fried in lots of butter and sprinkled with Parmesan cheese. If you prefer Italian cuisine, the Viennese prefer the Cantinetta, renowned for its excellent fish dishes.

In the Backerstraße, on a stretch not much longer than a hundred yards, there are bars and restaurants to satisfy every taste, pocket and frame of mind. After midnight, this small and usually quiet street looks more like a fairground. **Die Bar** is just around the corner in the Sonnenfelsgasse, and is frequented by the kind of ever-so-cool intellectual who knows it all and has seen it all. They usually just stare knowingly past each other. The tourist, not used to the pace of Viennese night life, usually gives up here. But this is where it all begins!

The Bermuda Triangle

Walk down Rotenturmstraße, past **Daniel Moser** (preferred by the sons of the upper classes and ambitious transvestites), then follow the noise. You can't miss it.

Rabensteig is a small square, surrounded by very old houses. On a warm summer's evening, it converts into one big garden. If you are lucky enough to get a seat, you can sit in the middle of the city, enjoy the mild evening, flirt a little and comment on the passers-by.

Inside the Weincomptoir.

Or you can go into **KrahKrah** (Croak Croak), choose between 40 different kinds of beer and eat one of their hot meat and garlic sandwiches on rye bread. In the **Rote Engel** (Red Angel) there's only bread and cheese on the menu to go with the wine by the glass, but there's live music every night. A strange steel construction stretches across the middle of the pub, but the guests sit squashed together on traditional Viennese coffee house furniture. The Rote Engel enjoys near-museum status nowadays, for it was the spark that ignited the Bermuda Triangle in the mid-70s.

From this point, bars and restaurants spread out like wildfire, all along the Seitenstettengasse as far as the Ruprechtskirche. The heavily armed policemen guarding the synagogue opposite the **Kaktus** add a somber note, however. The **Ma Pitom** is famous for its Italian and Jewish specialties. The

Hebrew name means, Why Suddenly. The top address on the Ruprechtsplatz is the **Salzamt** (Salt Trading Post).

The interior was designed by the Viennese star architect Hermann Czech, and has been photographed in detail for international decorating magazines. Plain wooden boxes hide the ventilation shafts under the ceiling, and among them hang the most elaborate Venetian chandeliers. The clientele is among the most chic in the city. The food is superb—the yuppie palate thrives on fried chicken and livers in red wine on a bed of lettuce, or terrine of broccoli with shrimps in herb sauce. Even the world-famous Austrian racing driver, Niki Lauda drops in occasionally. The Bermuda Triangle is dominated by those who are old enough to have made their pile already. The younger—and less well-off—Vespa and moped riders prefer to go to the "disco quarter" near the luxury hotels

The entrance to Figlmüller.

ZUM FIGLMÜLLER

SAS and **Marriot**. **Bora Bora** and **Wake Up** are an insider's tip to playboys with greying temples trying to chat up girls. After midnight, the people living here are robbed of their last bit of sleep by mopeds roaring down the streets. The "in" places are by no means confined to the city center. The **Europa** (District 7) is absolutely packed every night around midnight. The favorite drink at the L-shaped bar is tequila. Despite the name, the clientele of the **Titanic** seem to stave off any end-of-the-world mood quite successfully. In most guide books to Vienna you will find a long list under the heading "In-Lokale" of literally hundreds of bars, cafés, Beiseln and restaurants. It has become impossible to list them all. We recommend that you drift along with the crowd and try this or that restaurant for yourself. No-one, we can assure you, has ever died of thirst during this pleasant exercise.

Most of those revelers who have managed to stay awake till the early hours of the morning end up in the Linke Wienzeile in the **Café Dobner**, opposite the Naschmarkt. There is always a mixed clientele here—regular nightclubbers, elegant theater-goers, the odd down-and-out or scrounger. You can have a hot meal as early as four in the morning. Many a potential hangover has been held off by a steaming risotto or a small goulash plus a "Pfiff" (a small glass of beer).

The Beisel

There are a few quite distinct features that make up a Beisel, a paneled bar with wooden floorboards and brightly polished taps for draught beer, where you can drink a quick beer standing up, and a "parlor" with chequered tablecloths and a few withered plants struggling to survive in the tobacco

Left, "At Sophie's" at Naschmarkt. Right, in the garden of the Glacisbeisel.

smoke, and a grumpy, hasty waiter, usually addressed as "Herr Franz". There is a hand-written menu with a different main dish every day, and a landlady who is usually the best advertisement for the nourishing food prepared in the kitchen where she rules. A fading piece of card in the window announces the regular meeting of a local club on the premises. All this makes up the mixture that delights both regulars and passing trade.

A certain Ignaz Castelli, nicknamed "Professor of the Science of Frivolity" by the Viennese, had this to say about the Beisel in 1800: "There are small and rather shabby inns in the suburbs, called Beiseln by the lower classes, whose innkeepers keep one or two pretty, cheeky wenches and where two or three musicians play dance tunes every evening. There is no great variety of food—sausages, cheese, occasionally pork. During the day, the mostly rather buxom wenches pose outside the entrance and offer their services to the passing menfolk. Over their bosoms they wear silk kerchiefs, which reveal more than they cover".

The wenches, with or without kerchiefs, advertise their services in the personal columns of newspapers today, and the shabby inns have long become an honorable institution. Employees, pensioners, students and professors, dog owners and their pets all eat here. In a Beisel you get a good plain meal, none of the fancy stuff. A clear soup (with liver or semolina dumplings) for starters, followed by goulash or roast beef with vegetables, fish on Fridays or maybe even homemade noodles, followed by sweet plum or apricot dumplings. The worst enemy of these traditional inns is success. Once a Beisel has achieved a reputation for good food, people will start crowding in at lunchtime. The time will come when

The formidable landlady of the Pfudl.

the Beisel will be "promoted" to restaurant status. The menu of plain good cooking becomes internationally interesting with garnishes of pineapple or kiwifruit.

These days the Beisel has become an honorable name again, but it also appears on the front of some pseudo-rustic snackbars—avoid these traps. It's better to queue for a table at the Pfudl in the Backerstraße. Here, you can still enjoy a delicious and very traditional Viennese meal. The preparation is closely supervised by the landlady (the "Pfudlwirtin"). Not very far away is another good tip for gourmets, **Zu den drei Hackn**. In summer you can sit in the pleasantly shaded garden in front of the inn. The **Koranda** in the Wollzeile has a large, old-fashioned dining room, in which journalists, artists and young politicians season their meals with the latest in gossip. In August, when the temperature rises, the

Viennese flock to either the **Silberwirt** or the **Fasslwirt**, both in District 5. Their courtyards are shaded by enormous chestnut trees, sparrows fight over the crumbs on the gravel. Opposite the cemetery in Ottakring is another favorite Beisel with a typically Viennese atmosphere, the **Witwe Bolte**. The quiet drinker, sitting here with a quarter liter of Heuriger and a juicy piece of roast pork, soon realizes that life is well worth living.

An exceptional establishment is **Peter's Beisl**, also in Ottakring. In the bar, tired workers wash away the day's troubles, but in the dining room superb and very reasonably priced dishes of Viennese novelle cuisine are served. If you want to discover your very own Beisel, your best bet is to wander through the quiet suburban streets, eyes open, and follow your nose. When you smell fried onions and paprika, you're on the right track. If you see an elderly gent with his dachshund disappearing behind a plain wooden door, follow him. He knows the place.

Beisel on the fringe

To have fun at somebody else's expense, to eat well and to drink well—these are the three favorite pastimes of the Viennese. And nowadays they can indulge in all three at once. The fringe Beiseln (mainly cabaret) are in great demand , and it is advisable to reserve a table well in advance. If you visit the established Viennese theaters, you'll probably have to follow custom and squeeze yourself into a little black dress or half-choke yourself with a bow tie. Here, you can sprawl in jumper and jeans, and providing you can cope with the language, enjoy the abrasive cabaret on the stage. Eating, drinking and even smoking (unless the performer is still a bit hoarse from yesterday) are of course permitted. The waiters and waitresses, balancing plates and beer tank-

Inside one of the discos in the Bermuda Triangle.

ards, have perfected their timing to fit in with the performance. Strengthened in body and soul, guests leave the pub at closing time with the comfortable feeling of having indulged in physical and mental pleasures. The first of these busy establishments to spring up was the **Kulisse** in the Rosensteingasse in Hernals (District 17). It is an old suburban theater which was converted with some difficulty by three teachers, a cook and a photographer and opened in 1980. The repertoire includes Nestroy as well as social satire. Any cabaret artist who manages to pack the Kulisse to its full capacity of 220 seats can call himself or herself successful. A competitor to be reckoned with is the Spektakel near the Naschmarkt. There is less space, but the food is better. One of its stars is the wickedly ingenious Lukas Resetarits, known to the Viennese as the unconventional hero of a TV detective series. He shows the Vien-

nese heart of gold to be distinctly leaden, while the guests devote themselves to the food, laughing gives you an appetite. Other high points of the cabaret scene are the **Metropol**, a former dance café, and the **Kabarett Niedermaier**. The young woman who runs the latter organizes three "talent spotting" evenings a year for young entertainers. The **Simpl** in the Wollzeile offers traditional jokes, and is frequented by politicians trying to demonstrate that they do not take themselves too seriously. The Simpl is the last survivor of the heydays of Viennese cabaret, the years between the wars and again immediately after World War II. There is a Viennese saying: "When times are bad, the cabaret's good". In the years between the wars there were times when you could choose up to 25 cabaret establishments (mostly housed in cellars). Helmut Qualtinger, that imposing figure, revived cabaret after

The stage in the Metropol.

1945. Georg Kreisler, sitting tinkling harmlessly at the piano, fired many an acid remark which later found its way into the language as a proverb. Cabaret declined in popularity during the economic boom years. People took their work seriously, trying to grab a piece of the economic cake as living standards rose. Today, thank God, cabaret is back again. There's something for everyone, from the blackest of humor to feminist sketches. Cabaret is once more part of Viennese life.

Coffee houses, patisseries and other Viennese delicacies

At the crack of dawn the Viennese "Kaffeehauser" open their doors, there is a delicious aroma of freshly ground coffee, the baskets on the marble tables are filled with a vast variety of bread, buns and rolls, newspapers from all over the world are waiting, neatly sorted, for the guests. Vienna's coffee houses are often talked about, though actually indescribable, a much-loved institution. The writer Camillo Schaefer once said that the coffee houses represented "an oasis in the desert of life", essential for the thirst of every age and social class. The most colorful mixture can be found in the **Café Museum** in the Karlsplatz. Seated on red leather sofas and armchairs, councillors and students read or play chess, painters and sculptors from the nearby Academy of Visual Arts discuss their work. The walls are yellowed with cigarette smoke and covered with theatrical and art posters. The waiters take care of their guests, over and above the call of duty depending on the size of the tip. If you are lucky enough to get one of the window seats, you can enjoy a marvelous view of the newly re-gilded dome of the Secession building across the street. The Secession also houses, in

A patisserie in Oberlaa.

its cellar, a coffee house, the **Café in der Secession**, which presents a quite daring mixture of styles (traditional coffee house furniture, the walls tiled with garish Italian tiles). On warm summer evenings, you can dance the tango on the lawn outside, with the traffic roaring around you and the Karlskirche silhouetted against the darkening sky like a Baroque mirage.

The atmosphere in the **Landtmann** (right next to the Burgtheater), probably the most splendid of the coffee houses, is much more subdued. At lunchtime, it tends to be packed with politicians (the parliament and town hall are close by). Amongst them sit journalists with ears pricked for a good story and actors waiting to be recognized. The food is excellent, the prices reasonable. **Pruckl** in the Stubenring thrives on that slightly worn Viennese charm. Bridge is played here every Saturday afternoon, with the greatest concentration. Other coffee houses in the inner city which follow the old Viennese tradition are the **Diglas** (Wollzeile), with gigantic cakes on display, the **Frauenhuber** or the **Braunerhof**. If you want to enjoy some culture with your coffee, you could try the **Wortner** (Wiedner Hauptstraße) or the **Zartl** (Rasumofskygasse). They provide poetry readings and concerts in the evenings. The Alte Backstube (old bakehouse) in Josefstadt is coffee house and museum in one. While drinking hot chocolate with whipped cream you can admire old flour measures, bakery utensils and the oven that was first used 250 years ago.

The **Hawelka** in Dorotheergasse looks back on a glorious past. Here, you should ask for a "Buchtel", a kind of pastry, which is served hot after ten in the evening. If you prefer sour to sweet, or sweet-sour, you had better go to the **Trzesniewski** opposite and try one of their rolls with spicy fillings.

The "Konditoreien" (patisseries) are real temples for the sweet tooth. There is no clear distinction between a Kaffeehaus and a Konditorei, except perhaps that the clientele differs. Elegant ladies, reminiscing about the times when the black forest cherry cake was simply *enormous*, meet at **Lehmann** in the Graben or "Gerstner" in the Kartnerstraße, once suppliers to the imperial court. The mecca for everyone with a sweet tooth, however, is the **Demel** in the Kohlmarkt. It was founded 200 years ago. Its cakes, gateaux, confectionery and delicate salads are still among the finest on offer. Guests are still addressed in the old but proper fashion, in the third person, and waitresses in monasterial black serve "creme de jour" and keep the more easy-going tourists in check with stern glances. The icings on the cakes displayed in the window are shaped in the form of well-known Austrians such as the Emperor Franz Josef or Bruno

Kreisky, the former chancellor.

A bit of frivolity is essential, even when eating. The battle for the biggest Schnitzel has been won in style by **Figlmüller** (in the passage between the Wollzeile and Stephansplatz), where they are bigger than the plates they are served on. Disgusted vegetarians take refuge in the **Wrenkh** (District 15) and enjoy a healthy meal in a smokeless atmosphere, eating desserts sweetened with honey from Burgenland instead of sugar. This menu would lead to a revolt among the guests in the "authentic" Viennese pubs. Good roast pork just isn't a light meal, and chicken should be crisply fried in plenty of butter or oil. The traditional accompaniment is live zither music and Heuriger songs, occasionally a real gypsy violinist. The most popular places are **Piaristenkeller** in Josefstadt, **Mathiaskeller**, **Augustinerkeller** and **Zwolf-Apostel-Keller** in the inner city.

If you want to walk off some of the calories afterwards, take a look round some of the many Viennese art galleries. The exhibits range from Biedermeier watercolors to the products of the Jungen Wilden. The oldest one is the gallery **Wurthle** in the Weihburggasse. The Galerie nachst St. Stephan promoted avant garde art in the 60s. Video art can be seen at Grita Insam in the Kollnerhofgasse. The **Galerie Krinzinger** (Seilerstatte), with its exhibition area of over 6,666 sq ft (600 sq meters), could perhaps more rightly be called a museum. The ambitious Peter Pakesch values collaboration with young artists, and exhibits their work in his gallery in the Ballgasse.

Do not miss the **Dorotheum** (Dorotheergasse), pawn shop and auction house in one. Its popular name is Pfandl (from the German verb *verpfanden*, to pawn). The exhibits displayed on several floors range from period

Inside the famous Demel coffeehouse.

furniture to paintings, jewelry, porcelain, clothes and all sorts of nicknacks. Nostalgia fans can admire themselves in the decorative old mirrors, search wormy old desks for secret drawers, or sink into velour armchairs.

Gifts and souvenirs

The little antique shops between the Dorotheum and between the Hofburg have windows filled with glittering Jugendstil jewelry. Vienna offers souvenirs for every taste and pocket. From fine Augarten porcelain (preferably shaped into pirouetting Lipizzaner horses) to petit-point spectacle cases or to a "meter of love"—a fancy box, exactly one meter long and containing tiny, hand-made pieces of confectionery. The great traditional confectioner **Altmann & Kuhne** in the Graben produces this superb miniature confectionery. They lovingly pack it into little

boxes, cases and doll's hatboxes and export it all over the world. But the Viennese, too, like to spoil themselves by buying a little nougat or bitter chocolate drops here.

Elegant, handmade leather shoes are the speciality of **Scheer & Söhne**, **Matern** and **Nagy**, all three in the inner city. Stacked up on their shelves are the latest models used by many prominent personalities. **Milano and Goiserer**, newcomers amongst the expensive Viennese shoe shops, offer super-soft felt slippers and pumps made of bark decorated with exotic birds' feathers. Traditional costumes of exclusive design can be found at **Assasin** in the Judenplatz. They have a wide range of embroidered braces and colorful leather jackets with hartshorn buttons. The beautiful and rich shop at the elegant boutique **Schella Kahn** in the Singerstraße, it offers modern classics in quiet colors, with the emphasis on first-class materials and workmanship. Matching spectacles for the cosmopolitan couple can be found round the corner in the Liliengasse, at **Hartmann's**. Here the aids to vision are made of horn or super light pear or maple wood. You can also buy perfectly shaped combs, brushes and hair slides. Both fine jewelry and the latest craze are available at the **Galerie am Graben** and **V & V** in the Lindengasse. If you've lost your rocks (or had to take them to the Pfandl), there is a vending machine outside selling necklaces made of plastic diamonds.

Having completed your shopping trip and bought a few glittering things for yourself, you might fancy an evening of drinking champagne at one of Vienna's casinos. In the elegant atmosphere of the **Cercle**, the casino in the Karntner Straße, you can lose a fortune—or watch someone else losing it. Next door is the famous dressmaker **Adlmuller**, where the wives of politicians and primadonnas alike have

Mouth-watering display of confectionery in the Heiner.

themselves fitted with yards of taffeta for the annual Opera Ball. A visit to the nightclubs between St. Stephen's Cathedral and the Opera House can be as expensive as an evening in the casino. In the **Moulin Rouge** guests often wait in vain for the striptease show they expected. The Theater im Kopf is performing there at present, with *Waiting for Godot* or the feminist thriller *Extremities*. The landlord, Heinz Schimanko, perhaps the best known bald head in Vienna, is a fervent patron of the arts. Thanks to a few courageous individuals, Viennese fringe theater has been transformed from a dull desert to fertile meadow. In the very shadow of the Opera, the Burgtheater and the Theater in der Josefstadt, young ensembles have been formed that fearlessly blow the cobwebs off the classic pieces. The well-known and dedicated actress, Emmy Werner was one of the courageous ones and formed her own

group, Theater in der Drachengasse a few years ago. She was so successful that she was offered the post of director of the Volkstheater, the first woman in Vienna to be made director of one of the big established theaters.

The Viennese follow the appointment of theater directors like the plots of TV thrillers. Alas, an over-progressive spirit is all too easily indentified with the decline of Western civilization. Many directors are well and truly hated, only they don't know it.

Well, we have found out that the Viennese like to eat and drink well, that they like to go out, display themselves and conduct intrigues. But what about keeping fit in order to survive all this good living? The Viennese, the truth must be told, are not very fond of sports activities. This is often to the visitor's advantage. As one guide book ironically puts it: "There will be plenty of space in the swimming pools, espe-

Left, window shopping in the inner city. Right, Viennese petit-point embroidery.

cially in the water". If you want relaxing exercise, try the spectacular Amalienbad. You can splash around in the wonderful Jugendstil hall and watch the milky light fall through the glass roof onto the Turkish tiles. We also recommend a visit to the steam baths with their mosaic decorations. Snobs, fresh air fanatics and those who like betting head toward the Prater. There is trap racing in **Krieau** and horse racing in **Freudenau**. Freudenau, once the meeting place of high society, is still considered one of the most beautiful racecourses in the world. You can get the best view of the start from the white-painted roofed stands. At the end of every race there is a confetti snowstorm of torn-up tickets tossed away by disappointed losers. Elegant old gentlemen of the turf console themselves with champagne. The atmosphere recalls a long-lost world. The parkland around the racecourse is a golf course, the only

one in Vienna. On the Alte Donau, the old course of the Danube, is another favorite recreation center. With the skyline of the UNO-City in the background, you can surf, row, swim and go ice skating in the winter. The only drawback—the mosquitos love the place, too. The favorite sport of the Viennese, however, has always been and still is simply going for a walk. On a Sunday afternoon, couples, families and individuals stroll happily through the park of Schloß Schönbrunn, along the Danube Canal or along the Ring in the inner city. In imperial times the flower show in the Prater was one of the most important social events in spring. Today the Stadtfest (city festival), held on the first weekend in May, has become almost as great a tradition. Young and old swarm through the city, bent on enjoying themselves, and the police turn a blind eye. This is followed by the **Wiener Festwochen** (Vienna Festival)

Show-cases in the Dorotheum.

in June. It is traditionally opened with a ballet performance by the Ballet of the State Opera House in the Rathausplatz, unless it's a "washout" because of the weather. For a few weeks the city belongs to the artists and street performers. There are open-air theater performances and concerts, tradition and avant garde in peaceful co-existence. Vienna officially becomes what it is all the year round—one single stage.

Fasching—the season of balls

Vienna is at its liveliest when it's cold and wet, or "ungemütlich" outside. From November to February's Ash Wednesday, all the music and concert halls of a bygone Imperial splendor are filled again with the rhythm of the waltz, then they become again, what they once have been: playgrounds where the Viennese soul unfolds, where class, clan and family are forgotten, where joy, gaiety, merriment and frivolity reign supreme.

There is the Champagne ball, the Emperor's ball, the Hunter and Chimneysweeper's ball, the Thieve and the Opera ball. Nearly every group of people who, during the year, work together in (more or less) harmony has a place and time to meet to dance, drink and laugh.

If one doesn't own the essential ball dress, it doesn't matter, there are enough instituitions where you can lease them. The tailcoat for the Opera ball can be rented for a sum of US$200 a night. But the real Viennese doesn't mind paying, for him, the rest of the year is there to prepare for the season of balls, for the time when he can finally be what he was born for and when all these lifeless majestic structures of the city come to life again.

The Habsburgs did not always have the common touch that nostalgia makes them out to have possessed. For instance, they strictly forbade their subjects to enter the woods and meadows outside the city walls, as they preferred to keep them indulged in the imperial sport of hunting. This lasted until way into the 18th century. Not until the liberal Joseph II succeeded his mother Maria Theresia, was the Prater opened (in 1766) to all Viennese. Criticized for this decision by the aristocracy, he calmly retorted: "If I wanted to stay among my peers, I'd have to spend all day walking in the Kapuzinergruft" (where the Habsburgs are buried). The Viennese enthusiastically came en masse from the first day onwards. They spread out over the meadows and filled the shady corners. Shrewd businessmen sought an imperial license to sell coffee, tea and ice cream. The first simple merry-go-rounds, swings and bowling alleys were set up. On one stall "mechanical birds" were on display.

Growth of the Prater

The Viennese desire for the sensational led to the rapid growth of the Prater. Comic revues and shooting-galleries sprang up, there were firework displays, dwarfs and other human freaks—real or fraudulent—were exhibited and much admired. In 1855, the famous "Cafalatti", a wooden mandarin (30-ft, nine-meters high, with a long narrow pigtail) was set up in the center of one of the merry-go-rounds. The true symbol of the Prater, however, has always been the figure of Punch, lovingly known as "Wurstel" in Vienna. The Viennese look upon this tragicomical figure as a soulmate. Ill-treated by life, pursued by a crocodile, he struggles on from adventure to adventure and ends up as the winner after all, a Viennese Don Quixote.

The Prater was not only noise and public entertainment, but also peace and quiet. The secretive little lanes away from the commotion of the fairground were, and still are, favored by lovers. The giant Ferris wheel was erected in 1897, when the World Exhibition was held in Vienna. Some 200 ft (67 meters) high, it was at the time the highest Ferris wheel in the world. In the last days of World War II, the Prater was badly damaged. Reconstruction began in 1948, and it formed the location for Orson Welles' brilliant movie *The Third Man*. Today, the Prater is in danger of turning into an American-style theme park. Amusement arcades and peepshows have replaced the old-fashioned merry-go-rounds with their brightly painted wooden horses. Traditional delicacies have given way to fast food snackbars. If you want to catch something of the old atmosphere, take a trip on the Liliputbahn, a miniature train, into the the tangled greenery. Or walk along the main avenue of the Prater, a splendid street lined with giant trees, used every Sunday by thousands of Viennese for cycling. Afterwards, go to the Lusthaus (despite its name—house of pleasure—it's a highly respectable establishment) and take a break, restoring the worked-off calories with *guglhupf* and a *melange*.

The Bohemian Prater

In the south of Vienna, on the very edge of the tenth District of Favoriten, lies a very special street. On a clear day, the view of Vienna from the gently rolling slopes of the Laaerberg is superb. The sky above the sea of roofs and church towers is sprinkled with dots of colorful kites flown by children.

In this idyllic place, Bohemian brickmakers worked until well into the last century, under appalling, slave-like conditions. They made bricks for half the Habsburg empire and mostly slept in the open, using a brick for a pillow. The Bohemian immigrants provided plentiful and popular cheap labor in the factories and as cooks and maids in upper class households. Many a touch-

ing song was written about them, but they were mercilessly exploited. Today, many pages of the Vienna telephone directory still read like the telephone directory of Prague. The lyrics of one popular song of the post-war years were written with the help of the telephone directory. It consisted entirely of a list of names beginning with V—with such tongue-twisters as Vaclavik, Vrbka and the unsurpassable Vlk.

The Böhmische Prater (Bohemian Prater) is one of the few relics of the days when Bohemian immigrants lived here. Tucked away among allotments and birch woods are old-fashioned flimsy stalls. There is a smell of candy floss and Turkish delight. The oldest carousel in Europe is there, under a wooden canopy dating from 1840. It was placed under protection in 1985. The carved wooden horses all have a name. They are called Elfi, Herbert and Karli.

At the roulette table in the Cercle.

TRAVEL TIPS

GETTING THERE

BY AIR

There are connections to over 60 destinations all over the world and domestic flights to Graz, Linz, Salzburg, Klagenfurt and Innsbruck from Vienna Schwechat.

The information desk in the arrivals lounge is open between 9 a.m. and 10 p.m.

Airlines: There are 36 airlines operating from and to Vienna.

The biggest ones are:
Austrian Airlines
1, Kärntner Ring 18,
Tel. 6800

German Lufthansa
1, Opernring 1,
Tel. 563535

Swissair
1, Kärntner Ring 4,
Tel. 5871798

Air France
1, Kärntner Straße 49,
Tel. 526655

British Airways
1, Kärntner Ring 10,
Tel. 657691

Pan American
1, Kärntner Ring 5,
Tel. 526646

KLM
1, Kärntner Straße 12,
Tel. 5235250

Alitalia
1, Kärntner Ring 2,
Tel. 651707

Airport Schwechat
Schwechat is situated about 9.5 miles (15.2 km) to the east of Vienna and can be reached on the airport motorway in 25 min.

Information: Tel. 77702231

Express Coach Services operate between the airport and the southern and western rail terminals and the **City Air Terminal** outside the Hilton hotel between 6 a.m. and 7 p.m. During the evening and night, there is a bus connection after every scheduled flight arrival.

Information: Tel. 723534

Taxi Fares are approximately öS 350

Shuttle Service: Transport by mini bus to the airport from every major hotel, Tel. 6360190

Trains: Trains leave from Wien-Mitte (central station) every hour between 7.30 a.m. and 8.30 p.m.

BY RAIL

The two main railway stations linking Vienna with destinations in Europe are the "Westbahnhof" (western station) and the "Südbahnhof" (southern station). Trains from West Germany, France, Belgium and Switzerland arrive at Westbahnhof, those from Yugoslavia, Greece, Hungary and Italy at Südbahnhof.

International Intercity Trains:
Prinz Eugen: Hannover-Dortmund-Frankfurt-Vienna.
Ostende-Wien Express: Ostende-Brussels-Cologne-Vienna.
Arlberg Express: Paris-Basel-Zürich-Vienna.
Holland-Wien Express: Amsterdam-Cologne-Vienna.

Trains carrying cars run between Vienna and Düsseldorf, Cologne and Frankfurt. During the summer months, there is a ferry service on the Danube River from Passau to Vienna.

The main railway station for trains arriving from Czechoslovakia and East Germany is the "Franz-Josephs-Bahnhof".

Passenger Information
Tel. 835149/839574
Complaints
Tel. 245512
General Information
Tel. 7200
Westbahnhof Destinations
Tel. 1552
Südbahnhof Destinations
Tel. 1553
Reservations
Österreichisches Verkehrsbüro, 1. Opernring 5, Tel. 56000

BY ROAD

Most visitors to Vienna from the western parts of Europe approach the town on the "Westautobahn". Tourist Information at the end of the motorway, hotel bookings are also arranged. The same facilities are available when entering Vienna on the motorway coming from the south ("Südautobahn").

PARKING

You should avoid the center of Vienna if traveling by car. There are few parking facilities in the inner city, and a net of one-way streets make driving a nightmare. If it cannot be avoided, look out for the car parks but bear in mind that some of them are closed on weekends and during the night.

Car Parks in the Center of Town

City Parkhaus: (Stephansplatz), entrance Schulerstraße. Tel. 5122709, Mon.-Fri. 7.00 - 21.00, Sat. 7.00 - 14.00

Garage am Hof: Entrance Schottengasse, Freyung, Tel. 635571, open day and night, seven days a week.

Hoher Markt Garage: Entrance Marc-Aurel-Straße, Tel. 635825, from Mon.- Fri. 7.00 - 20.00

Franz-Josefs-Kai-Garage: Entrance Franz-Josefs-Kai, Tel. 631521, the first floor is open day and night, seven days a week.

Garage am Beethovenplatz: Entrance Johannesgasse, Tel. 735321, open day and night, seven days a week.

Kärntner Straße Tiefgarage: Entrance Kärntner Ring, Tel. 571597, open day and night, seven days a week.

Opernringhofgarage: Entrance Operngasse and Elisabethstraße, open day and night, seven days a week.

There are certain areas where parking is allowed for 1-1/2 hours when a parking disc is displayed. These can be purchased at tobacco shops ("Tabak-Trafik"). At night, during the winter months, it is forbidden to park in streets where the trams pass through. Where parking is not allowed, you may only stop for a maximum of 10 minutes. Illegal parking costs about öS 100. If your car was towed away, you must reclaim it at the nearest police station. Once the fine of öS 2000 (plus a handling fee) has been paid, the car can be collected at Wienerberg or Mannswörth. The fine for exceeding the speed limit is öS 200 (and more).

Breakdown Services
ÖAMTC: 1, Schubertring 1-3, Tel. 927651-0, emergency call 120 and 9540
ARBÖ: 15, Mariahilfer Straße 180, Tel. 782521-0, emergency call 123

Petrol stations open all night
1, Börsegasse 11
1, Franz-Josefs-Kai/Morzinplatz
3, Untere Viaduktstraße 47-49
4, Paulanergasse 13

TRAFFIC RULES AND REGULATIONS

At a roundabout you must give way to cars coming from the right. Approaching a junction you *must* get in lane. A rapid succession of flashing lights indicates that the lights are about to change to red. It is forbidden to use your horn in the town. Seat belts for the passenger's and driver's seat are obligatory, children under 12 are not allowed on the passenger seat. It is advisable to carry an international insurance card. Cars with foreign number plates must also display international registration plates.

Speed Limit: 80 miles (130 km) on the motorway, 60 miles (100 km) on country roads, 30 miles (50 km) in built-up areas.

TRAVEL ESSENTIALS

VISAS & PASSPORTS

In order to balance its trade deficits, Austria relies heavily on tourism. The procedures at passport controls and customs are therefore rather lax.

You will need a passport when entering Austria. Some nationalities must obtain a visa before entering. Contact the Austrian embassy in your country for details.

MONEY MATTERS

Currency

The Austrian Schilling (öS) is divided into 100 "Groschen". There are notes of 20, 50, 100 and 1000 Schilling, and coins of 2, 5, 10 and 50 Groschen.

At the date of publication the exchange rate was 22.15 Austrian Schilling to 1 Pound Sterling.

Foreign Currency

There is no limit on importing or exporting foreign currency. No more than 15.000 Austrian Shilling can be taken out of the country.

Banks

Banks are open from 0800 - 1230 hrs and 1330 - 1500 hrs Monday to Friday, and stay open until 1730 hrs on Thursdays. The main branches are open throughout lunch time.

Bureau de Change

Stephansplatz:	daily 0900 - 1730 hrs
Operngasse:	daily 0800 - 1900 hrs

Südbahnhof:	daily 0630 - 2200 hrs
Westbahnhof:	daily 0700 - 2200 hrs
City Air Terminal:	daily 0800 - 1230 hrs,
	1400 - 1800 hrs
Airport:	daily 0630 - 2300

Eurocheques must be made out in Schilling. Most credit cards are accepted by the big hotels and main shops in the inner city.

American Express
1, Parkring 10, Tel. 51511-0

Visa
1, Wipplingerstraße 4, Tel. 638751-0

Diners Club
4, Rainergasse 1, Tel. 65935-0

ANIMAL QUARANTINE

If you intend to bring any animals into Austria you need a veterinary document as proof of rabies vaccination.
Emergency service: Tel. 834303

CUSTOMS

No duty on items for personal use. (This includes two cameras, an 8-mm film camera or a video camera, a portable typewriter, a transistor radio, a portable television, a tape recorder and a record player.) If you exceed 17, 200 cigarettes or 50 cigars, two liters of wine and one liter of spirits are duty free.

VAT

Goods are either taxed with 20 percent VAT or a 32 percent so-called luxury tax. If you purchase goods exceeding the value of öS 1000, VAT is refunded when leaving the country. You must produce an invoice proving that VAT was deducted, together with a document called "U 34". Both must be obtained when purchasing the goods.

GETTING ACQUAINTED

ECONOMY

Vienna is the economic center of Austria. Industry: precision engineering, electrical, electronic, metal. With nearly two million visitors (25 percent of which are West Germans) a year, the biggest industry is tourism.
The seat of the Austrian parliament is Vienna. Vienna is also a Catholic archbishopric (ca. 150 clergymen) and the seat of a Protestant bishop.

GEOGRAPHY

The 23 Districts (Bezirke)

I	Innere Stadt (Inner City)
II	Leopoldstadt
III	Landstraße
IV	Wieden
V	Margareten
VI	Mariahilf
VII	Neubau
VIII	Josefstadt
IX	Alsergrund
X	Favoriten
XI	Simmering
XII	Meidling
XIII	Hietzing
XIV	Penzing
XV	Fünfhaus
XVI	Ottakring
XVII	Hernals
XVIII	Währing
XIX	Döbling
XX	Brigittenau
XXI	Florisdorf
XXII	Donaustadt
XXIII	Liesing

The border of the Inner City is the "Ringstraße" (ring road), or the "Kai". Grouped around it in a circle are the former suburbs, i.e. the districts II - IX plus Brigittenau. These are enclosed by the outer ring road, the former "Linienwall". The last ring around the town is formed by districts XX - XXIII. Brigittenau (XX) and Leopoldstadt (II) are situated on the island in the Danube. The street numbers of the streets leaving the inner ring road start at the ring. The street numbers along the ring road and the outer circle work clockwise. Even numbers are always on the right side of a street.

Postcodes work in the following manner: 1(0) + number of district + 0. District I therefore has the code: 1010, district XII the code 1120, etc.

CLIMATE

Average Temperatures

January	-1°C
February	2°C
March	5°C
April	8°C
May	14°C
June	16°C
July	20°C
August	25°C
September	15°C
October	9°C
November	4°C
December	2°C

Weather Forecast: Tel. 1566

CULTURE & CUSTOMS

Tipping, service charge (hotels, restaurants, etc.)
In most restaurants, the service charge will automatically be added to your bill. An additional tip of 10 percent, however, is usually expected for good service. Taxi drivers, hairdressers and tourist guides are some of the people who also expect a 10 percent tip for their services.

Power voltage of 200 volts is standard, so are Continental plugs.

HOLIDAYS

January 1, January 6, Easter Monday, May 1, Ascension Day, Whitsuntide Monday, Corpus Christi, August 15, October 26, November 1, December 8, 25 and 26.

FESTIVALS

Vienna is not just a musical city. Apart from opera and ballet performances and concerts, there is always a constant stream of world-famous exhibitions. However, Vienna's range of opera, operetta, classical concerts and ballet is greater than any other cosmopolitan city's. A few examples are the **Viennale Film Festival** (March); **Spanish Riding School** performances (March-June); **waltz music** and **operetta concerts** (April-Oct.).

The **Vienna Festival** takes place in May and June and is followed by the **Vienna Summer Music Festival**, which continues until the end of August. These festivals take place in a framework of **Schubert**, **Mozart** and **Haydn** concerts, which are held at various times throughout the year. An international **Youth Music Festival** and **concerts of sacred music** round off the year, culminating in **Advent and Christmas music**. In November, everyone gets the opportunity to indulge in a little fantasy and extravagance, for this is when the **Viennese Ball Season** begins: the Champagne Ball, the Imperial Ball, innumerable New Year Balls, the Vienna Philharmonica Ball and, in February, the Opera Ball. Tourists can purchase tickets to attend these balls too.

Apart from musical events, a large number of conferences, trade fairs and exhibitions are held in Vienna throughout the year. Two events to take note of are the **Viennese Art and Antiques Exhibition** and the **Viennese International Trade Fair**. The former takes place in spring and the latter in autumn,

U-BAHN AND S-BAHN MAP OF VIENNA

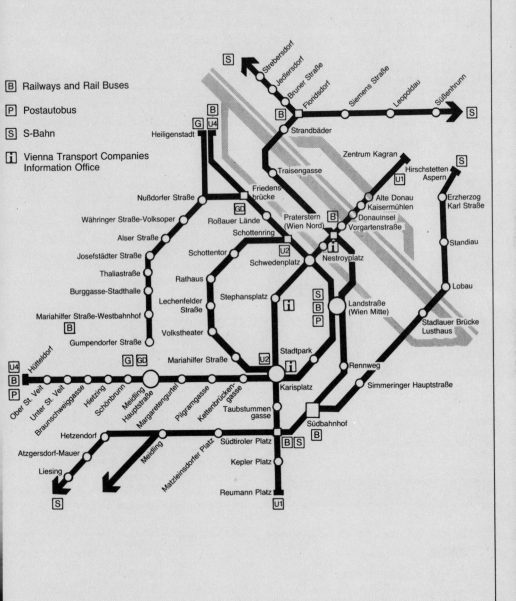

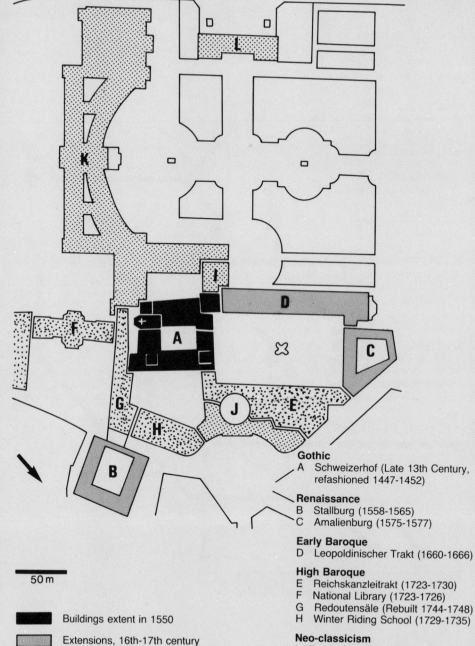

STAGES IN THE BUILDING OF THE HOFBURG

Gothic
A   Schweizerhof (Late 13th Century, refashioned 1447-1452)

Renaissance
B   Stallburg (1558-1565)
C   Amalienburg (1575-1577)

Early Baroque
D   Leopoldinischer Trakt (1660-1666)

High Baroque
E   Reichskanzleitrakt (1723-1730)
F   National Library (1723-1726)
G   Redoutensäle (Rebuilt 1744-1748)
H   Winter Riding School (1729-1735)

Neo-classicism
I   Zeremoniensaal (1802-1806)
L   Outer Burg Gate (1821-1824)

Historicism
J   Michaelertrakt (1889-1893)
K   Neue Hofburg (1881-1913)

50 m

Buildings extent in 1550

Extensions, 16th-17th century

18th century additions

New additions, 19th century

The Viennese Tourist Office publishes a calender of fairs and conferences which the visitor can use as a reference guide to look up the dates for various events

Wiener Fremdenverkehrsverband
(Viennese Tourist Office)
Kinderspitalgasse 5
A-1095 Wien.
Tel: 431608.

The Viennese Tourist Office will supply you with the following:

Vienna (illustrated brochure)
Jewish Vienna
Vienna waits for you (for young people)
Map of the city
List of museums
List of hotels
List of restaurants
List of youth hostels and camp sites
List of Heuriger
Art Nouveau in Vienna
Diary of forthcoming events
Calendar of conferences
Previews and programs for State Opera House and Volksoper
Programs for the Riding School and Vienna Boys' Choir
Monthly diary of events
Brochure of winter events, carnival and spring events
Vienna Festival program
Viennese Summer Music Festival—preview and program

Vienna Boys' Choir
2, Obere Augartenstrae 1, Tel: 334451/0
Order tickets for the performances in the Burgkapelle through theater ticket agencies.

RELIGIOUS SERVICES

Catholic (from 6.00) Tel. 51552/375
Protestant, Tel. 5128392
Jewish, Tempel Wien, 1, Seitenstettengasse 4, Tel. 361655
Altkatholische Kirche, 1, Wipplinger Straße 6, Tel. 637133
Wiener Islamisches Zentrum, 21, Am Hubertusdamm 17-19, Tel. 301389
Islamischer Gebetsraum, 9, Türkenstraße 13, Tel. 344625
Anglican Services, 3, Jauresgasse 17-19, Tel. 731575
Mormons, Tel. 373257
Methodists, Tel. 786367

COMMUNICATIONS

MEDIA

Cable television is an old hat in Vienna! English, West German, Swiss and, of course, Austrian stations can normally be received. Programs in English are broadcast by the radio station "Blue Danube" and by Radio Austria (ö 3).

International newspapers and magazines can be purchased at any newspaper shop in the inner city area. A large selection is available in Opernpassage. *The Herald Tribune* and the *Financial Times* are in the newspaper shops early in the morning.

Dailies

Arbeiter-Zeitung
Kronen-Zeitung
Kurier
Presse
Volksstimme
Wiener Zeitung

Local Papers/Magazines

Falter
Forum
Furche
Profil
Vienna Life
Wien Aktuell
Wiener

"Tabak Trafik"

All newsagents are called "Tabak Trafik". They are immediately recognizable: a red ring with a cigarette in the middle. They sell tobacco, cigarettes, stamps, newspapers/magazines and bus and tram tickets.

CONVENTIONS

Many national and international conventions, conferences, seminars etc. are held in Vienna each year. There are a total of 22 centers and 16 hotels (a further nine are being built) which offer satisfactory facilities for a convention of any size.

Information: Kongreßbüro, Wiener Fremdenverkehrsverband, 9, Kinderspitalgasse 5, Tel. 431608

POSTAL SERVICES

Hauptpostamt (main post office), 1, Fleischmarkt 19, Tel. 5127681 (open round the clock)

There are a total of 115 post offices and sub-post offices in Vienna, open 0800 - 1200 hrs and 1400 - 1800 hrs, Monday to Friday.

Postal rates:
Postcard (inland)   4 Schilling
Postcard (abroad) 5 Schilling
Letter (inland)   5 Schilling
Letter (abroad)   6 Schilling

Telephone Exchange:
Fernamt Wien, 1, Schillerplatz 4, Tel. 58844-0

Directory Inquiries:
National Dialling: 16
International Dialling: 08
Telegrams: 190

International Codes:
To Great Britain: 06
To The Republic of Ireland: 05

To Vienna from Great Britain: 01043222

EMERGENCIES

LOSS

Zentrales Fundbüro, 9, Wasagasse 22, Monday - Friday 0800 - 1300 hrs, Tel. 316611 (general), Tel. 9205 (trams), Tel. 9202 (documents)

MEDICAL SERVICES

Hospitals
Allgemeines Krankenhaus (general), 9, Alserstraße 4 + 9,
Spitalgasse 23, 9, Lazarettgasse 14, Tel. 4800
Krankenhaus der Barmherzigen Brüder, 2, Große Mohrengasse
9, (free treatment available for the poor), Tel. 241521-0
Allgemeine Poliklinik der Stadt Wien, 9, Mariannengasse 10, Tel. 425571-0
Ambulatorium Wien-Nord, 21, Karl-Aschenbrenner-Gasse 3, Tel. 383528-0
Ambulatorium Wien-Süd, 10, Wienerbergstraße 13, Tel. 623111-0
Kinderklinik Glanzing (children's), 19, Glanzinggasse 37, Tel. 474266-0
St. Anna Kinderspital (children's), 9, Kinderspitalgasse 6, Tel. 483577
Semmelweis-Frauenklinik (women's), 18, Bastiengasse 36-38, Tel. 471515

Accidents/Emergencies
1. Unfallchirurgische Ambulanz des AKH, 9, Alserstraße 4 Tel. 4800 (odd days)
2. Unfallchirurgische Ambulanz des AKH, 9, Spitalgasse 23, Tel. 4800 (even days)

Homeopathy
Institut fur Homöopathie, Krankenhaus Lainz, Pav. VII, 13, Wolkersbergenstraße 1, Tel. 841616
A list of all registered homeopathic doctors can be obtained here.

Acupuncture
Ludwig Boltzmann-Institut fur Akupunktur, 9,
Mariannengasse 10, Tel. 425571, daily 8.00 - 13.00
Further Information: Gesellschaft fur Akupunktur und Auriculotherapie, 12, Tivoligasse 65, Tel. 835440

Dental Treatment
Dial the emergency doctor (141) to receive details about dentists available over the weekend, or contact the dental department (Kieferchirurgie) of the Allgemeine Krankenhaus (AKH), Tel. 4800.
Universitäts-Zahnklinik (University Dental Hospital), 9, Währinger Straße 25a, Tel. 424636 (you will only be charged for material used, not for treatment as such).

Gynecologists
Psychosomatisch-Gynäkologische Ambulanz, 2,
Universitätsfrauenklinik, 9, Spitalgasse 23, Tel. 4800/3547
Abortion (if it is carried out during the first 12 weeks of pregnancy) is legal in Austria. The treament is private (ca. Shilling 4000)
Information: Familienplanung, 18, Währinger Gürtel 141, Tel. 346561, open 0800 - 1200 hrs Monday, Wednesday and Friday.

AIDS
Österreichische Aids-Hilfe, 8, Wickenburggasse 14, Tel. 486186-87

Venereal Diseases
Institut für Dermato-Venerologische Serodiagnostik im
Lainzer Krankenhaus, 13, Wolkersbergenstraße 1, Tel. 841616

Vaccination
Hygiene-Institut der Stadt Wien, 9, Kinderspitalgasse 15, Tel. 431595

Radio Emergency Calls

The Austrian Broadcasting Corporation will broadcast emergency calls during their program "Autofahrer unterwegs" (Driving along) from 12.00 - 13.00, on Radio 3 (ö 3), every half hour.

EMERGENCY CALLS

Ambulance: 144
Emergency Doctor: 141, daily from 1900 to 0700 hrs
Chemist: 1550
Psychiatrist: 9, Fuchsthalergasse 18, Tel. 318419
International Chemist: 1, Kärntner Ring 15, Tel. 5122825
Poisoning: 9, Lazarettgasse 14, Tel. 434343

GETTING AROUND

ORIENTATION

Vienna is not only the capital of Austria, but also one of the nine federal states of the republic. Population: 1,600,000, which means that every 4th Austrian lives in Vienna. There is a surplus of ca. 15 percent of women in Vienna. Height: ca. 530 ft. (160 meters) above sea level. Area: ca. 160 sq miles (400 sq km). Administration: 100 councillors (including the mayor), elected for five years.

Vienna is divided into 23 districts. Since 1919, socialist governments have prevailed. The standard of living is high. Fifteen percent of the ca. 900,000 work force are self-employed or freelance, 50 percent are employees or civil servants, 15 percent are manual workers. About one quarter of the 800,000 flats in Vienna are owned by the council—which means it is the biggest property owner in the world!

PUBLIC TRANSPORT

A car really is superfluous, and a lot of bother, in Vienna. The town has one of the best urban and regional transport systems. There are: **Underground**, **subway**, **fast subway**, **local** and **regional trains**, **trams** and **buses**.

There are three **underground lines**:

U1 Kagran -Reumannplatz
U2 Karlsplatz - Schottenring
U3 Heiligenstadt - Hütteldorf

and also two **Inner City lines:**

G   Heiligenstadt - Gumpendorferstraß

GD Friedensbrücke - Gumpendorfer-
straße

The **"Badner Lokalbahn"** (regional) runs a service between the Wiener Oper and Josephsplatz in Baden, near Vienna.

There are nine **subway lines** servicing the surrounding towns of Neusiedl am See, Neulengbach, Wiener Neustadt, Tulln and Mödling, apart from 21 **regional train services** to the provinces.

Whereas in many towns **trams** have long been abandoned, they enjoy right of way in Vienna. It is often faster to travel by tram than by car. There are 37 tram lines in addition to 80 **bus routes**. Red bus stops indicate that all buses will stop, blue stops are request stops only.

Maps can be obtained from the official Austrian tourist offices and tobacco shops ("Tabak-Trafiken").

The limited travel pass (**3-Tage-Wien-Netzkarte**), valid for three days, costs öS 92, an unlimited travel pass (**8-Tage-Streifenkarte**), valid for eight days and covering the provinces, is available for öS 200.

On Sundays, National Holidays and during school holidays, children under 15 travel free.

A single ticket costs öS 19. Ticket machines do not give change. Groups can hire **special tram coaches** for a nostalgic trip along the ring road or to Grinzing (Tel. 65930/2455).

There is a special bus for the Inner City district, the **Citybus**, servicing three different routes:

1A from Schottentor to Landstraße

2A from Schwedenplatz/Petersplatz to
Dr.-Karl-Renner-Ring

3A from Schottenring to Schwarzenbergplatz

TAXIS

You cannot hail taxis traveling along the streets. There are official taxi stands. In the inner city at:

Babenbergerstraße/Burgring

Dr.-Karl-Lueger-Ring

Hoher Markt/Marc-Aurel-Straße

Opernring/Operngasse/Schottenring/ Ringturm

Schwarzenbergplatz/Kärntner Ring

Stubenring/Dr.-Karl-Lueger-Platz

Radio Taxi: 3130

AUTOMOBILE HIRE

Avis, 1, Opernring 1, also at the airport, Tel. 7770/2700

Budget-Rent a Car, 3, Wien Hilton and airport, Tel.756565

Europcar, 6, Mollardgasse 15, Tel. 59771675

Hertz, 1, Kärntner Ring 17, Tel. 512877

Inter-Rent, 1, Schubertring 7, Tel. 756717

Reisemobil-Vermietung Benkö (caravans), 4, Rechte Wienzeile 21, Tel. 57119993

Rent a Bus, 12, Assmayergasse 60, Tel. 833223

Blecha, Exclusive Rent a Car (Rolls Royce, Bentley, Mercedes 600), 16, Lienfeldgasse 35, Tel. 453672

WHERE TO STAY

HOTELS

Accommodation (price per person at date of print) in Austria is graded in the following manner:

***** Luxury, öS 1000 to 3000
**** First class, öS 500 to 1000
*** Comfortable, öS 250 to 500
** Satisfactory service, öS 200 to 400
* Simple, basic facilities, öS 200 to 300

*****

Ambassador,
1, Neuer Markt 6,
Tel. 51466

Bristol,
1, Kärntner Ring 1,
Tel. 51516-0

Clima Villenhotel,
19, Nußberggasse 2c,
Tel. 371516

De France,
1, Schottenring 3,
Tel. 343540

Hilton Wien,
3, Am Stadtpark,
Tel. 752652

Im Palais Schwarzenberg,
3, Schwarzenbergplatz 9,
Tel. 784515

Imperial,
1, Kärntner Ring 16,
Tel. 50110

Inter-Continental Vienna,
3, Johannesgasse 28,
Tel. 7505-0

Vienna Marriott,
1, Parkring 12a,
Tel. 51518-0

Parkhotel Schönbrunn,
13, Hietzinger Hauptstraße 10-20,
Tel. 822676

Sacher,
1, Philharmonikerstraße 4,
Tel. 51456

SAS Palais Hotel,
1, Weihburggasse 32,
Tel. 51517-0

****

Amadeus,
1, Wildpretmarkt 15,
Tel. 638738

Am Parkring,
1, Parkring 12,
Tel. 526524

Am Schubertring,
1, Schubertring 11,
Tel. 721551-0

Am Stephansplatz,
1, Stephansplatz 9,
Tel. 53405-0

Capricorno,
1, Schwedenplatz 3-4,
Tel. 53331-0

Cottage,
19, Hasenauerstraße 12,
Tel. 312571-0

Graben,
1, Dorotheergasse 3,
Tel. 5121531

Kaiserin Elisabeth,
1, Weihburggasse 3,
Tel. 51526-0

König von Ungarn,
1, Schulerstraße 1,
Tel. 526520-0

Opernring,
1, Opernring 11,
Tel. 5875518

Rathauspark,
1, Rathausstraße 17,
Tel. 423661-0

Ring,
1, Am Gestade 1,
Tel. 637701

Römischer Kaiser,
1, Annagasse 16,
Tel. 5127751

***

Am Augarten,
2, Heinestraße 15,
Tel. 243240

Arabella Hotel Jagdschloß,
13, Jagdschloßgasse 79,
Tel. 843508

Austria,
1, Wolfengasse 3,
Tel. 51523

Capri,
2, Praterstraße 44-46,
Tel. 248404

Casino Zögernitz,
19, Döblinger Hauptstraße 76-78,
Tel. 364100

Kahlenberg,
19, Josefsdorf 1,
Tel. 321251

Kärntnerhof,
1, Grashofgasse 4,
Tel. 5121923

Monopol,
4, Prinz Eugen Straße 68,
Tel. 658526

Papageno,
4, Wiedner Hauptstraße 23-25,
Tel.656744

Post,
1, Fleischmarkt 24,
Tel. 51583-0

Savoy,
7, Lindengasse 12,
Tel. 934646

Schweizer Hof,
1, Bauernmarkt 22,
Tel. 5331931

St. James,
4, Waaggasse 15,
Tel. 5872408

Wandl,
1, Petersplatz 9,
Tel. 53455-0

**

Central,
2, Taborstraße 8a,
Tel. 242405

Faist,
18, Schulgasse 9,
Tel. 432405

Gabriel,
3, Landstraßer Hauptstraße 165,
Tel. 726754

Goldene Spinne,
3, Linke Bahngasse 1a,
Tel. 724486

Goldenes Einhorn,
5, Am Hundsturm 5,
Tel. 554755

Kugel,
7, Siebensterngasse 43,
Tel. 933355

Müllner Gasthof,
19, Grinzinger Allee 30,
Tel. 322317

Rathaus,
8, Lange Gasse 13,
Tel. 434302

Südbahn,
4, Weyringergasse 25,
Tel. 658590

Terminus,
6, Fillgradergasse 4,
Tel. 5877386

Urania,
3, Obere Weißgerberstraße 7,
Tel. 731711

Westend,
6, Fügergasse 3,
Tel. 5976729

Wilhelmshof,
2, Kleine Stadtgutgasse 4,
Tel. 245521

Zu den drei Kronen,
4, Schleifmöhlgasse 25,
Tel. 5873289

*

Franzenhof,
2, Große Stadtgutgasse 19,
Tel. 242237

Hospiz,
7, Kenyongasse 15,
Tel. 931304

Orient,
1, Tiefer Graben 30-32,
Tel. 637307

Stalehner,
17, Ranftlgasse 11,
Tel. 482505

Thalia,
16, Lindauergasse 2-6,
Tel. 424513

GUESTHOUSES

*** Comfortable, öS 250 to 600
** Clean, satisfactory service, öS 250 to
450
* Simple, basic facilities, öS 200 to 300

***

Am Operneck,
1, Kärntner Straße 47,
Tel. 5129310

Christina,
1, Hafnersteig 7,
Tel. 5331447

City,
1, Bauernmarkt 10,
Tel. 639521

Domizil,
1, Schulerstraße 14,
Tel. 5133093

Geissler,
1, Postgasse 14,
Tel. 5332803

Marc Aurel,
1, Marc-Aurel-Straße 8,
Tel. 5333640

Nossek,
1, Graben 17,
Tel. 5337041

Residenz,
1, Ebendorferstraße 10,
Tel. 434786

Schweizer Pension Solderer,
1, Heinrichgasse 2,
Tel.638156

Suzanne,
1, Walfischgasse 4,
Tel. 5132507

**

Acion,
1, Dorotheergasse 6-8,
Tel. 5125473

Ani,
9, Kinderspitalgasse 1,
Tel. 4265553

Austria,
9, Garnisongasse 7,
Tel. 422136

Columbia,
8, Kochgasse 9,
Tel. 426757

Felicitas,
8, Josefsgasse 7,
Tel. 427212

Kolpingwerk,
10, Sonnwendgasse 22,
Tel. 6042451

Liechtenstein,
9, Liechtensteinstraße 12,
Tel. 344186

Lindenhof,
7, Lindengasse 4,
Tel. 930498

Rose,
7, Zieglergasse 27,
Tel. 938416

Vera,
9, Alserstraße 18,
Tel. 432595

*

Esterhazy,
6, Nelkengasse 3,
Tel. 5875159

Mozart,
6, Theobaldgasse 215,
Tel. 5978505

Wild,
8, Langegasse 10/7,
Tel. 435174

All the hotels and guesthouses listed above are located in the inner city or very close to it. There is, of course, plenty of accommodation available in the outer districts and suburbs.

Further Information:

Wiener Fremdenverkehrsverband,
1095 Wien, Kinderspitalgasse 5,
Tel. 435974

Jugendgästehaus Wien 20,
Brigittenau, 20,
Friedrich-Engels-Platz 24,
Tel. 338294, open all year.

Jugendherberge Wien 7,
Neubau, 7, Myrthengasse,
Tel. 936316, open all year.

Jugendgästehaus der Stadt Wien,
Hütteldorf-Hacking, 13,
Schloßberggasse 8,
Tel. 821501, open all year.

City Hostel,
1, Seilerstätte 30,
Tel. 5128463, open 01/07 - 30/09.

Turmherberge Don Bosco,
3, Lechnerstraße 12,
Tel. 731494,
open March to November.

Kolpingfamilie Wien Meidling,
12, Bendlgasse 10-12,
Tel. 1835487, open all year.

Hostel Zöhrer,
8, Skodagasse 26,
Tel. 430730, open all year.

CAMPGROUNDS

Campingplatz der Stadt Wien West I, 14,
Hüttelbergstraße 40,
Tel. 941449, only open during the summer season.

Campingplatz der Stadt Wien, Wien West II, 14,
Hüttelbergstraße 80,
Tel. 942314, open all year.

Campingplatz der Stadt Wien, Wien-Süd, 23,
Breitenfurter Straße 269,
Tel. 869218,

grounds are open only during the summer season.

Schwimmbad Camping Rodaun, 23,
Wien-Rodaun, An der Au 2,
Tel. 884154,
only open during the summer season.

Campingplatz Schloß Laxenburg,
2361 Laxenburg, Erholungszentrum,
Tel. (2236) 71333,
only open during the summer season.

Private Accommodation can be booked through: Wiener Fremdenverkehrsverein, 1, Operngasse. Written enquiries: 1, Schottenring 28.

Reservation centers of the big hotel chains

Alba Hotels,
1, Neuer Markt 3,
Tel. 521594

Austria Hotels,
1, Schottenring 3,
Tel. 346386

CCA Hotels,
1, Mahlerstraße 6,
Tel. 528693

Clima Hotels,
4, Wiedner Hauptstraße 13,
Tel. 653273

Kremslehner Hotels,
9, Roosevelt Platz 16,
Tel. 427681

Novotels,
14, Autobahnstation Auhof,
Tel. 972542

Schick Hotels,
2, Taborstraße 12,
Tel. 24241

FOOD DIGEST

WHERE TO EAT

Restaurants in Hotels

Astoria
1, Führichgasse 1,
Tel. 51577-0

Bristol-Korso bei der Oper
1, Mahlerstraße 2,
Tel. 51516/546

Hilton-Rotisserie Prinz Eugen
3, Am Stadtpark,
Tel. 752652-0

Imperial-Restaurant Württemberg
1, Kärntner Ring 16,
Tel. 661765-0

Intercontinental im Vier Jahreszeiten
3, Johannesgasse 28,
Tel. 7505/143

Palais Schwarzenberg
3, Schwarzenbergplatz 9,
Tel. 784515

Sacher
1, Philharmonikerstraße 4,
Tel. 51456

Stadtkrug
1, Weihburggasse 3,
Tel. 5127955

Zu den 3 Husaren
1, Weihburggasse 4,
Tel. 5121092

Wiener Rathauskeller
1, Rathausplatz 1,
Tel. 421219

Zum Donnerbrunnen
1, Kärntner Straße 18,
Tel. 5131223

Griechenbeisel
1, Fleischmarkt 11,
Tel. 631941

Paulusstube
1, Walfischgasse 7,
Tel. 528136

Sanfter Heinrich
14, Höttelbergstraße 57,
Tel. 941397

Servus
6, Mariahilferstarße 57,
Tel. 573401

Zum weißen Rauchfangkehrer
1, Weihburggasse 4,
Tel. 523471

Schrammelbeisl
17, Kalvarienberggasse 51,
Tel. 424346

Walfisch
2, Prater 71b,
Tel. 245495
(March to September)

Piaristenkeller
8, Piaristengasse 45,
Tel. 429152

Vindobona Keller im Hilton
3, Am Stadtpark,
Tel. 752652-0

Zigeunerkeller Parkhotel Schönbrunn
13, Hietzinger Hauptstraße 10-20,
Tel. 822676
(Easter to November)

Urbani Keller
1, Am Hof 12,
Tel. 639102

Zur Agnes
19, Sieveringer Straße 221,
Tel. 441424

Balkan Grill
16, Brunnengasse 13,
Tel. 921494

Budva
1, Naglergasse 1,
Tel. 635246

Dubrovnik
3, Am Heumarkt 5,
Tel. 732755

Wiener Winzerhaus
1, Rotenturmstraße 17,
Tel. 639582

Restaurants with International Cuisine

Mattes
1, Schönlaterngasse 1,
Tel. 526275

Marriott-Symphonika
1, Parkring 12a,
Tel. 533611-0

Le Siècle
1, Weihburggasse 32,
Tel. 51517-0

Belvedere Stöckl
3, Prinz Eugen Straße 25,
Tel. 784198

Die Savoyengemächer
15, Schweglerstr. 37,
Tel. 921381

Zum König von Ungarn
1, Schulerstr. 10,
Tel. 525319

De France
1, Schottenring 3,
Tel. 343540

Steirereck
3, Rasumofskygasse 2,
Tel. 733168

Brodik
5, Wiedner Hauptstr. 130,
Tel. 557171

Himmelpforte
1, Himmelpfortgasse 24,
Tel. 531967

Prinz Eugen
4, Wiedner Gürtel 14,
Tel. 651741

Restaurants with Traditional Viennese Cuisine

Chez Rainer
4, Wiedner Hauptstraße 27,
Tel. 654646/325

Altwienerhof
15, Herklotzgasse 6,
Tel. 837145

Schubertstüberl'n
1, Schreyvogelgasse 4,
Tel. 637187

Beim Novak
7, Richtergasse 12,
Tel. 9332244

Bohemia
15, Turnergasse 9,
Tel. 836648

D'Rauchkuchl
15, Schweglerstraße 37,
Tel. 921381

Eckel
19, Sieveringer Str. 46,
Tel. 323218

Goldene Glocke
9, Neubaugasse 5,
Tel. 937499

Gösser Bierklinik
1, Steindlgasse 4,
Tel. 5333336

K. & K. Küche und Keller
7, Zollergasse 14,
Tel. 932480

Leupold - Zum Schottentor
1, Schottengasse 7,
Tel. 639381

Nicky's Kuchlmasterei
3, Obere Weißgerberstraße 6,
Tel. 724418

Regina
9, Rooseveltplatz 15,
Tel. 427681-0

Schöner
7, Siebensterngasse 19,
Tel. 937206

Stadtbeisl
1, Naglergasse 21,
Tel. 633323

Altenberg
1, Dorotheergasse 3,
Tel. 5121531

Zur Linde & Lindenkeller
1, Rotenturmstraße 2,
Tel. 51122192

Restaurants with a View

Donauturm
22, Donauturmstr. 4,
Tel. 235368

Römischer Kaiser
19, Neustift am Walde 2,
Tel. 441104

Cobenzl
19, Am Cobenzl 94,
Tel. 325120

"Beisel"

Alt Nußdorf
19, Nußdorfer Platz 4,
Tel. 371277

Alt Sievering
19, Sieveringer Straße 63,
Tel. 325888

Bastei Beisl
1, Stubenbastei 10,
Tel. 524319

Gasthaus Heidenkummer
8, Breitenfeldergasse 18,
Tel. 429163

Glacisbeisel
7, Messepalast,
Tel. 961658

Kern
1, Wallnerstraße 3,
Tel. 639188

Ofenloch
1, Kurrentgasse 8,
Tel. 638844-0

Schönbrunner Stöckl
13, Schloß Schönbrunn,
Tel. 834229

Figlmüller
1, Wollzeile 5,
Tel. 526177

Pfudl
1, Bäckerstraße 22,
Tel. 526705

Sailers Küchenbar
18, Gersthoferstraße 4,
Tel. 472121

Schmelzer Weinpresse
15, Schweglerstr. 37,
Tel. 921381

Strobl
17, Hernalser Hauptstr. 85,
Tel. 463316

Zipfer Stüberl
1, Dominikanerbastei 22,
Tel. 5127218

Zu den 2 Liesln
7, Burggasse 63,
Tel. 933282

Zur Stadt Krems
7, Zieglergasse 37,
Tel. 937200

Zur Stadt Paris
8, Josefstädterstraße 4,
Tel. 421467

Cellar Restaurants

Alte Schmiede
1, Schönlaterngasse 9,
Tel. 523495

Bastei Keller
1, Stubenbastei 10,
Tel. 524319

Melker Stiftskeller
1, Schottengasse 2,
Tel. 635530

Zwölf Apostelkeller
1, Sonnenfelsgasse 3,
Tel. 526777

Esterhazykeller
1, Haarhof 1,
Tel. 632567

Chinese Restaurants

Lotus Haus
1, Jasomirgottgasse 3,
Tel. 635577

Luo Chow
6, Kollergasse 4,
Tel. 566698

Peking
1, Färbergasse 3,
Tel. 6330044

Turandot
17, Dornbacher Straße 116,
Tel. 461535

Fish Specialities

Lindmayer - Zur Donauperle
2, Dammhaufen 50,
Tel. 742183

French Restaurants

Chez Robert
18, Gertrudplatz 4,
Tel. 433544

Salut
1, Wildpretmarkt 3,
Tel. 631322

Greek Restaurants

Der Grieche
6, Barnabitengasse 5,
Tel. 5877466

Diogenes
1, Landgerichtsstr. 8,
Tel. 426663

Mykonos
1, Annagasse 7,
Tel. 520243

Sirtaki
7, Kandlgasse 26,
Tel. 936462

Indian Restaurants

Rani
6, Otto Bauer Gasse 21,
Tel. 565111

Taj Mahal
9, Nußdorfer Straße 33,
Tel. 345101

Koh-i-noor
1, Marc-Aurel-Straße 8,
Tel. 631180

Italian Restaurants

Cantinetta Scaraboccio
1, Bäckerstr. 5,
Tel. 5127372

Grotta Azzurra
1, Babenbergerstr. 5,
Tel. 561144

Ristorante Guido
3, Ungargasse 21,
Tel. 733131

La Pizza
1, Führichgasse 1,
Tel. 526255

Ristorante Da Gino e Maria
4, Rechte Wienzeile 17,
Tel. 5874570

Trattoria San Stefano
1, Dorotheergasse 5,
Tel. 526793

Japanese Restaurants

Miksukoshi
1, Maysedergasse 5,
Tel. 5133008

Kosher

Arche Noah
1, Seitenstettengasse 2,
Tel. 631347

Orth. Kosher Restaurant
2, Hollandstraße 3,
Tel. 333565

Russian Restaurants

Feuervogel
9, Alserbachstr. 21,
Tel. 3410392

Boat Restaurants

MFS Theodor Körner
2, DDSG Schiffsstation,
Handelskai, Tel. 266536/503

DDS Johann Strauß
1, Donaukanal,
Am Salztorufer, Tel. 639367

Snack Bars

Chattanooga Snackbar
1, Graben 29a,
Tel. 523830

Trzesniewski
1, Dorotheergasse 1,
Tel. 523291

Turkish Restaurants

Kervansary
1, Mahlerstr. 9,
Tel. 5128843

Hungarian Restaurants

Csardasforstin
1, Schwarzenbergplatz 2,
Tel. 529246

Csardas im Hotel Hungaria
3, Rennweg 51,
Tel. 732521

Mathiaskeller
1, Maysedergasse 2,
Tel. 522167

Ungar Grill
7, Burggasse 97,
Tel. 936209

Vegetarian Restaurants

Estakost
9, Währinger Straße 57,
Tel. 4250654

Ring Restaurant Josephinum
9, Währinger Straße 33,
Tel. 433335

Siddharta
1, Fleischmarkt 16,
Tel. 531197

Vietnamese Restaurants

Vietnam
3, Löwengasse 21,
Tel. 726293

"Heuriger" Inns
(with live music)

Altes Preßhaus Grinzing
19, Cobenzlgasse 15,
Tel. 3222393

Das "Alte Haus" Rausch-Rode
19, Himmelstraße 35,
Tel. 323221

Grinzinger Hauermandl
19, Cobenzlgasse 20,
Tel. 323027

Grinzinger Weinbottich
19, Cobenzlgasse 28,
Tel. 324237

Landstraßer Stadtheuriger
3, Landstraßer Hauptstraße 28, and, 3,
Ungargasse 13,
Tel. 755575/513

Neustifter Weinfassl
19, Neustift am Walde 70,
Tel. 442140

Passauerhof Grinzing
19, Cobenzlgasse 9,
Tel. 326345

Schloß Thühnlhof
11, Münnichplatz 5,
Tel. 766207

10er Marie
16, Ottakringer Straße 224,
Tel. 463116

Zum Binder
16, Speckbachergasse 14,
Tel. 460230

Zum Martin Sepp
19, Cobenzlgasse 34,
Tel. 323233

Cafés, Coffee-houses

Imperial
1, Kärntner Ring 16,
Tel. 651765

Landtmann
1, Dr.-Karl-Lueger-Ring 4,
Tel. 630621

Sacher
1, Philharmonikerstr. 4,
Tel. 521487

Schloßcafe Parkhotel
Schönbrunn, 13,
Hietzinger Hauptstraße 10-20,
Tel. 822676

Bräunerhof
1, Stallburggasse 2,
Tel. 523893

Café Hawelka
1, Dorotheergasse 6,
Tel. 5128230

Central
1, Herrengasse 14,
Tel. 664176

Diglas
1, Wollzeile 10,
Tel. 528401

Dom-Café
1, Stephansplatz 9,
Tel. 635605

Dommayer
13, Auhofstraße 2,
Tel. 825465

Eiles
8, Josefstädterstraße 2,
Tel. 423410

Frauenhuber
1, Himmelpfortgasse 6,
Tel. 524323

Haag
1, Schottengasse 2,
Tel. 631810

Hübner's Café Stadtpark
3, Am Heumarkt 2a,
Tel. 734620

Hübner's Kursalon
1, Johannesgasse 33,
Tel. 732181

Hummel
8, Josefstädterstraße,
Tel. 425314

Marriott-Gartencafé
1, Parkring 12a,
Tel. 533611-0

Monopol
8, Florianigasse 2,
Tel. 422513

Mozart
1, Albertinaplatz 2,
Tel. 525616

Museum
1, Friedrichstraße 6,
Tel. 565202

1900
1, Fichtegasse 1,
Tel. 531437

Café Pavillon
19, Hartäckerstraße 80,
Tel. 472222

Prückl
1, Stubenring 24,
Tel. 526115

Raimund
1, Museumstraße 6,
Tel. 932582

Ritter
6, Mariahilfer Straße,
Tel. 578238

Schloßcafé Schönbrunn
13, Schloß Schönbrunn,
Tel. 831268

Schwarzenberg
1, Kärntner Ring 17,
Tel. 527393

Sirk
1, Kärntner Straße 53,
Tel. 51516-0

Sperl
6, Gumpendorferstr. 11,
Tel. 564158

Stadlmann
9, Währinger Str. 26,
Tel. 341308

Wunderer
14, Hadikgasse 62,
Tel. 822561

Zartl
3, Rasumofskygasse 7,
Tel. 725560

Zieher
3, Landstraßer Hauptstraße 82,
Tel. 7395003

Patisseries

Demel
1, Kohlmarkt 14,
Tel. 635516-0

Gerstner
1, Kärntner Straße,
Tel. 524963

Heiner
1, Kärntner Straße 21,
Tel. 526863, and,
1, Wollzeile 9, Tel. 524838

Kleine Konditorei im Hilton
3, Am Stadtpark,
Tel. 752652-0

Kurcafé Konditorei
10, Favoritenstraße 90,
Tel. 644445

Lehmann Louis
1, Graben 12,
Tel. 5121815

Schindler
3, Löwengasse 44,
Tel. 737200

Sluka
1, Rathausplatz 8,
Tel. 427172

DRINKING NOTES

Alte Backstube
8, Lange Gasse 34,
Tel. 431101

Alt Wien
1, Bäckerstr. 9,
Tel. 525222

Café Gulaschmuseum
1, Schulerstraße 20,
Tel. 5121017

Café Stein
9, Währinger Straße 6,
Tel. 317241

Friesz und Stirb
7, Stiftgasse 8,
Tel. 961660

Kajevski
1, Stubenring 4,
Tel. 638193

KrahKrah
1, Rabensteig 8,
Tel. 638193

Oswald & Kalb
1, Bäckerstraße 14,
Tel. 5121371

Pavillon Alt-Wiener Salettl
18, Hartäckerstraße 80,
Tel. 472222

Rincon Andino
6, Münzwardeingasse 2,
Tel. 576125

Ring
1, Stubenring 20,
Tel. 5129404

Roter Engel
1, Rabensteig 5,
Tel. 664105

Salzamt
1, Ruprechtsplatz 1,
Tel. 635332

Schmid-Hansl
18, Schulgasse 31,
Tel. 433658

Titanic
6, Theobaldgasse 11,
Tel. 5874758

Tunnel
8, Florianigasse 39,
Tel. 423465

Wiener
7, Hermanngasse 27,
Tel. 937228

Wunderbar
1, Schönlaterngasse 8,
Tel. 5127989

THINGS TO DO

TOUR GUIDES

Burgtheater and some theatrical workshops. They are organized by the "Bundestheaterverband" (Friends of the National Theaters).

Details: Führungsreferat, Bundestheaterverband, 1, Hanuschgasse 3, Tel. 5324/2613.

Guided theme tours, with qualified guides to show you around, are available through various parts of Vienna. The following is a selection only:

This is how Beethoven lived
The real Franz Schubert
Emperor Franz Joseph and Empress Elizabeth
The mysteries of the "Hofburg"
Commemorating famous composers
The New Treasury
Klimt, Schiele and other revolutionary artists
Jugendstil in Vienna
Viennese myths and legends
A Romantic tour round the old town
The old Viennese charm in the suburb of Spittelberg
Old houses, tranquil courtyards

A detailed brochure can be obtained from the Wiener Fremdenverkehrsverband (tourist office).

Private Guided Tours:
Johann Szegö, Tel. 4338922
Vienna Guide Service, 13, Montecuccoliplatz 1-3,
Tel. 742234

SIGHTSEEING TRIPS

Vienna Sightseeing Tours, 3, Stelzhamergasse 4, Tel. 724683
Cityrama Sightseeing Tours, 1, Börsengasse 1, Tel. 6366190
Alternative Stadtrundfahrten, 9, Kolingasse 6, Tel. 343384
Wiener Stadtrundfahrten, 1, Friedrich-Schmidt-Platz 1, Tel. 42800/2950
Fiaker Tours, leaving from Stephansdom, Heldenplatz and Albertinaplatz
Oldtimer Tramway, Tel. 954953
By aeroplane from the airport Schwechat, Tel. 679454
Boat trips, DDSG Reisedienst, Tel. 26259114

BOAT TRIPS

"Donaudampfschiffahrtsgesellschaft" (the famous DDSG),
2, Handelskai 265,
Tel. 266536

During the summer months, the DDSG provides boat trips on the routes listed below:
Vienna - Dürnstein - Vienna
Melk - Krems - Melk
Passau - Linz - Passau
Grein - Melk - Grein
Vienna - Bratislava - Vienna
There are discotheque and "Heuriger" trips in the evenings on the Danube and Danube Canal.
There is an express hovercraft ("ACC Donaupfeil") service to Budapest, leaving Vienna at 0810 hrs (from Schiffartszentrum), arriving in Budapest at 1250 hrs. The hovercraft leaves Budapest again at 1420, hrs and arrives back in Vienna at 1950 hrs. Single: öS 750. Return: öS 1400

Son et Lumiere
Schloß Belvedere, daily, May 15 - August 31, at 2100 hrs; September 1 - September 30 at 2000 hrs. Tickets: Österreich-Haus, 1, Josefsplatz 6; or at the box office, Tel. 783944

Spanische Hofreitschule (Vienna Riding School)
Tickets: Spanische Hofreitschule, 1,

Michaelerplatz 1, Tel. 5339031-0, or at the official box offices.

Seats: öS 200 to 600

Standing: öS 135 to 150

OTHER PLANS

Main Theater Box Office
Bundestheater, 1, Goethegasse 1, Monday - Saturday 0900 hrs - 1700 hrs, Sunday, Holiday 0900 - 1200 hrs, Tel. 514440

Others:
Austrobus, Tel. 564312
Donauzentrum, Tel. 233258
Elite Tours, Tel. 5122225
Kartenbüro Alserstraße, Tel. 429134
Kartenbüro Augustinerstraße, Tel. 5330961
Kartenbüro Flamm, Tel. 524225
Österreichisches Verkehrsböro, Tel. 58800-0

Clothes/Costume Hire
Belinda, 6, Amerlingstraße 9, Tel. 5738485
Elite, 7, Neustiftgasse 137/7, Tel. 935346
Jahoda, 4, Favoritenstraße 29, Tel. 657352
Lambert Hofer, 15, Hackengasse 10, Tel. 922120
Schmid, 6, Otto-Bauer-Gasse 19, Tel. 5799265

Evening dress
You need evening dress if you intend to go to the annual ball at the Opera, also for the opening night at the theater. In your spare time, however, no restrictions apply!

CULTURE PLUS

MUSEUMS

A booklet containing 14 tickets allowing entrance to all municipal and national museums can be purchased for öS 150.

Entrance for children under six and for groups of school children is free. In most of the national museums, there is no entrance fee on Friday mornings and on every first Sunday of every month.

Akademie der bildenden Künste, Gemäldegalerie (Art Gallery of the Academy of Arts), 1, Schillerplatz 3, Tel. 58816-0; Tuesday, Thursday, Friday1000 - 1400 hrs, Wednesdy 0900 - 1300 hrs and 1500 - 1800 hrs, Saturday, Sunday, Holiday 0900 - 1300 hrs

Graphische Sammlung Albertina, 1, Augustinerstr. 1, Tel. 53483; Monday, Tuesday, Thursday 1000 - 1600 hrs, Wednesday 1000 - 1800 hrs, Friday 1000 - 1400 hrs, Saturday, Sunday 1000 - 1300 hrs

Alte Backstube, 8, Lange Gasse 34, Tel. 431101, Tuesday - Saturday 0900 - 2400 hrs Holiday 1400 - 2400 hrs

Alte Schmiede, 1, Schönlaterngasse 9, Tel. 5128329; Monday - Friday 0900 - 1500 hrs

Bestattungsmuseum (Funeral Museum), 4, Goldeggasse 19, Tel. 651631/227; Monday - Friday 1200 - 1500 hrs, by appointment

Bundessammlung alter Stilmöbel (Collection of Antique Furniture), 7, Mariahilfer Str. 88, Tel. 934240; Tuesday - Friday 0800 - 1600 hrs, Saturday 0900 - 1200 hrs

Dom - und Diözesanmuseum (Ecclesiastical), 1, Stephansplatz 6, 1st floor, Tel. 51552/598; Wednesday - Saturday, 1000 - 1600 hrs, Sunday and on holidays 1000 - 1300 hrs

Ephesos Museum, Neue Burg, 1, Heldenplatz, Tel. 934541; Monday, Wednesday - Friday 1000 - 1600 hrs, Saturday, Sunday 0900 - 1600 hrs

Esperanto Museum, 1, Hofburg, Michaelertor, Tel. 5210415; Monday, Wednesday, Friday 0900 - 1530 hrs

Feuerwehrmuseum (Fire-brigade), 1, Am Hof 10, Tel. 636671; Sunday, Holiday 0900 - 1200 hrs

Fiakermuseum, 17, Veronikagasse 12, Tel. 432607; every 1st Wednesday of the month 1000 - 1300 hrs

Österreichisches Filmmuseum, 1, Augustinerstr. 1, Tel. 5337054; showing of historical films October - May 1800 and 2000 hrs

Sigmund-Freud-Museum, 9, Bergstr. 19, Tel. 311596; Monday - Friday 0900 - 1300 hrs, Sunday, Holiday 0900 - 1500 hrs

Uhrensammlung Sobek (Clocks), 18, Pötzleinsdorfer Str. 102, Tel. 473139; Tuesday - Friday 1000 - 1500 hrs, by appointment, guided tours Sunday 1500 hrs

Globenmuseum der Österreichischen Nationalbibliothek (Collection of Globes, National Library Museum), 1, Josefsplatz 1/3, Tel. 53410/297; Monday - Wednesday, Friday 1100 - 1200 hrs, Thursday 1400 - 1500 hrs

Glockenmuseum (Bells), 10, Troststr. 38, Tel. 6043460; Wednesday 1400 - 1700 hrs

Heeresgeschichtliches Museum (Army), 3, Arsenal, Objekt 18, Tel. 782303; daily, except Friday, 1000 - 1600 hrs

Hermesvilla, 13, Lainzer Tiergarten, Tel. 841324; Wednesday, Sunday, Holiday 0900 - 1630 hrs

Herzgruft der Habsburger in der Augustinerkirche (The Habsburg Tomb), 1, Augustinerstr. 3, Tel. 523338, by appointment only

Historisches Museum der Stadt Wien, 4, Karlsplatz, Tel. 658747; daily, except Monday, 0900 - 1630 hrs

Hofburg: Schauräume Kaiserappartements (Imperial Apartments), 1, Michaelerplatz, Tel. 5875554/515 Monday - Saturday 0830 - 1600 hrs, Sunday 0830 - 1230 hrs

Hoftafel und Silberkammer (Banqueting Hall and Silver Room), Hofburg, 1, Michaelerplatz, Tel. 5222345; Tuesday - Friday , Sunday 0900 - 1300 hrs

Kaisergruft (Imperial Vault), 1, Neuer Markt, Tel. 526853; daily 0930 - 1600 hrs

Kunsthistorisches Museum, 1, Maria Theresienplatz, Tel. 934541; Tuesday - Friday 1000 - 1800 hrs, open Saturday and Sunday 0900 - 1800 hrs

Waffensammlung, Sammlung alter Musikinstrumente (Weapons and Musical Instruments), Neue Burg, 1, Heldenplatz, Monday, Wednesday - Friday 1000 - 1600 hrs

Museum des Instituts für Geschichte der Medizin (History of Medicine), Josephinum, 9, Währinger Str. 25/1, Tel. 432154; Monday - Friday 1100 - 1500 hrs

Museum des österreichischen Freiheitskampfes (Austria's Fight for Freedom), Altes Rathaus, 1, Wipplingerstr. 8/3, Tel. 630731/332; Monday, Wednesday, Thursday 0800 - 1700 hrs

Österreichisches Museum für angewandte Kunst (Applied Art), 1, Stubenring 5, Tel. 725696; Thursday - Monday 1100 - 1800 hrs

Museum für Hufbeschlag, Beschir-

rung und Besattlung (Riding Equipment), 3, Linke Bahngasse 11, Tel. 735581; Monday - Thursday 1330 - 1530 hrs

Museum für Völkerkunde (Ethnological), Neue Burg, 1, Heldenplatz, Tel. 934541; Monday, Thursday, Friday, Saturday 1000 - 1300 hrs, Wednesday 1000 - 1700 hrs, Sunday 0900 - 1300 hrs

Neidhart-Fresken, 1, Tuchlauben 19, Tel. 6380452; daily, except Monday, 1000 - 1200 hrs and 1300 - 1630 hrs

Österreichisches Museum for Volkskunde (Folklore), 8, Laudongasse 15, Tel. 438905; Tuesday - Friday 0900 - 1600 hrs, Saturday 0900 - 1200 hrs, Sunday 0900 - 1300 hrs

Museum Moderne Kunst im Palais Lichtenstein (Modern Art), 9, Fürstengasse 1, Tel. 341259; open daily, except Tuesday, 1000 - 1800 hrs

Österreichische Nationalbibliothek (National Library), 1, Josefsplatz 1, Tel. 53410; Monday - Saturday 1100 - 1200 hrs, special exhibitions Monday - Saturday 1000 - 1600 hrs

Naturhistorisches Museum, 1, Maria Theresienplatz, Tel. 934541; daily, except Tuesday, 0900 - 1800 hrs

Niederösterreichisches Landesmuseum, 1, Herrengasse 9, Tel. 635711-3111

Österreichische Galerie, 3, Prinz-Eugen-Str. 27 (admin.), Tel. 784158-0

Museum mittelalterlicher österreichischer Kunst und Österreichisches Barockmuseum (Medieval and Baroque Art), Unteres Belvedere, Rennweg 6a

Österreichische Galerie des 19. und 20. Jahrhunderts (19th/20th Century Art), Oberes Belvedere, Prinz-Eugen-Str. 27 Galerie des 19. Jahrhunderts in der Stallburg, 1, Reitschulgasse 2, Tel. 526480; all open Monday, Wednesday, Thursday, Saturday, Sunday 1000 - 1600 hrs

Pathologisch-Anatomisches Bundesmuseum, 9, Spitalgasse 2, Tel. 438672; Thursday 0900 - 1100 hrs

Pratermuseum, 2, Hauptallee, Planetarium beim Riesenrad (in close proximity to the giant wheel), Tel. 249432; Saturday, Sunday, Holiday 1400 - 1830 hrs

Römische Baureste am Hof (Roman Ruins), 1, Am Hof 9, Saturday, Sunday, Holiday 1100 - 1300 hrs

Römische Ruinen unter dem Hohen Markt, 1, Hoher Markt 4, Tel. 658747; daily, except Monday, 1000 - 1215 hrs and 1300 - 1630 hrs

Sammlung Religiöse Volkskunst (Religous Folklore), 1, Johannesgasse 8, Tel. 5121337; Wednesday 0900 - 1600 hrs, Sunday 0900 - 1300 hrs

Weltliche und Geistliche Schatzkammer (Secular and Spiritual Treasury), Hofburg, 1, Schweizerhof, Tel. 5336046; Monday, Wednesday - Friday 1000 - 1800 hrs Saturday, Sunday 0900 - 1200 hrs

Schatzkammer des Deutschen Ordens (Treasury of the Teutonic Order), 1, Singerstr. 7, Tel. 5121065/6; daily 1000 - 1200 hrs, Tuesday, Friday, Saturday also 1500 - 1700 hrs

Secession, 1, Friedrichstr. 12, Tel. 5875307; Tuesday - Friday 1000 - 1800, Saturday, Sunday 1000 - 1600 hrs

Wiener Straßenbahnmuseum (Trams), 3, Erdbergstr. 109, Tel. 5873186

Tabakmuseum, 7, Messepalast, Mariahilfer Str. 2, Tel. 961716; Tuesday 1000 - 1900 hrs, Wednesday - Friday 1000 - 1500 hrs, Saturday, Sunday 0900 - 1300 hrs

Technisches Museum, 14, Mariahilfer Str. 212, Tel. 833618; Tuesday - Friday, Sunday 0900 - 1600 hrs, Saturday 0900 - 1300 hrs

Österreichisches Theatermuseum, 1, Hanuschgasse 3, Tel. 5122427; Tuesdays and Thursdays from 1100 - 1200 hrs and only by appointment

Schloß Schönbrunn, 13, Schönbrunner Schloßstraße, Tel. 833546; daily 1000 - 1600 hrs

Uhrenmuseum der Stadt Wien (Clocks), 1, Schulhof 2, Tel. 5332265; daily, except Monday, 0900 - 1215 hrs and 1300 - 1630 hrs

Virgilkapelle, 1, Stephansplatz (underground station), daily, except Monday, 1000 - 1215 hrs and 1300 - 1630 hrs

Weinbaumuseum (Viniculture), 19, Döblinger Hauptstr. 96, Tel. 3610042; Saturday 1530 - 1800 hrs, Sunday 1000 - 1200 hrs

Zirkus- und Clownmuseum, 2, Karmelitergasse 9, Tel. 3468615; Wednesday 1730 - 1900 hrs, Saturday 1430 - 1700 hrs, Sunday 0900 - 1200 hrs

---

HOUSE MUSEUMS (COMMEMORATIVE)

All these museums are open daily, except on Mondays, from 1000 - 1215 hrs and 1300 - 1630 hrs

Beethoven Gedenkstätte "Pasqualithaus", 1, Mölkerbastei 8, Tel. 6370655

Beethoven Gedenkstätte "Eroicahaus", 19, Döblinger Hauptstraße 92

Beethoven Gedenkstätte "Heiligenstädter Testament", 19, Probusgasse 6

Mozartwohnung "Figarohaus", 1, Domgasse 5, Tel. 5240722

Johann-Strauß-Wohnung, 2, Praterstr. 54, Tel. 240121

Schuberts Sterbezimmer (The room Schubert died in), 4, Kettenbrückengasse 6, Tel. 5739072

Haydn-Wohnhaus und Brahms-Gedenkraum, 6, Haydngasse 19, Tel. 561307

Schubert Museum (Schubert's birthplace), 9, Nußdorfer Straße 54, Tel. 3459924

There is a museum in each of the 23 districts. In each of these museums, an emphasis is placed on both local and regional history.

ART GALLERIES

The following is a selection of the numerous and excellent art galleries which can be found all over Vienna. They will give you a fair impression of what Vienna has to offer in this respect. All of these galleries are located in the inner city area, and most of them are situated just behind St. Stephen's Cathedral:

Galerie Amer, 1, Tuchlauben 17, Tel. 634662

Galerie Ariadne, 1, Bäckerstraße 6, Tel. 5129479

Galerie am Graben, 1, Graben 7, Tel. 523999

Galerie Contact im Palais Rottal, 1, Singerstr. 17, Tel. 5129880

Galerie Julius Hummel, 1, Bäckerstraße 14, Tel. 5121296

Galerie Krinzinger, 1, Seilerstätte 16, Tel. 5133006

Galerie nächst St. Stephan, 1, Grönangergasse 1, Tel. 5121266

Galerie Peter Pakesch, 1, Ballgasse 6, Tel. 524814

Galerie Würthle, 1, Weihburggasse 9, Tel. 5122312

CONCERTS

Vienna is the home of at least 20 orchestras. When they are not on a world tour, they perform in the various concert halls and churches in Vienna itself. During the so-called "Musical Summer" months, the orchestras give numerous outdoor concerts, either at historic sites or in one of Vienna's beautiful parks.

Bösendorfer Saal, 4, Graf-Starhemberg-Gasse 14, Tel. 656651

Hofburg Redoutensäle, 1, Josefsplatz, Tel. 5873666

Konzerthaus, 3, Lothringerstr. 20, Tel. 721211

Musikverein, 1, Bösendorferstraße 12, Tel. 658190

Großer Sendesaal des ORF, 4, Argentinierstr. 30a, Tel. 65950

Sophiensäle, 3, Marxergasse/Blattgasse, Tel. 722196

Staatsoper Wien, 1, Opernring 2, Tel. 51444/2660

Volksoper Wien, 9, Währinger Str. 78, Tel. 51444/2662

Wiener Kammeroper, 1, Fleischmarkt 24, Tel. 5120100-0

LITERATURE

Alte Schmiede (Kunstverein Wien), 1, Schönlaterngasse 9, Tel. 528329

IDI, Internationales Dialekt-Institut, 18, Maynollogasse 3/13, Tel. 4348233

Jerry's Verein für kulturelle Kommunikation, 19, Geistingergasse 1/6/9, Tel. 3637885

Österreichischer P.E.N. Club, 1, Bankgasse 8, Tel. 634459

Österreichischer Schriftstellerverband, 5, Kettenbröckengasse 11/1, Tel. 564151

Shakespeare & Co., 1, Sterngasse 2, Tel. 664376

CULTURAL INSTITUTES

Afro-Asiatisches Institut, 9, Türkenstr. 3, Tel. 344625

Albert Schweitzer Haus, 9, Schwarzspanierstr. 13, Tel. 425265

Amerlinghaus, 7, Stiftgasse 8, Tel. 936475

Café America Latina, 5, Turmburggasse 7, Tel. 579269

Dramatisches Zentrum, 7, Seidengasse 13, Tel. 961556-0

Institut Francais de Vienne, 9, Währinger Straße 30, Tel. 316503

Internationales Kulturinstitut, 3, Ungargasse 43, Tel. 733454

Internationales Kulturzentrum, 1, Annagasse 20, Tel. 526951

Musisches Zentrum, 8, Zeltgasse 7, Tel. 483250

Rosa Villa, Kommunikationszentrum für homosexuelle Männer und Frauen (Center for Homosexual Men and Women), 6, Linke Wienzeile 102, Tel. 568150

Frauenkommunikationszentrum (Center for Women), 9, Währinger Straße 9, Tel. 485642

Frauencafé (Café for Women), 8, Langegasse 11, Tel. 438678

THEATERS

Tickets: The Austrian Tourist Office does not accept bookings for theaters. Theater tickets can be booked from abroad by writing to: Bundestheaterverband, Goethegasse 1, 1010 Wien. Please book at least 14 days in advance.

The box office for all except privately run theaters—the "Bundestheaterkasse"—is in Hanuschgasse 3, Tel. 51444-0. Tickets can be booked at this office seven days in advance.

Tickets for the private theaters (and privately organized concerts) can be obtained at the so-called **"Kartenbüros"**, or at the respective box offices.

Standard price categories

Staatsoper:	category I: up to öS 800
	category VI: up to öS 1800
Volksoper:	category I: up to öS 250
	category IV: up to öS 500
Burgtheater:	up to öS 500
Akademietheater:	up to öS 500
Theater in der Josefstadt:	up to öS 490
Kammerspiele:	up to öS 440
Volkstheater:	up to öS 470
VT Studio:	up to öS 125
Theater an der Wien:	up to öS 540
Raimundtheater:	up to ös 520
Musikverein:	öS 40 to 450
Konzerthaus:	öS 60 to 750
Burgkapelle:	öS 50 to 120

NATIONAL THEATERS

Akademietheater, 3, Lisztstraße 1, Tel. 51444/2658

Burgtheater, 1, Dr.-Karl-Lueger-Ring 2, Tel. 51444/2656

Staatsoper, 1, Opernring 2, Tel. 51444/2655

Volksoper, 9, Währinger Straße 78, Tel. 51444/2657

PRIVATE THEATERS

Dramatisches Zentrum, 7, Seidengasse 13, Tel. 961556-0

Ensemble Theater im Treffpunkt Petersplatz, 1, Petersplatz 2, Tel. 663200, 522852

Kammeroper, 1, Fleischmarkt 24, Tel. 5122461

Kammerspiele, 1, Rotenturmstraße 20, Tel. 632833

Der Kreis, 9, Porzellangasse 19, Tel. 349187

Raimundtheater, 6, Wallgasse 18-20, Tel. 576626

Serapionstheater, 20, Wallensteinplatz 6, Tel. 334231

Theater an der Wien, 6, Lehargasse 5, Tel. 58830-0

Theatergruppe 80, 6, Gumpendorfer Str. 67, Tel. 565222

Theater in der Josefstadt, 9, Josefstädter Str. 26, Tel. 425127

Volkstheater, 7, Neustiftgasse 1, Tel. 932776

FRINGE THEATERS

Ateliertheater, 6, Linke Wienzeile 4, Tel. 5878214

Domino Musiktheater, 1, Annagasse 20, Tel. 5122499

Drachengasse-2-Theater, 1, Fleischmarkt 22, Tel. 5131444

Experiment am Liechtenwerd, 9, Liechtensteinstraße 132, Tel. 314108

Graumanntheater, 15, Graumanngasse 39, Tel. 834663

International Theater, 9, Porzellangasse 8, Tel. 316272

Intime Bühne, 1, Franz-Josefs-Kai 29, Tel. 632434

Kleine Komödie, 1, Walfischgasse 4, Tel. 524280

Pradler Ritterspiele, 1, Bibergasse 2, Tel. 525400

Spielraum, 15, Palmgasse, Tel. 80873525

Theater am Schwedenplatz, 1, Franz-Josefs-Kai 21, Tel. 6320973

Theater beim Auersperg, 8, Auerspergstr. 17, Tel. 430707

Theater Brett, 6, Münzwardeingasse 2, Tel. 5870663

Theater "Die Tribüne", 1, Dr.-Karl-Lueger-Ring 4, Tel. 638485

Theater Forum, 9, Porzellangasse 50, Tel. 315421

Tschauners Stehgreiftheater, 16, Maroltingergasse 43, Tel. 924605

Vienna's English Theater, 8, Josefsgasse 12, Tel. 421260

VT Studio im Konzerthaus, 3, Lothringer Str. 20, Tel. 734300

DANCE THEATER

Tanztheater Wien, 7, Burggasse 38/10, Tel. 963934

PUPPET THEATERS

Arlequin Marionettentheater, 1, May-sedergasse 5, Tel. 526471

Domino, Schwarzes Theater Sihouetten, Nesher-Puppentheater, 1, Sonnenfelsgasse 3/2b, Tel. 5122499

Karagöz, Türkisches Schattentheater, 3, Kundmanngasse 9/15 Tel. 7227555

Urania Puppenspiele, 1, Uraniastraße 1, Tel. 726191

WHAT'S ON

The main cultural attractions in Vienna are without doubt opera, concert and ballet performances. There are other highlights, however: the annual film festival in March (**Viennale Film Festival**), the spectacular horse shows at the **"Spanische Reitschule"** (March - June) or the many art exhibitions of international fame.

Music, however, rules. There are the **Walzer- und Operettenkonzerte** (waltzing you through from April to October), the **Wiener Festwochen** in May and June, followed by the **Wiener Musik-Sommer** that lasts till the end of August. All year round, numerous concerts and festivals are held in memory of **Schubert**, **Mozart** and **Haydn**. The musical festival for the young (**Jugendmusikfest**) takes place later in the year, just before carol-singing dominates streets and concert halls (**Adventmusik vor Weihnachten**). November in Vienna is far from being dull and grey. It sees the beginning of a time dedicated to the famous Viennese Balls (Wiener Bälle)—for example, the "Imperial Ball", the "Champagne Ball", the "Ball of the Viennese Philharmonic Orchestra", the fancy dress balls during carnival time (usually January and February) and the "Opera Ball" (February).

Many national and international conventions, trade fairs, etc., are also held in Vienna all year round—for example, the International Trade Fair (**Internationale Messe**) in spring and the Arts and Antiques Fair (**Wiener Kunst- und Antiquitätenmesse**) in autumn.

Detailed information and programs are

available from the tourist office (Wiener Fremdenverkehrsband).

● **Meditation Centers**

Astro Box, 7, Burggasse 9, Tel. 961147

Buddhistisches Zentrum, 1, Fleischmarkt 16, Tel. 527146

Center für Vedic Studies, 1, Am Lugeck 1-2, Tel. 529825

Institut für Autogenes Training, 6, Lehargasse 1/2, Tel. 5748034

Internationale Meditationsgesellschaft, 1, Biberstr. 22, Tel. 5127859

Tai-Chi-Verein Shambala, 8, Josefstädter Str. 5/13, Tel. 484786

Zentrum für Rebirthing, 15, Dingelstedtgasse 42/8, Tel. 831663

NIGHTLIFE

DISCOS

Atrium
4, Schwindgasse 1,
Tel. 653594

Bijou Bar im Parkhotel Schönbrunn
13, Hietzinger Hauptstraße 10-20,
Tel. 822676

Camera
7, Neubaugasse 2,
Tel. 9397142

Can-Can
9, Währinger Gürtel 96,
Tel. 424705

Capt'n Cook
1, Franz-Josefs-Kai 23,
Tel. 631381

Monokel
4, Margaretenstr. 42,
Tel. 5728515

Move
8, Daungasse 1,
Tel. 433278

Terrassencafé
19, Cobenzlgasse 11,
Tel. 321203

U4
12, Schönbrunner Straße 222,
Tel. 858313

LIVE MUSIC

Audi Max
6, Getreidemarkt 9,
Tel. 563574-0

Casablanca
15, Goldschlagstr. 2,
Tel. 925616

Café Wortner
4, Wiedner Hauptstraße 55,
Tel. 653291

Jazz-Leitl
16, Habichergasse 15,
Tel. 950721

Metropol
17, Hernalser Hauptstraße 55,
Tel. 433543

Miles Smiles
8, Lange Gasse 51,
Tel. 4284814

Opus One
1, Mahler Str. 11,
Tel. 5230895

Willy's Rumpelkammer
16, Lerchenfelder Gürtel,
Tel. 921336

BLUES

After Midnight
4, Mühlgasse 15,
Tel. 577444

Jonathan Seagull
8, Stolzenthalergasse 14,
Tel. 434197

COUNTRY & WESTERN

Gärtnerinsel
6, Magdalenenstr. 2,
Tel. 562169

Café Verde
7, Gardegasse 3,
Tel. 939171

Nashville
5, Siebenbrunnengasse 5a,
Tel. 557389

NIGHTCLUBS
(WITH LIVE SHOWS)

Casanova Revue-Bar-Theater
1, Dorotheergasse 6-8,
Tel. 5129845

Eden Bar Cabaret
1, Liliengasse 2,
Tel. 527450

Eve-Bar-Cabaret
1, Führichgasse 3,
Tel. 525452

Fledermaus
1, Spiegelgasse 2,
Tel. 528438

Moulin Rouge
1, Walfischgasse 11,
Tel. 5122130

Renz
2, Zirkusgasse 50,
Tel. 243135

NIGHTCLUBBING

Jazzland
1, Franz-Josefs-Kai 29,
Tel. 632575

Jazz Spelunke
6, Dürergasse 3,
Tel. 570126

Klimt Bar im Hilton
3, Am Stadtpark,
Tel. 752652-0

La tou tou Bar
10, Kurbadstr.8,
Tel. 681631

Porta
1, Schulerstrase 6,
Tel. 5131493

Queen Anne
1, Johannesgasse 12,
Tel. 5120203

Tenne
1, Annagasse 3,
Tel. 525708

Wurlitzer
1, Schwarzenbergplatz 10,
Tel. 640311

Into the early morning hours

Beatrixstüberl
3, Ungargasse 8,
Tel. 725876

Café Drechsler
6, Linke Wienzeile 22,
Tel. 5878580
(opens at 0400hrs)

Café Kammerspiele
1, Rotenturmstr. 25,
Tel. 632110

Spiel-Casino Wien
1, Kärntner Straße 41,
Tel. 524836
(open daily from 1700 hrs)

Spiel-Casino Baden
Baden bei Wien, im Kurpark,
Tel. 02252-4496
(daily from 1600 hrs)

"HEURIGER" INNS

Note that not all "Heuriger" inns are open all year round. If you require additional information, details are available from the Austrian Tourist Offices.

●**Grinzing**

Bach-Hengl
19, Sandgasse 7,
Tel. 323084

Berger Raimund
19, Himmelstraße 29,
Tel. 3220703

Rockenbauer Otto
19, Sandgasse 12,
Tel. 3219722

Rauscher Franz
19, Langackergasse 5a,
Tel. 325465

Ruckenbauer Franz
19, Sandgasse 6,
Tel. 321455

●**Heiligenstadt-Nußdorf**

Brunner Willibald
19, Hackhofergasse 7,
Tel. 3718262

Greiner
19, Kahlbergstr. 17,
Tel. 372131

Mayer am Pfarrplatz
19, Beethovenhaus, Pfarrplatz 3,
Tel. 371287

Welser Karl und Werner
19, Probusgasse 12,
Tel. 371302

●**Jedlersdorf**

Bernreiter Gertrude
21, Amtsstraße 24,
Tel. 393680

Binder Peter
21, Jedlersdorferstr. 151,
Tel. 394144

Lentner Karl
21, Amtsstr. 44,
Tel. 395123

Siebert Ploiner
Brünner Str. 91,
Tel. 394292

●**Mauer**

Edlmoser Karl
23, Maurer Lange Gasse 123,
Tel. 888680

Grausenburger Leopold
23, Maurer Lange Gasse 101a,
Tel. 881354

Lindauer Josef
23, Maurer Lange Gasse 83,
Tel. 885172

Familie Stadlmann
23, Maurer Lange Gasse 30,
Tel. 8827125

● **Neustift am Walde**

Altes Werkel
19, Mitterwurzergasse 22,
Tel. 442196

Bachmann Franz
19, Rathstraße 4,
Tel. 442720

Friseurmüller
19, Hameaustr. 30,
Tel. 441414

Fuhrgassl-Huber
19, Neustift am Walde 68,
Tel. 441405

● **Sievering**

Dietz Helene
19, Sieveringer Straße 269,
Tel. 442243

Haslinger Eva
19, Agnesgasse 3,
Tel. 441347

Koller Franz
19, Sieveringer Straße 269,
Tel. 442224

Muhr Christine
19, Windhabergasse 34,
Tel. 325851

Schreiber Gustav
19, Sieveringer Str. 158,
Tel. 325851

● **Stammersdorf**

Brunnhuber Anton
21, Herrenholzgasse 42,
Tel. 394295

Ehringer Theresia
21, Stammersdorfer Str. 20,
Tel. 2247864

Fritsch-Wanderer
21 Stammesdorfer Str. 67,
Tel. 394191

Klager Franz
21, Stammesdorfer Str. 14,
Tel. 391356

● **Strebersdorf**

Andrea Franz
21, Rußbergstraße 88,
Tel. 3917223

Riegler
21, Rußbergstr. 29,
Tel. 3928413

Seiwerth Karl
21, Langenzerdorferstr. 58,
Tel. 3918242

Traxler Frieda
21, Fillenbaumgasse 27,
Tel. 391402

CABARETS

Cabaret Fledermaus
1, Spiegelgasse 2,
Tel. 528438

Casanova Revuetheater
1, Dorotheergasse 8,
Tel. 528438

Freie Bühne Wieden
4, Wiedner Hauptstr. 60b,
Tel. 562122

Hernalser Stadttheater im Metropol
17, Geblergasse 50,
Tel. 433543

Heurigenkabarett "Spitzbuben"
19, Hackhofergasse 13,
Tel. 371285

Kabarett & Komödie am Naschmarkt
6, Linke Wienzeile 4,
Tel. 572275

Kabarett Niedermair
8, Lenaugasse 1a,
Tel. 484492

Kabarett Simpl
1, Wollzeile 36,
Tel. 524742

Kulisse
17, Rosensteingasse 39,
Tel.453870

Spektakel
5, Hamburger Straße 14,
Tel. 5870653

Tabor Brettl im Bayrischen Hof
2, Obere Augartenstraße 5,
Tel. 355110

Theater Forum
9, Porzellangasse 50,
Tel. 315421

SHOPPING

SHOPPING AREAS

If shopping is your forte, make a note in your diary that the most elegant and expensive shops, as well as art galleries and antique shops can be found in the inner city area between Hofburg, Graben and Kärntner Straße.

Opening hours (shops) are Monday - Friday, usually from 0900 - 1800 hrs, Saturdays 0900 - 1230 hrs.

CLOTHES

Classic:
E. Braun & Co., 1, Graben 8
Elmar Garzon, 1, Naglergasse 19
Erwin & Georg Grüener, 1,
Kohlmarkt 5
Etoile, 1, Lugeck 3
House of Gentlemen, 1, Kohlmarkt 12
Knize, 1, Graben 13
Lady Ascot, 1, Kohlmarkt 2
Linnerth, 1, Lugeck 1-2
Striberny, 1, Führichgasse 2

Avant Garde:
Schella Kann, 1, Seilerstätte 15 + 1,
Singerstraße 6/2/8
Steinegg Angelike, 1, Salzgries 18/98
Szekely Peter, 1, Führichgasse 10/6/5

Young:
Ciau-Ciau, 1, Tuchlauben 17
Guys & Dolls, 1, Schultergasse 2
Judengasse Drei, 1, Judengasse 3
Lilli Pilli, 1, Bäckerstraße 10
Lord Rieger, 1, Judengasse 11
My Market, 1, Singerstraße 4

MISCELLANOUS

- **Bags**
  Rada, 1, Kärntner Straße 8

- **Hats**
  Cilly, 1, Petersplatz 2

- **Shoes**
  Angelo, 1, Seilergasse 1
  Bellezza, 1, Kärntner Straße 45
  D'Ambrosio, 1, Bauernmarkt 1
  Map-Stiefelkönig (boots), 1,
  Kupferschmiedgasse, 2

- **Jewelry**
  Carius Binder, 1, Kärntner Straße 17
  Cartier, 1, Kohlmarkt 4
  Galerie am Graben, 1, Graben 17
  Hammermüller, 1, Wipplingerstraße 31
  Schullin, 1, Kohlmarkt 17

- **"Loden"**
  Lanz, 1, Kärntner Straße 10
  Nagy, 1, Wollzeile 36
  Plankl, 1, Michaelerplatz 6

- **Embroidery**
  Smejkal, 1, Kohlmarkt 9
  Stransky, 1, Hofburgpassage 2

- **Handicraft**
  Österreichische Werkstätten,
  1, Kärntner Straße 6

- **Records**
  Carola, 1, Albertinapassage

- **Prints, Posters**
  Durst, 1, Schottengasse 2

- **Antiques**
  Alt Wien Kunst, 1, Bräunerstr. 11
  Antiquitäten Bednarczyk, 1,
  Dorotheergasse 12
  Antiquitäten Feldbacher, 1,
  Annagasse 6
  Art und Interieur, 1, Seilerstätte 28
  Wiener Interieur, 1, Dorotheergasse 14

- **Second-Hand Bookshops**
  Aichinger, Bernhard & Co.,
  1, Weihburggasse 16

Böhlau, 1, Dr.-Karl-Lueger-Ring 12
Bourcy und Paulusch, 1 Wipplinger
Straße 5
Bücher Ernst, 6, Gumpendorfer
Straße 82
Der Buchfreund W. Schaden, 1,
Sonnenfelsgasse 4

- **Bookshops**
  Berger, 1, Kohlmarkt 3
  Braumüller, 1, Graben 22
  English Bookshop Heidrich, 1,
  Plankengasse 7
  Gerold, 1, Graben 31
  Gottschalks Bücher-Basar, 1,
  Krugerstr. 10
  Herrmann, 1, Grünangergasse 1
  Hintermayer, 7, Neubaugasse 290
  Octopus, 1, Fleischmarkt 16

- **Art Bookshop**
  Galerie Image, 1, Ruprechtsplatz 4

- **Newspapers, Magazines**
  H. Winter (International Press), 6,
  Mariahilfer Straße 77-79
  Morawa, 1, Wollzeile 11

- **Maps**
  Freytag & Berndt, 1, Kohlmarkt 9

Department Stores
Gerngross, 7, Mariahilfer Straße 38-48
Steffl, 1, Kärntner Straße 19

- **Musical Instruments**
  Musik Goll, 1, Babenbergerstraße 1-3
  Musikhaus Doblinger, 1,
  Dorotheergasse, 10

MARKETS

Markets are held daily in almost every district in Vienna. Special markets operateonly on Tuesdays and Fridays. The most famous of these markets is the "Naschmarkt". Near the Naschmarkt, a flea market is set up every Saturday at 4/5, Wienzeile, Kettenbrückengasse.

In addition to these, there are the seasonal fairs and markets (the **"Jahrmärkte"**), for example:

Allerheiligenmarkt (All Saints), in front of Zentralfriedhof, gates 1 - 3.

Christkindlmarkt (Christmas), in December, in front of the townhall.

Fastenmarkt (Lent), 17, Kavalerien-berggasse/St. Bartholomäus Platz.

Firmungsmarkt (Confirmation), at Whitsuntide, at Stephansplatz.

Sports

PARTICIPANT

- **Bowling**
  Bowlinghalle Prater, 2, Prater Hauptallee 124, Tel. 346461
  Bowlinghalle am Postsportplatz, 17, Schumanngasse 107, Tel. 464361

- **Iceskating**
  Eislaufverein, 3, Lothringerstr. 22, Tel. 736353

- **Water Sports**
  Donauinsel, Tel. 42800/3110
  Freizeitzentrum Neue Donau, Tel. 227730 (surf board hire)
  Schistek, Tel. 227730 (surf board hire)
  Surfgarage Hofbauer, Tel. 236733
  Surfschule Hawaii, Tel. 227730
  Tauchschule Peter's Club, Tel. 230609 (diving)

- **Angling**
  Information: Tel. 432176

- **Nudist Colonies**
  Danube, left embankment, northern part

- **Cycling**
  Cyclodrom BMX Bahn (BMX track)
  Radverleih Hammermayer (bicycle hire)
  Radverleih Luef, Tel. 388698

- **Tennis**
  2, Prater 21, Tel. 246384
  2, Prater, Kriau, Tel. 248261
  3, Arsenalstr. 1, Objekt 3-5, Tel. 782132
  3, Landstraßer Hauptstraße 63-65, Tel. 725435

3, Lothringer Straße 22, Tel. 736553
3, Sechskrügelgasse 4, Tel. 738182
7, Lindengasse 9, Tel. 933289
7, Mariahilfer Straße 80, Tel. 9330154

- **Golf**
Osterreichischer Golfverband, Haus des Sports, Tel. 6552163
Golf course, 2, Freudenauerstraße 65a

SWIMMING BATHS

- **Open-air Swimming Pools** (May - September 9.00 - 19.00):
  Stadionbad, 2, Prater, Meiereistraße
  Laaerbergbad, 10, Ludwig-von Höhnel-Gasse 2
  Theresienbad, 12, Hufelandgasse 3
  Hietzinger Bad, 13, Atzgersdorfer Straße 14
  Schönbrunner Bad, 13, Schloßpark
  Neuwaldegger Bad, 17, Promenadegasse 58
  Schafbergbad, 17, Josef-Redl-Gasse 1
  Krapfenwaldbad, 19, Krapfenwaldgasse 65-73

- **Open-air swimming pools along the Danube**
  Angeliebad, 21, An der Oberen Alten Donau
  Gänsehäufl, 22, Moissigasse 21
  Städtisches Strandbad Alte Donau, 22, **Arbeiterstrandbadstraße** 91

- **Bathing places along the Danube**
  Lobau, via Hubertusdamm
  Donauinsel, north side and south side

- **Indoor swimming pools with sauna**
  Amalienbad, 10, Reumannplatz 9
  Dianabad, 2, Lilienbrunnengasse 7-9
  Jörgerbad, 17, Jörgerstraße 42
  Oberlaa Thermalbad, 10, Kurbadstraße 14

interested in horse racing should attend the races in Krieau and Freudenau.

Further Information

Sportstelle der Stadt Wien, 8, Friedrich-Schmidt-Platz 5, Tel. 42800-5
Haus des Sports, 4, Prinz-Eugen-Straße 12, Tel. 653742

SPECTATOR

Avid football fans can watch football matches at the "Praterstadion", while those

LANGUAGE

Viennese for Visitors

The Viennese use "Schönbrunner-deutsch" for all official and semi-official purposes. The structure and most of the vocabulary are identical with standard High German, though the Viennese accent is distinctive. The everyday Viennese dialect, however, diverges considerably from High German in grammar and vocabulary. We have prepared a short list of specialized Viennese words that the visitor may come across—most of them associated with eating and drinking!

Achterl
small glass of wine (1/8 litre)

Beisel, Beisl
small restaurant

Brauner
coffee with very little milk

Einspänner
coffee in a glass with cream

Gruß Gott
hello (standard greeting)

Guglhupf
type of cake

Heuriger
new wine

Indianer
small chocolate cake

Kapuziner
coffee with little milk

Jause
afternoon meal

Melange
coffee, half milk and half coffee

Obstler
type of spirit

Obers
cream

Paradeiser
tomatoes

Powidl
plum puree

Schlagobers
whipped cream

Schwarzer
black coffee

Trafik
tobacconist's shop

Viertel
large glass of wine (liter)

Zuagraster
visitor, tourist

FURTHER READING

History

A.F. Pribram: *Austria-Hungary and Great Britain, 1908-14*. Greenwood Press, London.

Barbara Jelavich: *Austria, Empire and Republic*. Cambridge University Press.

J.W. Mason: *Dissolution of the Austro-Hungarian Empire*. Longman.

Fritz Judtman: *Mayerling: the Facts behind the Legend*. Harrap 1971.

George E. Berkley: *Nightmare in Paradise: Vienna and its Jews*. California University Press.

Biography, Autobiography

Ernest Jones: *The Life and Work of Sigmund Freud*. Penguin

Alma Mahler: *Gustav Mahler - Memories and Letters*. Collins.

W.A. Mozart: *Letters*. Edited by Hans Mersmann. Dover Publications.

Nicholas Henderson: *Prince Eugene of Savoy*. Weidenfeld

Stefan Zweig: *The World of Yesterday*. New York 1943.

Edward Crankshaw: *Maria Theresia*. Constable.

Literature

Peter Branscombe (ed.): *Austrian Life and Literature—Eight Essays*. Scottish Academic Press.

Mark G. Ward (ed.): *From Vormärz to Fin de siècle—Essays in 19th Century Austrian Literature*. Lochee Publications.

William M. Johnstone: *The Austrian Mind—An Intellectual and Social History 1848-1938*. University of California Press.

Arthur Schnitzler: *La Ronde and Other Plays* (translations). Carcanet Press.

Art and Architecture

Carl J. Friedrich: *The Age of the Baroque, 1610-1660*. Greenwood Press, London.

Anthony Blunt (editor): *Baroque and Rococo*. Granada.

Christa Witt-Dorring: *Vienna in the Age of Schubert—the Biedermeier Interior*.

Kirk Varnedoe: *Vienna 1900—Art, Architecture, Design*.

Food

Gretel Beer: *Austrian Cooking*. Andre Deutsch.

USEFUL ADDRESSES

TOURIST INFORMATION

Austrian National Tourist Offices Abroad

30 St. George's St,
London W1R OAL,
Tel. 629-0461

The Lodge,
Ardoyne Ho, Pembroke
Park, Ballsbridge,
Dublin 4,
Tel. 683321

500 Fifth Ave.,
Suite 2009-2022,
New York 10110,
Tel. 9446880

11601 Wilshire Blvd.,
Los Angeles 90025,
Suite 2480,
Tel. 4773332

Östereichische Fremdenverkehrswerbung,
Rossmarkt 12,
6000 Frankfurt/Main,
Tel. 293673

Neue Hard 11,
8037 Zürich,
Tel. 443331

Office Nationale Autrichien du Tourism,
47 Ave. de l'Opera,
75002 Paris,
Tel. 47427857

Ente Nazionale Austriaco per il

Tourismo,
Via Barberini 29,
00187 Roma,
Tel. 4754658

Tourist Information in Vienna

Offizielle Tourist-Information
Opernpassage,
Tel. 431608/435974,
daily 0900 - 1900 hrs

Österreich Information
4, Margaretenstraße 1,
Tel. 5872000, 0900 - 1700 hrs
Monday to Friday

Wiener Fremdenverkehrsverband
9, Kinderspitalgasse 5,
Tel. 435974/431608

Stadtinformationen
Rathaus,
Tel. 438989

Jewish Welcome Service
1, Stephansplatz 10,
Tel. 638891

The Vienna Tourist Office

Address: **Wiener Fremdenver-kehrsverband**, Kinderspitalgasse 5, 1095 Wien; Tel. 431608

The following brochures and leaflets can be obtained free from the tourist office:

Vienna in pictures
"Jewish Vienna"
"Vienna waits for you"
(for the younger ones)
Map of the town
List of museums
List of hotels
List of restaurants
List of youth hostels and camping sites
List of "Heuriger" inns
"Wien live" (for the younger ones)
Jugendstil in Vienna
What's on in Vienna
List of conventions/trade fairs
Programs for coming events at the Staatsoper and Volksoper

Programs: Spanish Riding School/Viennese Boys' Choir
What's on this/next month
What's on in winter/spring and during carnival
Music Festivals
Program: Wiener Musik-Sommer

Viennese Boys' Choir

2, Obere Augartenstraße 1,
Tel. 334451-0

Tickets for the performances in the "Burgkapelle" can be obtained from the general box offices.

Useful Telephone Numbers

Directory Enquiries	16
Direct Dialing Abroad	08
Police	133
Emergency	144
Emergency Doctor	141
Emergency Poison Cases	434343
Red Cross	9626
Accommodation	424225
Radio Taxi	6282, 9101, 4369, 3130
Lost Property	316611, 9211
Flight Information	7770-2231
Buses, Coaches	733535
Weather Forecast	1566
Trains	7200

EMBASSIES & CONSULATES

Council for the Arts	42800-2874
Great Britain	731575
USA	315511
Canada	633691
China	315511
India	658666-0
Indonesia	342533
Ireland	754246
Israel	311506
Malaysia	651142-0
New Zealand	526636
Republic of Ireland	722657-0
South Africa	326493-0
Thailand	348361-0

International Organizations

The Vienna International Center for the United Nations, abbreviated UNO-City, was built in 1973-76. It is the seat of many international organizations: the **IAEO** (Nuclear Energy), the **UNIDO** (Industrial Development), the **CSDHA** (Social Development, Humanitarian Affairs), the **UNCITRAL** (International Trade Laws), the **UNRWA** and **UNHCR** (Palestinian and other refugees), and others.

UNO-City is exterritorial, even Austrians must show a valid passport before being allowed to enter.

UNO-City is also the headquarters of **OPEC** and the International Music Center.

MISCELLANEOUS

Alcoholics Anonymous
17, Geblergasse 45/3, Tel. 438164

Babysitter
Babysitter-Zentrale, 16, Herbststraße 6-10, Monday - Friday from 0800 - 1430 hrs, Tel. 951135

Libraries
Österreichische Nationalbibliothek, 1, Josefplatz 1, Tel. 521684
Graphische Sammlung Albertina, 1, Augustinerstraße 1, Tel. 525769
Bibliothek der Österreichischen Akademie der Wissenschaft, 1, Dr.-Ignaz-Seipel-Platz 2, Tel. 51581/257
Universitätsbibliothek, 1, Dr.-Karl-Lueger-Ring 1, Tel. 4300/2372

Couriers
AAB Botendienst, Tel. 462506
ARGE Funkbotendienst, Tel. 765577
Blitzkurier, Tel. 346505

German Classes
Amerlinghaus, 7, Stiftgasse 8,
Tel. 936475

Auction House
Dorotheum, 1, Dorotheergasse 20, Tel. 51560-0, auctions are held daily from 1400 hrs; first viewing is from Monday - Friday 1000 - 1800 hrs, Saturday 0830 - 1200 hrs

Bicycle Hire

Bicycles can be hired at the following addresses for öS 30/per hour or öS 70/per day. Bicycles can also be hired at some railway stations (öS 60/per day) by producing an identity card/passport. They can be returned at any station.

Information: Tel. 565051/5507

1, Franz-Josefs-Kai, at Salztorbrücke, Tel. 663422

2, Prater 133, Tel. 2409494

2, Vivariumstraße 8, Tel. 266644

10, Waldgasse 47, Tel. 6410113

19, Heilgenstädter Straße 180, Tel. 374598

22, Linkes Ufer Wehr 1, Tel. 231171

22, Neue Donau, Reichsbrücke, Tel. 236518

ART/PHOTO CREDITS

INDEX

A

B

I

J

K

R

S

T

U

INSIGHT *Pocket* GUIDES

EXISTING & FORTHCOMING TITLES:

• •

United States: **Houghton Mifflin Company, Boston MA 02108**
Tel: (800) 2253362 Fax: (800) 4589501

Canada: **Thomas Allen & Son, 390 Steelcase Road East**
Markham, Ontario L3R 1G2
Tel: (416) 4759126 Fax: (416) 4756747

Great Britain: **GeoCenter UK, Hampshire RG22 4BJ**
Tel: (256) 817987 Fax: (256) 817988

Worldwide: **Höfer Communications Singapore 2262**
Tel: (65) 8612755 Fax: (65) 8616438

"I was first drawn to the Insight Guides by the excellent "Nepal" volume. I can think of no book which so effectively captures the essence of a country. Out of these pages leaped the Nepal I know – the captivating charm of a people and their culture. I've since discovered and enjoyed the entire Insight Guide Series. Each volume deals with a country or city in the same sensitive depth, which is nowhere more evident than in the superb photography.**"**

Sir Edmund Hillary